Study Guide to accompany

*A*bnormal Psychology and Modern Life

Eighth Edition

Robert C. Carson

James N. Butcher

James C. Coleman

Mary P. Koss

University of Arizona

Scott, Foresman and Company

Glenview, Illinois
Boston
London

ISBN 0-673-18933-3

345678-MKN-91908988

Preface

In most schools abnormal psychology is one of the most popular courses offered. Commonly, there are students enrolled in this course whose major fields are quite diverse and who have taken only an introductory course in psychology. These students sometimes feel at a disadvantage competing with upper-level psychology majors. In addition, abnormal psychology can be a tricky subject . The familiarity of the subject matter and its high relevance to real life may give some students the feeling that they "understand" the material only to find out at examination time that they do not "know" the material the way the instructor expected.

This study guide has been developed to assist you in learning the material presented in the textbook. It has been designed to help you overcome any lack of experience you may have in approaching psychological material and to make you familiar with the kind of information you should really know in order to do well on exams. It is written in a straightforward and serious style, minimizing games and other gimmicks. Most students find the textbook, *Abnormal Psychology and Modern Life,* so full of case histories and examples that they become interested in and motivated to learn the material without any outside props. What students *do* need is help to decide what to learn and an organized place to write down the information which can be used as notes from which to study for examinations.

HOW TO STUDY

Many teachers recommend the following approach to studying course material:

1. Skim major headings and read chapter summaries.

2. Read and highlight (underline) important sections of the text.

3. Outline the important points you have highlighted in your reading. (Psychological studies show that putting material into your own words helps you to learn and retain the information better.)

4. Study from your text notes and class notes for exams--not from your textbook. Start studying a few days in advance. (Studying from your underlined text is confusing, not as effective, and may make you feel more anxious and unprepared.)

This study guide has been written as a check on the appropriateness of your Stage 2 reading. It indicates the terms and concepts many teachers feel are most important in the text. Do you seem to be underlining the same points? If not, the guide will help you pick up on points you have overlooked rather than have you wait until exam time for this feedback. The most important function of the study guide, however, is as a substitute for the difficult and time-consuming outlining recommended in Stage 3. In the study guide, you will find that a lot of the choosing and organizing of the material has been done for you. Also, whenever possible, the charts have been constructed to help you consolidate and learn the material. You have been given the general outlines. Your job is to fill in the specific information so you can prepare a complete and efficient set of notes to use in studying for examinations.

HOW TO USE THIS STUDY GUIDE

The study guide follows the sequence of the textbook and uses the same chapter headings and section headings. Each study guide chapter consists of five sections.

1. Chapter Overview

This short section is designed to prepare you to begin the chapter. Rather than just summarizing what the chapter is about (the text chapter summaries do this), the overview is designed to orient you to the purpose and some of the implications of the material you are about to read. It is designed to alert you to the overall importance of the chapter so you will, hopefully, feel motivated to start reading it. It is recommended that you first read the overview, then read the chapter summary in the textbook. Next skim the chapter by reading the major section headings so you get a mental picture of the overall organization of the chapter. Now go back to the beginning of the chapter and begin reading and highlighting the text. After you have done this, you are ready to begin filling in the study guide sections.

2. Learning Objectives

This section presents the specific factual and conceptual knowledge that is to be learned in the chapter. Once you have finished reading the text and have finished the relevant sections in the study guide, you should have all the information accumulated to meet the objectives. Your only remaining task is to memorize the material to prepare for examination. Keep in mind that the learning objectives are often used by instructors as a guide to the selection of relevant examination items.

3. Terms You Should Know

Here you will find listed all the major terms introduced in the chapter along with a page reference on which to find the definition of the term in the textbook. To assist your locating the terms, care has been taken to ensure that they are listed in exactly the same form or wording as in the textbook. Many of the terms can also be found in the glossary at the back of the textbook. However, it is still a good idea to look up the definition of the term within the chapter to be certain you know the context in which the term appeared. In the space provided, write out a brief definition of each term.

4. Concepts to Master

Each major section heading in the text is treated as a concept and is numbered consecutively. Under each numbered concept are specific points of information identified by small letters. Each requires that you provide some information. You may have to write a short answer, complete a chart, match two columns, or fill in blanks. The page reference tells you where to find the requested information. The language of the questions parallels as much as possible that used in the textbook to make it easier for you to locate the answer in your book.

The concepts have been chosen so that you have a guide to the most important topics in the chapter. The specific questions help you identify the factual knowledge you should learn about each topic. To complete the requested information, go to the referenced page, locate the appropriate section and read it over, then write a correct response in your own words in the study guide. As much space as possible has been provided for you to write in your answers, but in some cases you may have to continue on a separate page. Answer the questions carefully, completely, and accurately, and you will complete a detailed outline for each chapter that you can use instead of the textbook to study efficiently for examinations.

At the end of the concepts section, you will notice that there are some concepts whose numbers are in parentheses . This indicates that this concept is based on one of the text's highlights. Many instructors assign these highlights optionally. Therefore, they have been placed together at the end of the concept section so you can easily skip them if your teacher won't be using them.

5. Chapter Quiz

Each study guide chapter concludes with a short self-test of multiple-choice items. The self-test will not only allow you to assess your mastery of the chapter, it will allow you to get a feeling for some of the types of questions that may appear on your course examinations. Complete the self-test items after you have completed the study guide terms and concepts sections and after you are about halfway into your studying for the examination. Look up the correct answer to each item. Go back to the referenced page for each item you missed and read over the correct answer. Then try to analyze why you made the mistake. Didn't you know the material? (If not, try to study more.) Did you misinterpret the item? (Try to read each item very carefully and make sure you know the definitions of all the terms introduced in the chapter. During tests remember you can usually ask your instructor to define a word you don't know as long as it is not a technical term you were supposed to learn.) Up to 10 of the items in each quiz were taken directly from the test item file for the textbook that you instructor may be using.

HOW TO PREPARE FOR EXAMS

Many students become anxious about their performance on tests and this tension becomes increasingly greater as the exam time becomes nearer. Research suggests that the most effective preparation is accomplished under moderate levels of anxiety. Therefore, do not leave all your studying until the last minute when tension renders your behavior disorganized and less effective. Read the text and complete the study guide on an ongoing basis during the term, and aim to complete these tasks several days before the exam.

Plan to study for a few hours each day on the several days before the scheduled exam. Study from your completed study guide and your class notes, not from your textbook. Re-reading the textbook is time consuming and inefficient. If you've been conscientious in completing the study guide, it contains the material you need to learn. Start with the "Terms You Should Know" section. Cover the definition and try to recite it from memory. (If you have a private study area, it's even more effective to say the definition out loud.) Go back over the list and cover each term successively. Read the definition and try to recall the term to which it applies. This general approach is to be used with the "Concepts to Master" section as well. Cover the answers you have written and try to generate them from memory. Continue to review the study guide until you can reproduce all the correct answers from memory.

Whether your teacher will be using multiple-choice or essay exams doesn't affect how you will prepare--both types of testing require a command of the basic facts. Good, well-prepared students come out on top no matter what form of testing the instructor uses. Some students may argue that memorization isn't necessary for multiple-choice tests which only require recognition of the right response. This is untrue. Instructors purposely write the wrong answers to look and sound plausible. If you don't know the facts, you'll be misled by these distractors.

CONCLUSION

I've been a teacher of abnormal psychology for fifteen years. The suggestions I have made and the way I've set up this study guide reflect an approach that has helped many of my students. I hope the guide helps you build a good foundation of knowledge about abnormal behavior that you can add to in years to come through your personal experiences, reading, and new scientific developments you become aware of through the media.

Good luck,
Mary P. Koss

Contents

Part Three: ASSESSMENT, TREATMENT, AND PREVENTION

Chapter 1

Abnormal Behavior in Our Times

OVERVIEW

It has been said that psychology "has a long history but a short past." This is certainly true of abnormal psychology. Although examples of bizarre behavior are seen throughout history, and considerations of why people act as they do have appeared and reappeared in literature and philosophy, scientific study of abnormal behavior really only began around 1900. Chapter 1 begins with a discussion of modern life and its hassles. In such a world, is it any wonder that abnormal behavior exists? Then, the meaning of the term "abnormal" is discussed along with a description of contemporary procedures to classify the different ways psychological disturbance may be expressed. Finally, the value of scientific data is emphasized and research methods utilized to study behavior are described.

LEARNING OBJECTIVES

1. List some popular plays, movies, and books that describe abnormal behavior and explain why such sources are often inaccurate.

2. Describe two broad perspectives on abnormal behavior and explain how each views the goals of therapy.

3. List three aspects of abnormal behavior that must be considered by those who wish to understand it.

4. List several reasons why a classification system is needed in abnormal psychology and explain the meaning of validity and reliability in reference to such a system.

5. Differentiate between the DSM and ICD classification systems and describe the five axes of DSM-III.

6. Compare DSM-III and DSM-III-R and describe two limitations of DSM classifications and labeling in general.

7. Explain why the observation of behavior is basic to all forms of psychological inquiry.

8. Explain why research on groups of people is usually preferred to single case studies and why those groups must be representative of larger populations.

9. Explain why correlational research cannot establish cause and effect but has been extremely useful in epidemiologic research.

10. Explain why experimental studies are often inappropriate for abnormal psychology and indicate how analogue studies have been used in their place.

11. Describe the clinical case study and explain why it is easy to draw erroneous conclusions from this method of research.

12. Compare the advantages and disadvantages of retrospective and prospective research in abnormal psychology.

13. List and explain three concepts about the study of abnormal psychology on which this text is based.

14. List and describe three broad approaches to the classification of abnormal behavior and some of the assumptions underlying each.

15. Explain why the authors prefer a prototypal model of classification to the categorical one that is not in place.

TERMS YOU SHOULD KNOW

abnormal psychology (p. 8)

clinical psychology (p. 8)

psychiatry (p. 8)

social work (p. 8)

psychopathology (p. 8)

abnormal (p. 8)

reliability (p. 10)

validity (p. 10)

Diagnostic and Statistical Manual (DSM-III) (p. 10)

operational criteria (p. 10)

axes (p. 11)

organic mental disorders (p. 11)

substance use disorders (p. 11)

disorders of psychological or sociocultural origin (p. 11)

disorders usually arising during childhood or adolescence (p. 11)

acute (p. 11)

chronic (p. 11)

episodic (p. 12)

patient (p. 16)

client (p. 16)

hypotheses (p. 17)

sample (p. 18)

representative (p. 18)

control group (p. 18)

criterion group (p. 18)

correlation (p. 18)

path analysis (p. 19)

epidemiologic research (p. 19)

experimental method (p. 20)

analogue studies (p. 21)

learned helplessness (p. 21)

waiting list control group strategy (p. 22)

statistical control (p. 22)

clinical case study or N = 1 experiment (p. 22)

retrospective research (p. 23)

at risk (p. 23)

prospective studies (p. 23)

categorical model (p. 25)

dimensional approach (p. 25)

CONCEPTS TO MASTER

1. Abnormal behavior in our times
   The authors note that the present times are characterized by a large number of anxious, unhappy, bewildered people.
   a. What are some of the characteristics of our society that lead to these feelings?

   (pp. 3-4)

   b. Certain human behaviors "reveal" the stress of our times. Examples are massive amounts of:

      1. _____, alcoholic or otherwise, prescription and nonprescription, that we as a society consume. Other indications of widespread stress can be found in nonchemical activities such as involvement among youth in
      _____ (p. 4)
      2. How many people are affected by mental disorders compared to the number of people affected by physical disorders? (p. 4)

      3. President Carter's Commission on Mental Health concluded that eventually one person in _____ requires professional treatment for emotional disorders.
      (p. 5)

2. Popular views of abnormal behavior
   a. What major point about abnormal behavior is illustrated by the many examples obtained from historical documents which the authors present? (p. 6)

b. Several literary works have been highly critical of treatment in mental hospitals. Give
    two examples of such works.   (pp. 9-10)

3. What do we mean by "abnormal behavior"?
    a. What is the literal meaning of the word *abnormal* ?   (p. 8)

    b. What is the "cultural relativist" view of abnormal behavior as described by
        Ullman and Krasner?   (p. 9)

    c. When one accepts the view that behavior is abnormal if--and only if-- society labels
        it so, two serious conclusions result: (p. 9)

        1. There is one set of values that is good for everyone.
        2. Therefore, the task of psychotherapy is to_____
            _____.

    d. The authors of the text maintain that the best criterion for determining the normality of
        behavior is whether it fosters the well-being of the individual and, ultimately, of the
        group. This view is referred to as the abnormal as _____
        view.   (p. 9)

    e. How do the authors justify considering prejudice, discrimination, waste of natural
        resources, and polluting the environment as forms of "abnormal behavior"?
                                                                            (p. 9)

    f. What are the two value assumptions on which abnormal as maladaptive view rests?
                                                                            (p. 9)

        1.

        2.

g. What are the concerns of mental health personnel within an "abnormal-behavior-as-maladaptive-behavior" framework?   (p. 9)

4. The need for classification
    a. What does "classification" in abnormal psychology involve?   (p. 10)

    b. What are two mundane, or practical, reasons for making diagnostic classifications?
                                                                             (p. 10)

        1.

        2.

    c. Reliability means that a classification can be applied in a standard way by various users and validity means that a classification is meaningful. Fill in each term in the correct blanks below: (p. 10)

        _____ presupposes (or requires beforehand)

        _____.

    d. Regarding the Diagnostic and Statistical Manual of Mental Disorders (DSM-III):

        1. A distinct feature of DSM-III is "operational criteria." What does this mean?
                                                                             (p. 10)

        2. If operational criteria are achieved, reliability of diagnosis is greatly improved. On the other hand, the use of strict criteria causes much abnormal behavior to _____. For example, DSM-III diagnostic criteria for schizophrenia have resulted in a substantial improvement in reliability but in the process some 50% of formerly diagnosed schizophrenic patients were "lost " to other diagnoses.   (p. 10)

3. Identify the five axes of DSM-III: (p. 11)

   Axis I

   Axis II

   Axis III

   Axis IV

   Axis V

4. Axis I and II list the mental disorders.
   Place the following terms under their appropriate headings: mental
   retardation, alcohol abuse, psychophysiologic disorders, affective disorders,
   Alzheimer's disease, schizophrenia, autism, and anxiety disorders.   (p. 11)

Category	**Examples**
organic mental disorders	
substance use disorders	
disorders of psychological or sociocultural origin	
disorders arising during childhood or adolescence	

5. Place the following diagnostic terms under the correct axis: (a) Diabetes; (b) Level of psychosocial stressors: 5 (severe); (c) Psychological factors affecting physical condition; (d) Bi-Polar Affective Disorder (depressed); (e) Global functioning: 6 (moderate severity); (f) dependent personality disorder.

                                                                                    (p. 13)

Axis I
1.

2.

Axis II
1.

Axis III
1.

Axis IV
1.

Axis V
1.

6. Why do some clinicians object to the use of Axes IV and V on insurance forms?
                                                                                    (p. 13)

7. Soon after the publication of DSM-III, work began on DSM-III-R (the R stands for revised). Which of the following is the explanation of this rapid pace of change?
                                                                                    (p. 14)
    a. acceleration in the rate of new knowledge about abnormal behavior
    b. rapidity with which the inadequacies of the diagnostic system have been found

8. The authors list two limitations of DSM-III. Explain each: (p. 15)
    a. DSM-III just names.

    b. DSM-III only covers individual behavior.

9. The authors of the text indicate that the process of labeling, no matter what classification system is used, has drawbacks.   (p. 15)
   a. First, when a label has been assigned to a person, what may happen to the professionals who are treating the person?

   b. Second, how might labels affect the patients themselves?

5. Observation of behavior
   a. Abnormal behavior shares with the rest of psychology a focus on _____.
   As scientific data, however, self-observation of one's own behavior is limited because:
                                                                                          (p. 17)

      1.

      2. Even if a person is cooperative and sincere, he or she may be unable to make certain observations.

   b. Psychologists observe behavior. To make sense of observed behavior, they generate more or less reasonable _____ to help explain the behavior. A psychologist may observe some symptoms and guess that "schizophrenia" is the entity or hypothetical construct that caused the symptoms. This demonstrates the process of inference in psychology.   (p. 17)

6. Sampling and generalization
   Research in abnormal psychology is concerned with gaining enhanced _____ and where possible _____ of abnormal behavior. One strategy of research is the single case study, the major limitation of which is that we can't know for sure if observed characteristics are related to the disorder, to unique characteristics of the person with the disorder, or a(an) _____. To overcome these limitations, a representative _____ is usually studied rather than single cases and often both a group of people with the disorder (the criterion group) and a group of comparable people who do not have the disorder (the _____ group) are studied.   (p. 18)

7. Correlation and causation

Variable A is poor communication with the child. Variable B is a cranky withdrawn child. Variable C is a power failure. Finding that variable A and B are correlated with each other does not mean that variable A caused variable B. It is also possible that: (pp. 18-19)

a. B caused A: The cranky child frustrated the parents who gave up being understanding.

b. Both A and B are caused by C: Power failure and loss of air-conditioning caused both the cranky child and the crabby parents.

c. With correlational data, a statistical technique called _____ can be used to explore cause and effect relationships.

d. Some very useful research is correlational. For example, we have learned much from_____ research which focuses on the pattern of disease distribution.

8. Experimental strategies

Match the following terms and definitions: (pp. 21-22)

Term	**Definition**
1. waiting list control	a. Therapist intensively studies a client's background.
2. N = 1 experiment	b. Mathematical corrections are made for uncontrolled group differences.
3. experimental method	
4. statistical control	c. The study of behavior that isn't actually pathological but is similar to it.
5. analogue study	d. Treatment is withheld for a period of time.
6. comparative outcome research	e. All factors are controlled except for the one of interest.
	f. A study that compares two or more treatments.

9. Retrospective versus propsective strategies
    Describe the strengths and limitations of each of the following methods: (p. 23)

Method	Strengths	Limitations
case study method	sometimes results in useful insights	1.
retrospective research	standard method of clinical inquiry	1. hard to disentangle cause and effect 2. disordered person may not be accurate 3.
prospective research	cause and effect can be determined with greater confidence than in retrospective studies	1. uncertainty about what constitutes risk 2. risk factors may interact with other variables 3.

10. Orientation of the book
    a. What is involved in a "scientific approach"?   (p. 23)

        What does it mean to "take a critical and evaluative attitude toward research findings"?   (p. 24)

    b. How can a student develop an awareness of "common human concerns"?   (p. 24)

    c. How do the authors of the text view mentally disordered persons in order to respect their dignity?   (p. 24)

11. Unresolved issues
    a. DSM-III is based on symptoms of illness. It is referred to as a categorical model which assumes that all human behavior can be divided into normal and abnormal, and within the abnormal there exist nonoverlapping types of behavior. This is one of the three approaches to classification noted by Widiger and Allen. Describe the other two approaches: (pp. 25-26)

       1. What would a dimensional approach to classification be?

       2. What would a prototype approach to classification be?

    b. There are advantages to a prototype approach over a categorical approach. List the advantages of the prototype approach and then explain why this approach is not used in the text even though the authors believe it is superior. (p. 26)

(12.) Extimated prevalance of major maladaptive behavior patterns in the United States
    a. Assuming a population of 220 million, approximately 1 person in _____ suffers from minor emotional problems such as "demoralization" while 1 person in _____ experiences serious problems such as schizophrenia. (p. 4)

    b. Define the following terms: (p. 4)

       1. Incidence

       2. Prevalence

(13.) Some popular myths and misconceptions concerning mental disorder and abnormal behavior: (p. 7)
    a. Former mental patients are no more dangerous than people in general.
                                                                    TRUE OR FALSE

    b. Everyone shares a potential for becoming disordered.   TRUE OR FALSE

    c. Mental disorders are natural adaptive processes.   TRUE OR FALSE

(14.) Politics and the DSM-III-R
       The controversy over the self-defeating personality reveals the intrusion of nonscientific concerns into the classification process. Explain. (p. 14)

(15.)   Mental illness as a myth
       a. Describe Szasz's view of mental illness. (p. 16)

       b. What do Sarbin and Mancuso (1980) mean when they say that schizophrenia is a "moral verdict"? (p. 16)

(16.)   Patients in state and county mental hospitals from 1880 to 1970
       a. What has happened to the number of persons confined to state and county mental hospitals over the last 20 years? (p. 20)

       b. What are the four reasons mentioned by the authors that account for the above changes? (p. 20)

          1.

          2.

          3.

          4.

CHAPTER QUIZ

1. According to the 1978 report of the Commission on Mental Health, one person in _____ living in the United States will at some time require professional treatment for emotional disturbances. (p. 5)

    a. three   c. seven
    b. five   d. nine

2. Cultural relativists like Ullmann and Krasner maintain that abnormal behavior is that which is: (p. 9)

    a. deviant from social expectations.
    b. illegal according to the law of the land.
    c. immoral by religious standards.
    d. psychologically maladaptive.

3. Under the social deviation view of abnormality, a psychotherapist's task is to help patients:
    (p. 9)

    a. actualize their own potentials.
    b. become more moral in their outlook.
    c. conform to societal norms.
    d. foster their own well-being.

4. The word *abnormal* literally means behavior that: (p. 8)

    a. deviates from society's norms.
    b. interferes with the well-being of the individual.
    c. is "away from the normal."
    d. is undesirable.

5. The authors of the textbook maintain that the best criteria for determining the normality of behavior is: (p. 9)

    a. deviance from the norm.
    b. adaptivity of the behavior in furthering individual and group well-being.
    c. variance from societal expectations.
    d. the operational criteria listed in the DSM-III-R.

6. When different observers agree on the classification of certain abnormal behaviors, the system is said to be: (p. 10)

    a. diagnostic.   c. standardized.
    b. reliable.   d. valid.

7. The first three axes of the DSM-III-R assess: (p. 11)

    a. how well the individual is coping.
    b. stressors that may have contributed to the disorder.
    c. the person's present condition.
    d. the prognosis of the disorder.

8. Many clinicians object to the inclusion of an _____ diagnosis on insurance forms because it violates the client's confidentiality.   (p. 11)

    a. Axis I   c. Axis III
    b. Axis II   d. Axis IV

9. DSM-III-R's major categories of mental disorders include: (p. 11)

    a. organic mental disorders.   c. adjustment disorders.
    b. schizophrenic disorders.   d. psychosexual disorders.

10. Which of the following terms refers to a mental condition of relatively short duration?
                                                                              (p. 11)
    a. episodic   c. chronic
    b. acute   d. factitious

11. In order to make sense of observed behavior, psychologists generate more or less plausible
    ideas called: (p. 17)

    a. constructs.   c. principles.
    b. hypotheses.   d.   theories.

12. Researchers in abnormal psychology usually place the *least* reliance upon data gathered
    from: (pp. 17-18)

    a. large groups.   c. single case studies.
    b. representative samples.   d. small groups.

13. Which of the following may be safely inferred when a sizeable positive correlation is found
    between variables x and y?   (pp. 18-19)

    a. People high on x will usually be high on y.
    b. People low on x will usually be high on y.
    c. x causes y.
    d. y causes x.

14. Comparative outcome research features: (p. 22)

    a. a "waiting list control group."
    b. correlations of two or more behaviors in the same group.
    c. one experimental and one control group.
    d. two or more treatments in different equivalent groups.

15. A psychologist identifies 50 children who have schizophrenic mothers. At adolescence, the
    researcher compares those who break down with those who don't. This is an example of
    a _____ study.   (p. 23)

    a. clinical case   c. prospective
    b. comparative outcome   d. retrospective

2

Historical Views of Abnormal Behavior

OVERVIEW

Abnormal behavior has fascinated humankind from its beginning, and various explanations of the cause of such behavior have developed over the course of history. It's important to know what a particular group of people thought about the cause of bizarre behavior, since beliefs usually predict the way people treat mentally ill people. An understanding of the older viewpoints presented in this chapter helps in understanding why scientists working at the beginning of this century believed there was the need for drastic changes in thinking.

LEARNING OBJECTIVES

1. Give two examples of the treatment of abnormal behavior that probably took place about 3000 B.C. and before.

2. Describe early beliefs in demonology and explain the reasons why exorcism was used as a cure.

3. Describe Hippocrates' system of classifying mental disorders in ancient Greece and indicate some of the treatments he advocated.

4. Describe some conclusions that Plato and Aristotle reached about mentally disturbed people and explain how both anticipated some of Freud's ideas.

5. List four Greeks and Romans who continued in the Hippocratic tradition after 120 B.C. and describe some of the contributions each made to the understanding and treatment of abnormal behavior.

6. Describe the treatment of mental patients in Islamic countries around 792 A.D. and list the mental disorders described by Avicenna in The Canon of Medicine.

7. Compare two conflicting views of abnormal behavior that coexisted during the Middle Ages and describe the dance manias that occurred widely in Europe.

8. Describe some of the treatments for mental disorders that were used by the clergy during the Middle Ages.

9. Explain the supposed connection between mental illness and witchcraft and comment on the accuracy of this assumption.

10. Give several examples of people who, during the latter part of the Middle Ages, began to question witchcraft and demon possession as reasons for abnormal behavior.

11. Describe the treatment that mental patients received in early "insane asylums" in Europe and the United States.

12. Detail the events that led up to the founding of the Gheel Shrine in Belgium and describe its operation today.

13. Describe the humanitarian reforms in the treatment of mental patients that were instigated by Philippe Pinel, William Tukel, Benjamin Rush, and Dorothea Dix.

14. Describe the attitudes about mental health that existed near the end of the nineteenth century and show how Clifford Beers' efforts influenced the treatment of mental patients.

15. List some events beginning the the late nineteenth century that illustrate the increase of scientific research into the causes of mental abnormalities.

16. List and explain several weaknesses of the kind of retrospective research which attempts to produce an accurate history of mental illness and its treatment.

TERMS YOU SHOULD KNOW

trephining (p. 30)

Edwin Smith papyrus (p. 30)

exorcism (p. 31)

shamans (literal meaning: priests who use magic) (p. 31)

mass madness (p. 35)

tarantism (p. 35)

St. Vitus's dance (p. 35)

lycanthropy (p. 37)

humanism (p. 39)

bodily magnetism (p. 40)

Bedlam (p. 41)

San Hipolito (p. 41)

The Public Hospital (p. 42)

Gheel Shrine (p. 43)

La Bicetre (p. 43)

moral management (p. 45)

alienists (p. 47)

Journal of Abnormal Psychology (p. 50)

(general paresis) (p. 49)

(Spirochaeta pallida) **or "spirochete"** (p. 49)

CONCEPTS TO MASTER

1. Abnormal behavior in ancient times (up to 3000 B.C.)
    a. How were mental disorders treated by Stone Age cave dwellers?   (p. 30)

    b. Would you consider this treatment humane or cruel?   (p. 30)

    c. Describe what we have learned about ancient views of abnormal behavior by the discovery of the Edwin Smith papyrus.   (p. 30)

2. Demonology, gods, and magic
    a. To what did the early writings of the Chinese, Egyptians, Hebrews, and Greeks attribute abnormal behavior? (p. 30)

    b. What was the primary type of treatment used by these ancient peoples and which members of the community were charged with carrying out the treatment? (p. 31)

3. Early philosophical and medical concepts (400 B.C. to A.D. 200)
    a. Hippocrates stated, "For my part, I do not believe that the human body is ever befouled by a God." He is considered the "father of modern medicine," and is credited in your text with five important new ideas that contributed to the development of abnormal psychology. Complete this listing of his important contributions. (pp. 31-32)

        1. He saw the _____ as the central organ of intellectual activity and viewed mental disorders as due to brain pathology.

        2. He emphasized the importance of heredity, predispositions, and head injuries as causes of abnormal behavior.

        3. He classified all mental disorders into three general categories: mania, _____, and phrentis--which means "brain fever."

        4. He considered _____ to be important in understanding the person.

        5. He advocated treatment methods that were far advanced over the exorcistic practices of his time. For the treatment of _____ he prescribed a regular and tranquil life, sobriety, abstinence from all excesses, a vegetable diet, celibacy, and exercise.

    b. Hippocrates wrongly believed in the existence of four bodily _____ or "humors" which could cause mental disorder when disturbed. (pp. 31-32)

    c. Plato is credited with originating ideas with relevance to the legal status of the insane and community treatment of the mentally disordered. What were his ideas? (p. 33)

d.   Match the following persons with their major contributions: (pp. 33-34)

Name   **Major Contribution**

1.   Aristotle (384-322 B.C.)   a.   Advanced our understanding of the anatomy of the
                                                        nervous system based on dissections of animals.
                                                        The dark ages of abnormal psychology began with
                                                        his death around A.D. 200

2.   Asclepiades (ca. 124 B.C.)   b.   Described thinking as directed toward
                                                        attainment of pleasure and elimination of
                                                        pain.

3.   Cicero (106-43 B.C.)   c.   Saw mental disorders as extensions of normal
                                                        bodily processes.

4.   Aretaeus (A.D. 50-130)   d.   Believed that bodily ailments, as well as
                                                        mental disorders, could result from emotional
                                                        factors.

5.   Galen (A.D. 130-200)   e.   Noted the difference between acute and chronic
                                                        conditions as well as the differences among
                                                        illusions, hallucinations, and delusions.

6.   Avicenna (AD 980-1037)   f.   An outstanding figure of Islamic medicine, called
                                                        the "prince of physicians."

e.   Roman medicine as practiced by the Roman people was practical and reflected
pragmatism, which is the idea that the truth of a belief is determined by its
consequences. This treatment ended with the death of Galen in 200 A.D. and the "dark
ages of abnormal psychology" began. Describe the treatment received by mentally
disordered persons during the Roman empire.   (p. 34)

f.   The first mental hospital was established in the city of _____
(Turkey) in A.D. _____. The more scientific aspects of Greek and Roman
medicine survived only in Islamic countries.   (p. 34)

4. Conflicting views during the Middle Ages (6th to 15th centuries)
    a. The Middle Ages in Europe lasted from about A.D. 500-1500. The Middle Ages can be characterized as a relative _____ in respect to scientific thinking about the causes of abnormal behavior or enlightened treatment of mentally disordered persons.   (p. 35)

    b. How were the dancing manias, which were considered "abnormal behavior," related to ancient Greek religious practices?   Why were these behaviors attributed to symptoms of a spider bite rather than being viewed as religious practices?
                                                                                    (pp. 35-36)

    c. The occurrence of mass madness peaked in the 14th and 15th centuries. Why was mass madness so common during these years?   (pp. 36-37)

    d. During the sixteenth century, Teresa of Avila, a Spanish nun who later became a saint, explained hysteria among a group of cloistered nuns as *comas enfermas* which is translated "as if sick." Explain what she meant by this term.   (p. 38)

5. Witchcraft and mental illness: fact or fiction? (15th and 16th centuries)
    Most of the victims persecuted or killed for witchcraft were women "with a sharp tongue and a bad temper." Historians have suggested that women accused of being witches were not mentally ill. Do the authors of the text give an alternate explanation?
                                                                                    (p.39)

6. Growth toward humanitarian approaches (16th and 17th centuries)
    a. The reappearance of humane treatment of disturbed persons can be attributed to four persons. They were _____, who was the first physician known to speak out against witchcraft;   (pp. 39-40)
        _____, who insisted that dancing mania was a disease and also advocated treatment by "bodily magnetism," later called hypnosis;   (p. 40)
        _____, who was scorned by his peers and whose step-by-step rebuttal of witchcraft was banned by the church; and finally,   (p. 40)

_____, who wrote that witches were but victims of melancholy, a thesis that was rejected, banned, and burned by King James I of England.   (p. 40)

    b. King James I of England came to the rescue of demonology but by that time, many of the clergy also were beginning to question the practices. One of these clergy was St. _____ who said, "Mental disease is no different to bodily disease and Christianity demands of the humane and powerful to protect, and the skillful to relieve the one as well as the other."   (p. 41)

7. Establishment of early asylums and shrines (the 16th and 17th centuries--into the 18th century-- 1773-- in the United States)
    a. Henry VIII of England established a mental hospital in 1545 called St. Mary of Bethlehem, which soon became known as _____, adding a new word to our language.   (p. 41)

    b. The first hospital in the United States devoted exclusively to the mentally ill was _____, which was constructed in Williamsburg, Virginia in 1773. It is now a museum devoted to the subject of the treatment of mental illness.   (p. 42)

    c. Describe the atmosphere and treatment methods of these early "hospitals."
                                                   (pp. 41-42)

    d. The _____ shrine was one of the few enlightened settings where humane care of disturbed persons was practiced during this period. This colony has continued their work to the present day. Describe their current activities.   (p. 43)

8. Humanitarian reform (the 19th century)
    a. Humanitarian reform of mental hospitals received its first great impetus from the work of _____ of France. Why is his work referred to as an "experiment"?   (p. 43)

b. Pinel's work was begun at _____ hospital and later at
_____ hospital which have become known as the first "modern"
hospitals for the care of the insane. (p. 43)

c. The first trained nurses and supervisors were introduced at the _____
in 1841 by Samuel Hitch. (p. 44)

d. _____ was a famous American physician who wrote the first
textbook on psychiatry in the United States. He introduced the treatment approach
known as moral management. (p. 45)

e. During the years between 1833-1853, moral management resulted in a discharge rate
of _____ percent among patients who had been ill one year or less and
_____ percent among patients who had been ill longer than one year.
(pp. 45-46)

f. Moral management, despite its high degree of success, was abandoned by the late
1800s. Your text presents five reasons for this loss of influence. Complete the list.
(p. 46)

   1. Ethnic and racial predjudice that came with the increased size of the immigrant
      population.

   2.

   3.

   4.

   5. Advances in biology and medicine fostered the hope that all mental disorders would
      ultimately yield to biologically based treatment.

g. The tireless work of Dorthea Dix was honored by the United States Congress with a
resolution in 1901 labeling her as "among the noblest examples of humanity in
all history." What type of conditions did she find in state institutions at the beginning
of her career and how did she attempt to change them? (p. 47)

9. Changing attitudes toward mental health (the 20th century)
   What was the subject of Clifford Beers' book, *A Mind that Found Itself*?
   (pp. 47-48)

10. Growth of scientific research
   a.   How did the discovery of the cause of general paresis lead to the development of false expectations among researchers?   (p. 48)

   b.   The first clinic to treat behavior disorders from a psychological perspective was founded by _____ at the University of Pennsylvania in 1896.
                                                                                      (p. 49)

11. Unresolved issues
     Study of attitudes and treatment of mentally disordered persons in former eras is difficult. A primary difficulty is that we cannot rely on direct observation but have only historical documents from the period to study. Describe the problems of "propoganda" and "bias" in the interpretation of historical documents.   (p. 50)

(12.)   Early views of mental disorders in China
   a.   From earliest times, Chinese understanding of mental disorders was based on natural causes, on the concept of yin and yang. Describe how this concept explained the development of mental disorders.   (p. 36)

   b.   Around 200 A.D. Chung Ching, who has been called the Hippocrates of China, wrote two well-known medical works. Complete the following description of the views he expressed in these works.   (p. 36)

       1.   The primary cause of mental disorders is....

       2.   Organ pathology can also be caused by...

       3.   Emotional balance can be regained through...

   c.   How does the "dark ages" for the mentally ill in China compare to the dark ages in Europe?   (p. 36)

(13.) Events leading to the discovery of organic factors in general paresis
General paresis was described as a specific type of mental disorder by Bayle in the
year _____. The correlation between having had syphilis and later
appearance of general paresis was made by Esmarch and Jessen in the year
_____. Final verification that it was Spirochaeta pallida, or the
syphilitic spirochete, which was the brain-damaging agent in general paresis was
made by two scientists named _____ and
_____ in 1913.   (p. 49)

CHAPTER QUIZ

1. Which of the following is thought to contain the earliest description of the brain?

(p. 30)

   a. the Ebers papyrus   c. the Old Testament
   b. the Edwin Smith papyrus   d. the Rosetta Stone

2. Hippocrates erroneously held which of the following beliefs?   (p. 31)

   a. The brain is the central organ of human activity.
   b. Head injuries may cause sensory and motor distorders.
   c. Dreams are important in understanding the personality.
   d. There are basically four types of body fluids.

3. Plato and Aristotle anticipated Freud in their emphasis on: (p. 33)

   a. humane treatment.
   b. behavoir as motivated by "natural appetites" toward the attainment of pleasure and
       elimination of pain.
   c. the use of insanity as an excuse for crime.
   d. psychological factors, such as frustration and conflict, as causes of disturbed behavior.

4. The Greek physician Galen's most important contribution to abnormal psychology was his
    description of: (p. 34)

   a. the anatomy of the nervous system.
   b. medicinal herbs that could soothe mental patients.
   c. new treatments for the mentally disturbed.
   d. symptoms of common mental disorders.

5. The "Dark Ages" in the history of abnormal psychology began with the: (p. 34)

   a. "Black Death" of the fifteenth century A.D.
   b. death of Galen in 200 A.D.
   c. fall of Rome in the fifth century A.D.
   d. Roman monarchs around 100 A.D.

6. The physician who kept Greek and Roman medical concepts alive in Islamic countries after the fall of Rome was: (p. 34)

   a. Agrippa.   c. Asclepiades.
   b. Aristotle.   d. Avicenna.

7. The manual prepared by Sprenger and Kiaemer as a complete guide to the detection and punishment of witches was called the: (p. 40)
   a. *Summes Desiderantes Affectibus.*   c. *Deception of Demons.*
   b. *Mallus Maleficarum.*   d. *Discovery of Witchcraft.*

8. In 1584, Oxford-educated Reginald Scot wrote *Discovery of Witchcraft* in which he stated that: (p. 40)

   a. demons, devils and evil spirits did not cause mental disorders.
   b. mental disorders were caused by witches.
   c. the clery invented witchcraft.
   d. witchcraft was discovered by King James I.

9. The word *bedlam* originated from a(an):   (p. 41)

   a. ancient Greek term for "disturbance of biles."
   b. contraction for St. Mary of Bethlehem mental hospital.
   c. description of mass madness in the Middle Ages.
   d. practice of burning witches in their beds.

10. In 1780, treatment of mental patients at the Williamsburg, Virginia, hospital was designed to: (p. 42)

   a. force patients to leave.   c. save inmates' souls from hell.
   b. intimidate patients.   d. surround inmates with love.

11. An institution noted for kindness and humanity in the care of the mentally ill was: (p. 43)

   a. The Gheel Shrine, Belgium.   c. St. Mary of Bethlehem, London.
   b. La Maison de Charenton, Paris. d. San Hipolito, Mexico.

12. In 1805, Pierre was sent to La Bicetre mental hospital because of his bizarre delusions. Since this hospital was then administered by Philippe Pinel, he was probably treated:

(p. 43)

a. as a beast or prisoner.
b. by clerical exorcists.

c. by letting out his red bile.
d. in a humanitarian fashion.

13. The founder of American psychiatry is: (pp. 44-45)

a. William Turke.
b. Lightner Witmer.

c. Benjamin Rush.
d. Dorothea Dix.

14. Pinel and Tuke's moral management in mental hospitals was based on the idea that abnormal behavior is: (p. 45)

a. a result of sinful living.
b. due to possession of the devil.

c. related to an immoral balance of the humors.
d. the result of severe psychological stress.

15. All of the following are reasons that have been offered as explanations for the abandonment of moral therapy in the latter part of the nineteenth century except: (p. 46)

a. a rising tide of racial and ethnic prejudice.
b. overextension of hospital facilities.
c. general loss of faith among the general population.
d. belief that mental disorders would yield to physical solutions.

3

Biological, Psychosocial, and Sociocultural Viewpoints

OVERVIEW

The models of abnormal behavior are discussed in this chapter. The biological viewpoint focuses on irregularities in the biochemical functioning of the brain to explain mental disorders. Beginning with the work of two men, Pavlov and Freud, the psychosocial model has grown to include the psychoanalytic, behavioristic, humanistic, and interpersonal viewpoints. The sociocultural viewpoint reminds us that humans are social beings and our behavior cannot be fully understood without reference to the values and practices of the group in which we live. Previously, clinicians believed that they had to declare allegiance to one viewpoint or another, but it now widely recognized that no one model can adequately explain every aspect of every form of abnormal behavior. Consequently, one needs to assess and deal with the interaction of biological, psychosocial, and sociocultural factors to develop the total clinical picture.

LEARNING OBJECTIVES

1. Summarize the events that led up to the discovery that brain pathology could cause mental disorders and explain the difference between its answers to the "how" and "why" of causation.

2. Explain how Emil Kraepelin's Lehrbuch der Psychiatrie contained the forerunner of today's DSM-III-R classification system.

3. Compare some positive and negative consequences of the medical model of abnormal behavior and show how it was carried over into some nonbiological viewpoints on the nature of mental disorders.

4. Compare and contrast modern biological views of mental disorders with the early "brain pathology" point of view.

5. Summarize some of the findings of behavior geneticists that have increased our understanding of the causes of mental disorders.

6. Describe two types of biophysical therapy that arose in the 1930s and 1950s that have had a great impact on abnormal behavior.

7. Explain how mesmerism and the "Nancy school" became the early roots of psychoanalysis.

8. Describe several events in Sigmund Freud's professional career that moved him toward the development of psychoanalysis.

9. Describe the interaction of the id, ego, and superego in Freud's conception of personality.

10. Describe three sources of anxiety described by Freud and explain the function of the ego-defense mechanisms.

11. List and describe Freud's five stages of psychosexual development and their effects on personality.

12. Summarize some of the newer psychodynamic perspectives developed by Anna Freud, Melanie Klein, Margaret Mahler, and Otto Kernberg.

13. Describe two of Freud's most outstanding contributions to our understanding of normal and abnormal behavior, and list several criticisms of his approach.

14. Show how the discoveries of Ivan Pavlov, John Watson, and B.F. Skinner gave rise to the behavioral perspective on abnromal behavior.

15. Define each of the following and explain its importance for abnormal psychology: *classical conditioning, operant conditioning, reinforcement, generalization, discrimination, modeling, shaping,* and *learned drives.*

16. Contrast the focus of cognitive-behavior clinicians with that of the behavioristic therapists.

17. Explain three themes underlying the humanistic view of psychopathology, and summarize its impact on the field.

18. Explain how the work of Alfred Adler, Eric Fromm, Karen Horney, and Erik Erikson became the roots of the interpersonal perspective on psychopathology.

19. Describe the major features of Harry Stack Sullivan's interpersonal theory of personality.

20. List and describe several recent contributions of the social sciences and psychiatry to the interpersonal perspective and evaluate its impact on our views of psychopathology.

21. Explain the difficulties encountered in sociocultural research and summarize some findings that have helped us understand the impact of sociocultural forces on psychopathology.

22. Explain what is meant by an interdisciplinary approach to psychopathology and list three sets of determinants that may be considered.

23. Compare the advantages and disadvantages of adherence to a given theoretical position in the face of new viewpoints on psychotherapy and evaluate the adoption of an eclectic stance as a solution to such problems.

TERMS YOU SHOULD KNOW

paradigm shifts (p. 53)

eclectic (p. 54 and p. 88)

medical model (p. 55)

symptom-underlying cause point of view (p. 55)

neurological diseases (p. 56)

electroconvulsive therapy (ECT) (p. 57)

psychosocial (p. 58)

pyschoanalytic perspective (p. 58)

psychoanalysis (p. 58)

psychodynamic approaches (p. 58)

mesmerism (p. 59)

The Nancy School (p. 60)

cathartic method (p. 61)

unconscious (p. 61)

free association (p. 61)

id (p. 62)

life instincts (p. 62)

libido (p. 62)

death instincts (p. 62)

pleasure principle (p. 62)

primary process (p. 62)

ego (p. 62)

secondary processes (p. 62)

reality principle (p. 62)

superego (p. 62)

intrapsychic conflicts (p. 63)

anxiety (p. 63)

reality anxiety (p. 63)

neurotic anxiety (p. 63)

moral anxiety (p. 63)

ego defense mechanisms (p. 63)

unconscious (p. 63)

repressed (p. 63)

oral stage (p. 63)

anal stage (p. 63)

phallic stage (p. 63)

latency stage (p. 63)

genital stage (p. 63)

fixated (p. 63)

Oedipus complex (p. 64)

castration anxiety (p. 64)

Electra complex (p. 64)

introjection (p. 65)

object-relations (p. 66)

separation-individuation (p. 66)

behaviorism (p. 67)

conditioning (p. 67)

classical (or respondent) conditioning (pp. 67-68)

operant (or instrumental) conditioning (pp. 68-69)

unconditioned stimulus (p. 68)

unconditioned response (p. 68)

conditioned response (p. 68)

reinforcement (p. 69)

reinforcer (p. 70)

intermittent reinforcement (p. 70)

extinguishes (p. 70)

avoidance conditioning (p. 70)

generalization (p. 70)

discrimination (p. 70)

selective reinforcement (p. 70)

modeling (p. 71)

shaping (p. 71)

primary drives (p. 71)

secondary drives (p. 71)

systematic desensitization (p. 71)

behavior-modification techniques (p. 72)

humanistic perspective (p. 74)

self (p. 75)

interpersonal perspective (pp. 77-78)

significant others (p. 79)

"good me" (p. 79)

"bad me" (p. 79)

self-system (p. 79)

"not me" (p. 79)

personifications (p. 80)

social-exchange view (p. 80)

social roles (p. 80)

games people play (p. 80)

attribution theory (p. 81)

evaluations (p. 81)

expectations (p. 81)

interpersonal accommodation (p. 81)

cultural relativism (p. 84)

dramatization (p. 86)

epidemiology (p. 87)

high risk groups (p. 87)

prognosis (p. 87)

interdisciplinary approach (p. 87)

CONCEPTS TO MASTER

1. Biological, psychosocial, and sociocultural viewpoints
    a. Thomas Kuhn, an historian who focuses on scientific progress, has noted that theoretical orientations in science typically remain strong even in the face of contrary evidence or alternate explanations. A theory typically lasts until a fundamental insight is achieved that appears to resolve problems left unsolved by existing theories. The new insights, also called _____ shifts, are complete reorganizations of the way people think about a particular issue or field of science.   (p. 53)

    b. In the study of abnormal psychology, we are still awaiting a new fundamental insight. In the meanwhile, competing viewpoints exist. Therefore, the authors of the text have had to be _____, which means to select what appears to be best from various viewpoints. It is up to each student to select a particular preference, if any, after he or she becomes more knowledgeable about the field.   (p. 54)

2. The biological perspective
    a. The extreme biological viewpoint, held by many medical practitioners, states that abnormal behavior is the product of _____ in the brain or elsewhere in the central nervous system. In such a viewpoint, neither psychological factors nor the psychosocial environment of the individual are believed to contribute to the causes of mental disorder.   (p. 54)

    b. In 1845 William Griesinger published the first systematic presentation that insisted that all mental disorders could be explained by brain_____.
    Recent discoveries of the role of the spirochete in general paresis and work by _____ on senile psychoses enhanced the attractiveness of a biological view.   (p. 54)

    c. A dominant role in the early development of the biological viewpoint was played by _____ who developed a system of classification which was contained in his 1883 textbook. He looked upon each type of mental disorder as separate and distinct from the others and believed that the outcome of a given type of disorder could be _____ even if it could not yet be controlled. (p. 55)

d. These early biological successes in understanding mental disorders led to unfortunate consequences. They enhanced the belief that all mental disorders had an underlying physical cause and much of the psychiatric enterprise developed around a medical model which is now stubbornly entrenched. Unfortunately, we now know that the vast majority of abnormal behavior is not associated with physical damage to the brain. The medical model has also influenced psychosocial theorizing. Describe how it has done so.

(p. 55)

3. Modern biological thinking
   a. A patient has the delusion that he is Napoleon. The delusion is the impairment. The specific idea that he is Napoleon is the content of the impairment. How does this delusion reveal that biological causes must interact with experience?   (p. 56)

   b. Indicate whether the following statements about heredity and abnormal behavior are true or false: (pp. 56-67)

      1. Behavior is never determined exclusively by genes; rather biochemical processes are genetically programed and influence an organism's physical and behavioral adaptation to the environment.   TRUE OR FALSE

      2. There is evidence that heredity is an important determinant of some mental disorders such as depression, schizophrenia, and alcoholism.   TRUE OR FALSE

      3. Some behavioral differences are thought to be linked to sex hormone levels.
                                                                       TRUE OR FALSE

      4. Research by Pogue-Geile and Rose (1985) involving longitudinal study of identical twins disputed a genetic influence on personality dimensions including social maladjustment, depression, unusual thinking, and anxiety as measured by the Minnesota Multiphasic Personality Inventory (MMPI).   TRUE OR FALSE

   c. In earlier years, biological interventions had not proven successful at curing many patients. Then, beginning in the 1930's, a new biological therapy was introduced that produced significant behavioral changes. The therapy was called _____
   _____.   (p. 58)

d. How does ECT work?   (p. 58)

e. Describe the overall impact of biological thinking on our views of psychopathology.
(p. 58)

4.   The psychodynamic perspective
a. Who took the first systematic steps toward understanding psychological factors in
mental disorders?   (p. 58)

b. How is "mesmerism" related to the development of hypnosis?   (pp. 58-59)

c. Liebeault and Bernheim found that hypnosis "cured" a patient who had hysteria
for some time. What theory about hypnosis and hysteria did they develop as a
result?   (p. 60)

d. What was the impact of the widespread recognition that hysteria was a psychologically
caused disorder?   (p.60)

e. Freud developed the "cathartic method," using hypnosis differently from the French
doctors. How did Freud use hypnosis with his early patients?   (p. 61)

5. Basics of the psychoanalytic perspective
   a. Fill in the empty spaces in the following chart with the correct psychodynamic
      concepts.   (pp. 62-63)

Subsystem	Principle of Operation	Type of Thinking	Purpose	Type of Anxiety Generated
id	operates according to _____ principle	engages in mental images and fantasies referred to as _____ thinking	source of two types of instinctual drives: a._____ b._____	generates _____ anxiety that results from impulses, which if expressed, would be punished in some way.
ego	operates according to _____ principle	uses reason and intellectual resources to deal with external world, which is referred to as _____ _____ thinking	mediates between the _____ and the _____ in such a way as to insure that needs are met and survival assured	generates _____ anxiety that arises from threats in the external world
super-ego	operates according to _____ principle	mental representation of the taboos and moral values of society	operates through the _____ to inhibit desires that are considered wrong or immoral	generates _____ anxiety that arises from feelings of guilt

   b. Anxiety is a warning of impending danger as well as a painful experience, so it motivates
      people to do something about it. The ego can cope with anxiety in basically two ways.
      First, the ego can cope with anxiety by rational measures. If these are not effective or
      sufficient, the ego resorts to _____. These alleviate the
      painful anxiety, but they do so by pushing painful ideas out of consciousness, which
      leads to a distorted view of reality.   (p. 63)

   c. An important psychoanalytic concept is the unconscious. What types of memories,
      desires, and experiences exist in the unconscious?   (p.63)

desires, and experiences exist in the unconscious?   (p.63)

d.   An individual is unaware of unconscious material until it is expressed. How is it
     expressed?   (p.63)

e.   Freud viewed personality development as a succession of stages, each characterized
     by a dominant mode of achieving sexual pleasure. Fill in the empty spaces on the
     following chart regarding psychosexual stages.   (p. 63)

Stage	Ages	Source of Gratification
oral		
anal	2-3 years	
phallic		self-manipulation of the genitals
latency		
genital		

f.   Each stage of development places demands on the individual and arouses conflicts that
     must be resolved. One of the most important conflicts that occurs during the phallic
     stage is the Oedipus complex. Give the following information about it: (pp. 63-64)

     1.   What is the role of castration anxiety in the Oedipus complex?

     2.   What is considered to be its proper resolution if development proceeds normally?

     3.   Describe the Electra complex which is the female form of the Oedipus complex.

6. Newer psychodynamic perspectives
   a. Contemporary theorists including Freud's daughter Anna have further developed
      psychoanalytic thought. In contemporary psychodynamic approaches the focus in not on
      the ego or on the id. Rather it is on the _____.
      (p. 65)

   b. Object-relations theory is based on the concept of _____
      which refers to the incorporation into memory of symbols that represent images and
      memories of persons the child viewed with strong emotions.　　　(pp. 65-66)

   c. Describe the general notions of object-relations theory as developed by Melanie Klein
      and others in England.　　　　　　　　　　　　　　　　　　(p. 66)

   d. The work of Margret Mahler in the United States added insights to object-relations
      theory. Describe her concept of separation-individuation which is said to be essential
      for the achievement of a mature personality.　　　　　　　　　(p. 66)

   e. Otto Kernberg describes the result of poor early relationships which he labels the
      "borderline personality." What is the chief characteristic of the borderline
      personality and what is thought to be the cause of this condition?　　(p. 66)

7. Impact on our views of psychopathology
   a. Freud's views replaced brain pathology with exaggerated ego defenses against anxiety as
      the cause of at least some mental disorders. He greatly advanced our understanding of
      both normal and abnormal behavior. Two of his most noteworthy contributions were:
      (p. 66)

      1.

      2.

b. Eight major <u>criticisms</u> have been made of the psychodynamic perspective. Following are four of them. Fill in the remaining four. (p. 67)

  1. Psychoanalysts overemphasize the sex drive

  2. Undue pessimism about human nature

  3. Exaggeration of the role of the unconscious

  4.

  5.

  6.

  7.

  8. Therapy takes months, even years, and is very expensive

8. The behavioristic perspective
  a. Behavioral psychologists believe that the data used by psychoanalysts including material obtained by free association and dream analysis is unacceptable scientifically. What data do behaviorists prefer? (p. 67)

  b. The roots of the behavioristic approach can be traced to a Russian physiologist named _____, but the elaboration of the approach is credited to a young American psychologist named _____. (p. 67)

  c. Watson believed that if psychology were ever to become a true science, it must abandon the subjectivity of inner sensations and limit itself to what could be objectively observed. Thus, he changed the focus of psychology to the study of _____ behavior, an approach he called *behaviorism*. (p. 67)

  d. Watson focused his attention on stimulus conditions and their behavioral consequences. Two other psychologists, including E.L. Thorndike and _____ instead focused on the influences of behavioral consequences in producing certain outcomes. (p. 68)

  e. The book, *Personality and Psychotherapy*, written by John Dollard and _____ reinterpreted psychoanalytic theory in the terminology of classical and operant conditioning. This book laid the groundwork for an all-out behaviorist assault on psychodynamic doctrines. (p. 68)

9. Basics of the behavioristic perspective
    a. Place the following statements under the type of learning they describe: (pp. 68-69)

        1. Through conditioning, a response may come to be elicited by a wide range
            of stimuli.
        2. As we mature, this type of learning becomes more important.
        3. Many responses, particularly those related to fear or anxiety, are learned through
            this type of learning.
        4. In this type of learning, the response typically precedes the stimulus.
        5. As we grow, this type of learning becomes an important mechanism for
            discriminating the desirable from the undesirable.

        Respondent Conditioning   **Operant Conditioning**

        1.   1.

        2.   2.

                                                       3.

    b. A learned response is most difficult to extinguish when it has been established by
        what schedule of reinforcement? Circle the correct answer.   (p. 70)

        1. High rate of reinforcement

        2. Intermittent reinforcement

    c. Avoidance learning allows an individual to anticipate an adverse event and respond
        in such a way as to avoid it. A boy who has been bitten by a vicious dog may develop a
        conditioned avoidance response in which he consistently avoids all dogs. How does
        developing a phobia of dogs lessen anxiety?   (p. 70)

    d. Match the following terms and examples: (pp. 70-71)

        Term   **Example**

        1. discrimination   a. A person, previously bitten, avoid dogs.

        2. generalization   b. An occasional win at gambling keeps the
                                              behavior going.

        3. intermittent reinforcement   c. A person, beaten as a child by an authoritarian
                                              father, has an involuntary fear of anyone in
                                              authority.

4. reinforcement   d. A child performs a response that in the past produced candy.

5. negative reinforcement   e. A child performs a response that in the past avoided spanking.

6. avoidance conditioning   f. A child learns that only although red and green strawberries look somewhat similar, only red ones taste good.

7. shaping   g. A mute schizophrenic is reinforced for slight lip movements.

8. modeling   h. Children of parents who smoke, smoke at higher rates as adults than children of parents who don't smoke.

e. List some examples of the following types of drives: (p. 71)

Primary drives   **Secondary drives**

f. Since the 1950's, psychologists have "rediscovered the mind." What does this mean?
                                                                           (p. 71)

g. As a result, clinicians have simply shifted their focus from overt behavior to the underlying _____ assumed to be producing the behavior. Then, the clinical goal becomes one of altering maladaptive _____ rather than maladaptive behavior.   (p. 71)

10. Impact of behavioristic approach on our views of psychopathology
    a. Behaviorists believe that maladaptive behavior develops in two general ways. What are they?   (pp. 71-72)

        1.

        2.

b. Complete the following listing of the strengths and criticisms of behaviorism:

(p. 72)

Strengths

1. preciseness and objectivity

2.

3. demonstrated effectiveness

Criticisms

1. overly concerned with symptoms, ignores values and meaning

2.

3. generally, denies the possibility of choice and self-direction, although Bandura stated in 1974 that human beings do have a capacity for self-direction.

11. The humanistic perspective
    a. What is the focus of the humanistic perspective?   (p. 74)

    b. The humanistic approach has been called the third force in contemporary psychology. The humanistic approach, identified with the work of psychologists such as Gordon Allport, Abraham Maslow, and _____, recognizes the importance of learning and other psychological processes but it focuses, usually optimistically, on the future rather than on the past. How is the humanistic perspective in disagreement with: (p. 74)

        1. The behavioristic approach

        2. Psychoanalytic theory

    c. There are the three "underlying themes and principles" that characterize the humanistic approach. Complete this listing of them: (pp.75- 77)

        1. Emphasis on the concept of "self" as a unifying theme

        2.

        3.

d. The following statements are Carl Rogers' "propositions" about the self-concept. Fill in the missing words.   (p. 75)

1. Each individual exists in a private world of which the _____ is the center.

2. The most basic striving of the self is toward maintenance, enhancement, and _____ of the _____.

3. The individual reacts to situations in terms of the way he or she _____ them.

4. Perceived threat to the self is followed by _____.

5. The individual's inner tendencies are toward _____ and wholeness. Under normal conditions, we behave in rational and constructive ways.

12. Impact of the humanistic view on our views of psychopathology
    a. What has been the major impact of the humanistic approach on our thinking about abnormal behavior?   (p. 77)

    b. Humanists generally believe that psychopathology is caused by the blocking or distortion of natural tendencies toward_____.   (p. 77)

    c. The authors criticize the humanistic approach. Complete their set of three criticisms: (p. 77)

        1.

        2. Lacks scientific rigor

        3. Goals are grandiose

13. The interpersonal perspective
    a. Theorists who share an interpersonal perspective believe that abnormal behavior is best understood by analyzing a person's _____ both past and present.   (p. 78)

    b. The roots of the interpersonal perspective lie in the psychodynamic movement, but the views have been most fully developed by four theorists who rebelled from the Freudian mold including: (p. 78)

        1. Erik Fromm, who focused on dispositions that people adopt in their interactions.

2. Karen Horney, who vigorously rejected Freud's demeaning female psychology.

3.

4. Harry Stack Sullivan, who maintained that the term personality was best defined in terms of an individual's characteristic way of relating to others.

c. Harry Stack Sullivan believes that development proceeds through various stages, involving different patterns of _____.   (p. 79)

d. Sullivan believed that *personifications* determine how we perceive our current relationships. Personifications are developed in childhood. Describe how a child comes to label some of his or her personal tendencies as: (pp. 79-80)

   1. "Good me"

   2. "Bad me"

   3. "Not me"

e. Respond to the following questions regarding several other interpersonal theories:
                                                                    (pp. 80-81)

   1. The social exchange view (Thibault and Kelly, 1959) suggests that we form relationships with each other for what purpose?

   2. In relationships we each have *social roles* and *role expectations*. What are these?

   3. Berne has identified the "games people play." What are two purposes of "interpersonal games"?

   4. Why are the "attributions" we make important to make it possible to predict what we and others are likely to do in the future?

   5. When two persons evolve patterns of communication and interaction that enable them to attain common goals and meet mutual needs, the process is called

   _____.

14. Impact (of the interpersonal perspective) on our views of psychopathology
   a. The interpersonal perspective views unsatisfactory _____
       as the primary cause of maladaptive behavior.   (pp. 81-82)

   b. Supporters of the interpersonal perspective believe that it could be used to increase the
       reliability and validity of psychological diagnosis. How would this be accomplished?
                                                                         (p. 82)

   c. What is the focus of therapy from the interpersonal perspective ?   (p. 83)

15. Emergence of the the sociocultural viewpoint
   a. To demonstrate a convincing link between sociocultural factors and personality
       development, children would have to be randomly assigned to be reared in diverse
       circumstances. Yet, this type of controlled study is impossible. Why?   (p. 83)

   b. Cross-cultural research can be a substitute for laboratory studies but it is plagued
       with four difficulties. Complete the list of difficulties: (p. 84)

       1. Language and thought systems differ among countries

       2. Political and cultural climates may prevent objective inquiry

       3.

       4.

   c. Malinowski, in his book *Sex and Repression in Savage Society*, found little evidence
       among the Trobriand Islanders of oedipal conflict. He therefore concluded:
                                                                         (p. 84)

   d. This and other studies led to the formulation of "cultural relativism." Explain
       this doctrine.   (p. 84)

e. Is cultural relativism a widely accepted doctrine today? YES OR NO   (p. 84)

f. There are types of serious disorders found among all peoples of the world. What features lead behavior to be considered abnormal in any society?   (p. 84)

g. However, there is evidence that culture does influence the particular form a mental illness takes. For example: (p. 86)

    1. How do Irish and Italians differ in response to illness?

    2. Are strong guilt feelings always associated with depression in all parts of the world?

16. Sociocultural influences in our own society
    a. Respond to the following questions regarding the research of Faris and Dunham (1939), Jaco (1960), and others: (pp. 86-87)

    1. What did these researchers find about the relationship of schizophrenia and place of residence?

    2. Information about "high risks" can be learned from "epidemiological" studies such as this one including high risk areas, people, and _____.

    3. How can this information be used?

    b. Explain what Lennard and Bernstein (1969) meant by their comment, "Therapeutic or damaging potentials often inhere in social contexts rather than in individuals..."
        (p. 87)

17. Toward an interdisciplinary approach
    a. It is increasingly apparent that an interaction of biological, psychosocial, and sociocultural factors causes abnormal behavior. A viewpoint which integrates these factors is called the _____ approach.   (p. 87)

    b. What has been accomplished on a practical level by this approach?   (pp.87-88

18. Unresolved issues
   a. Describe the advantages of theoretical integrity, that is to say, adherence to one and only one systematic viewpoint.   (p. 88)

   b. Indicate the drawbacks of rigid adherence to a particular viewpoint which excludes other possible explanations.   (p. 88)

   c. Psychology is characterized by a confusing array of theories. Some psychologists have responded to this overabundance of perspectives by adopting a(an) _____ stance. This solution still falls short of the real need, however, which is to develop a single unified viewpoint that is both comprehensive and internally consistent and accurately reflects what we know to be true from past research.   (p. 88)

(19.)   Summary chart of ego defense mechanisms
        Place the ego defense mechanisms in the appropriate blanks in the following chart:
                                                                              (p. 64)

**acting out
denial of reality
fantasy
repression
rationalization
projection
reaction formation
displacement
intellectualization
undoing
regression
identification
compensation
splitting**

Ego Defense Mechanism   **Example**

1. _____   a. A student explains to the teacher why he has neglected studies for cultural pursuits.

2. _____   b. An office worker goes home and is unreasonably angry with her family after being criticized.

3. _____

    c. Man scheduled to be executed says, "So they'll kill me, and that's that."

4. _____

    d. "Conquering hero" and "suffering hero" are two common patterns.

5. _____

    e. A little boy reverts to bedwetting when the new baby comes home.

6. _____

    f. A student fails an examination and believes the teacher is to blame.

7. _____

    g. College grads are terribly upset if their college doesn't have a winning team.

8. _____

    h. Terminally ill persons go through a stage where they refuse to believe they are dying.

9. _____

    i. A soldier develops amnesia after seeing a friend killed.

10. _____

    j. People become zealous crusaders, often referred to as the "reformed sinner syndrome."

11. _____

    k. A child-abusing parent brings home presents.

12. _____

    l. Wilma Rudolph, crippled and unable to walk until she is eight years old, becomes an Olympic track winner.

13. _____

    m. A man does not recognize the individual qualities of women. Instead he views them as angels or whores.

14. _____

    n. Unhappy at work, a man cheats on his wife.

(20.) Some behavior modification techniques based on learning principles
Match the following three columns: (p. 74)

Technique	Learning Principle	Example
1. shaping	1. avoidance behavior	1. Physician gave himself a shock when he craved a drug

2. use of negative reinforcement	2. reinforcement to modify covert behavior	2. Child ate favorite food while a rabbit was in the background
3. cognitive re-structuring	3. reinforcement of successive approximations	3. Subjects learned what to say to themselves during anxiety-arousing situations
4. desensitization	4. an established behavior pattern is no longer re-inforced	4. Any degree of masculine behavior was rewarded in a feminine boy
5. withdrawal of reinforcement	5. conditions that evoke avoidance behavior are paired with positive stimuli	5. Parents showed children less attention when they engaged in self-injurious behavior

(21.)   The existential perspective
   a.   What does the existential perspective emphasize?   (p. 76)

   b.   How does this emphasis differ from the humanistic approach?   (p. 76)

   c.   What is the difference between the existential concepts of "existence" and "essense"?
      What creates our essence?   (p. 76)

   d.   What is the "will-to-meaning?"   (p.76)

   e.   Explain the significance of death in existential thinking?   (p. 76)

(22.) Toward an interpersonal diagnostic system
   a. Clemore and Benjamin (1979) argue that three serious flaws remain in DSM-III.
       What are they?   (p. 82)

       1.

       2.

       3.

   b. Describe how they suggest the dimensions of autonomy-interdependence, friendliness-
       hostility, and dominance-submission could be used to build a diagnostic system.
                                                                              (p. 82)

(22.) Unusual patterns of behavior that are considered to be culture bound
       Give descriptions and the countries in which each of the following disorders has
       been observed: (p. 85)

       1. Windigo

       2. Latah

       3. Amok

       4. Koro

       5. Kitsunetsuki

CHAPTER QUIZ

1. In most cases the discovery of the organic bases of mental disorders failed to address the _____ behind causation. (p. 55)

    a. how
    b. what
    c. where
    d. why

2. Emil Kraepelin's textbook, *Lehrbuch der Psychiatrie*, not only emphasized the importance of brain pathology in mental disorders, but also described a(an): (p. 55)

    a. method of brain dissection.
    b. system of classification.
    c. treatment for general paresis.
    d. type of senile psychosis.

3. Which of the following explains the relationship between genetics and abnormal behavior? (p. 56)

    a. Abnormal behavior is inherited from parents.
    b. Children learn mental disorders from their parents.
    c. Genes affect biochemical processes which alter behavior.
    d. Psychological trauma causes changes in the genes.

4. Joseph Breuer introduced the *cathartic method* of treating mental patients. It consisted of: (p. 61)

    a. asking hypnotized patients to talk freely about their problems.
    b. giving patients strong laxatives to clean out their systems.
    c. telling patients to scream until they felt relaxed.
    d. using a catheter to remove yellow bile.

5. According to Freud's psychoanalytic perspective, the source of all instinctual drives is the: (p. 62)

    a. ego.
    b. id.
    c. libido.
    d. superego.

6. Which type of anxiety is a signal to the ego that an unacceptable impulse is threatening to break out? (p. 63)

    a. reality anxiety
    b. neurotic anxiety
    c. moral anxiety
    d. free-floating anxiety

7. Margaret Mahler focused on the process by which children come to understand that they are different from other objects. This process involves a developmental phase called:

    (p. 66)

    a. assimilation-accommodation.
    b. introjection-identification.
    c. introversion-extroversion.
    d. separation-individuation.

8. The form of learning where an individual learns to achieve a desired goal is: (pp. 68-69)

    a. respondent conditioning.
    b. operant conditioning.
    c. modeling.
    d. avoidance conditioning.

9. Rewarding a behavior that is in the right direction even though it does not reflect the final form is: (pp. 70-71)

    a. intermittent reinforcement.
    b. generalization.
    c. discrimination.
    d. shaping.

10. The behavioristic tradition has been criticized for: (pp. 71-72)

    a. its precision and objectivity.
    b. its research orientation.
    c. failure to demonstrate effectiveness.
    d. overconcern with symptoms.

11. The major impact of the humanistic perspective on our views of psychopathology is its emphasis on: (p. 77)
    a. building one's courage to face frustration.
    b. moving people from maladjustment to adjustment.
    c. our capacity for full human functioning.
    d. replacing negative self-talk with positive self-cognitions.

12. Harry Stack Sullivan noted that we sometimes screen out of consciousness some especially frightening aspect of our self-experience and perceive it as: (p. 79)

    a. "bad me."
    b. "good me."
    c. "not me."
    d. "vulnerable me."

13. Research by Malinowski and Benedict concluded that what is considered abnormal in one society may be considered normal in another. This led to a(an) _____ position concerning abnormal behavior.   (p. 84)

    a. cultural relativism
    b. genetic transmission
    c. racial separatist
    d. universalized

14. Epidemiological studies which have linked psychopathology with social class are:

(p. 86)

    a.   based on controlled experimentation.
    b.   correlational in nature.
    c.   establishing a clear-cut cause-effect relationship.
    d.   good examples of analogue studies.

15. According to the authors, the problematic proliferation of diverse viewpoints about psychopathology can best be solved by:

(p. 88)

    a.   adhering to a single point of view for consistency's sake.
    b.   becoming an eclectic.
    c.   developing a unified point of view.
    d.   divorcing oneself from all major perspectives.

4

Causal Factors in Abnormal Behavior

OVERVIEW

The potentials for maladaptive outcome within the normal developmental process are discussed in depth in this chapter. A large number of research studies are introduced in the chapter to illustrate the current state of knowledge regarding biological, psychosocial, or sociocultural factors that may, directly or indirectly, cause various types of abnormal behavior. The chapter can seem overwhelming at first, because so many potential causal factors are discussed. Luckily, not all are applicable to any single client that one deals with clinically.

LEARNING OBJECTIVES

1. Define and differentiate between the following types of causes of abnormal behavior: *primary, predisposing, precipitating, and reinforcing.*

2. Explain how feedback and circularity can cause a vicious self-regulating system of abnormality.

3. Explain the two major components of the diathesis-stress model of maladaptive behavior.

4. Explain and illustrate two types of genetic endowment that may cause abnormal behavior.

5. Explain and illustrate three types of consititutional disability that can act as causes of maladaptive behavior.

6. Describe two types of brain dysfunction that can cause abnormal behavior.

7. Explain how deprivation of visceral needs and nonoptimal levels of stimulation may cause maladaptive behavior.

8. Describe five learning-based differences that make some children better prepared than others for further learning and personal growth.

9. List and illustrate six basic psychological strivings that characterize all of us and explain how the blocking of any of them may make us more vulnerable to abnormal behavior.

10. Explain how conflicts between biological needs and self-motives may contribute to maladaptive behavior, and show how a hierarchy of motives may limit this interaction.

11. Explain and illustrate ways that our construction of reality, unconscious aspects of motivation, and one's lifestyle may act as causes of maladaptive behavior.

12. Explain how institutionalization, deprivation in the home, and early trauma can be causes of abnormal behavior.

13. Explain the bidirectionality of parent-child relationships and describe six major inadequacies in parenting which may be causes of maladaptive behavior in children.

14. Describe five pathogenic family structures and explain how each may contribute to the causes of abnormal behavior.

15. List some advantages and disadvantages of juvenile peer relationships and summarize the results of research on the functions of popularity, status invariance, and rejection in producing maladaptive behavior in adulthood.

16. Explain and illustrate ways that the sociocultural environment shapes one's personality.

17. List and illustrate five types of societal influences that are especially potent causes of abnormal behavior.

18. Explain how current research methods in abnormal psychology make it difficult to clearly establish the causes of maladaptive behavior and summarize the problem that this presents for the clinician.

TERMS YOU SHOULD KNOW

vulnerabilities (p. 91)

etiology (p. 92)

primary cause (p. 92)

predisposing cause (p. 92)

precipitating cause (p. 92)

reinforcing cause (p. 93)

causal pattern (p. 93)

feedback (p. 94)

diathesis (p. 94)

diathesis-stress model (p. 94)

stress (p. 94)

stressor (p. 94)

genetic inheritance (p. 96)

chromosomal anomalies (p. 96)

faulty genes (p. 96)

autosomes (p. 96)

sex chromosomes (p. 96)

X chromosome (p. 96)

Y chromosome (p. 96)

Down's syndrome (p. 96)

trisomy (p. 96)

Klinefelter's syndrome (p. 96)

XO (p. 97)

XXX (p. 97)

Turner's syndrome (p. 97)

genetic faults (p. 97)

genes (p. 97)

Deoxyribonucleic acid or DNA (p. 97)

dominant gene (p. 98)

recessive gene (p. 98)

polygenetic (p. 98)

proband or index case (p. 98)

monozygotic (or identical) twin (p. 98)

concordance rates (p. 98)

constitutional (p. 99)

physique (p. 99)

congenital defect (p. 99)

low birth weight (p. 100)

primary reaction tendencies (p. 101)

neurotransmitter (p. 102)

steady states or homeostasis (p. 102)

hospitalism syndrome (p. 105)

cognitive map (p. 106)

self-identity (p. 106)

self (p. 106)

assimilated (p. 107)

accommodation (p. 107)

cognitive dissonance (p. 108)

effectance motivation (p. 110)

hierarchy of motives (pp. 110-111)

motive pattern (p. 111)

level of aspiration (p. 111)

parental deprivation (p. 112)

institutionalization (p. 113)

affectionless psychopathy (p. 113)

failure to thrive (p. 114)

parental rejection (p. 114)

psychic trauma (p. 115)

autistic (p. 116)

discordant family (p. 122)

disturbed family (p. 122)

marital schism (p. 122)

marital skew (p. 122)

disrupted family (p. 123)

inadequate family (p. 124)

antisocial family (p. 124)

social roles (p. 128)

androgyny (p. 128)

future shock (p. 132)

CONCEPTS TO MASTER

1. Causal factors in abnormal behavior
    a. All of us have vulnerabilities and could break down psychologically under some
        circumstances.   TRUE OR FALSE   (p. 91)

    b. Some respected scientists have suggested that severe mental breakdowns might often be
        due to bad luck in life.   TRUE OR FALSE   (p. 91)

2. Primary, predisposing, precipitating, and reinforcing causes
    Read the following vignette and determine the primary cause (if there is one),
    predisposing cause, precipitating cause and reinforcing cause of the
    husband's depression: (pp. 92-93)

    This is a story about a farm family with a husband, wife, and three teen-age children.
    They farm land that has been in their family for three generations although some of it
    was lost during the great depression when the husband was a boy. At the encouragement
    of the government, the family has borrowed money to buy more land and update their
    machinery. The result is $300,000. in debt.   Then farm prices fall and the money they
    receive for their crops no longer pays the interest debt. By taking a job in town, the
    husband brings in money that allows the family to get by but the livestock must be sold
    to settle back taxes. Finally, he becomes ill and has to quit working. One of the children
    who has left home returns to run the farm.   Although no serious physical disorder can
    be found, the husband continues for many months to suffer from fatigue and has lost
    interest in life.

3. Feedback and circularity ("vicious circles") in abnormal behavior
    Label the following diagrams with the appropriate term from the following:
                                                                                        (p. 94)

    cause and effect relationship , causal pattern, feedback loop

    1. A + B + C   =   condition Y   _____

    2.   _____

    3. X   condition Y   _____

4. A disthesis-stress model
    a. Fill in the same word in both blanks: Most mental disorders can be viewed as the
        product of stress operating on an individual who has a _____

for the particular type of disorder that emerges. Often the factors that contribute to the development of a _____ are in themselves potent stressors.

(p. 94)

b. One way of viewing vulnerability is as a lack of resources needed to overcome challenges.   TRUE OR FALSE (p. 94)

c. For causes within the person, the authors use the terms diathesis, vulnerability, or predisposition. For causes outside the person in his or her current life, the authors use the term_____.   (p. 94)

5. Genetic endowment
   a. A fertilized human egg contains 46 chromosomes arranged in 23 pairs. Twenty-two pairs, called _____, determine general anatomical and physiological characteristics. The remaining pair, called _____ chromosomes,   determines the individual's sex.   (p. 96)

   b. Name the conditions, mentioned in the text, that result from: (pp. 96-97)

      1. trisomy (extra chromosome) #21   _____

      2. extra X chromosome in a male child   _____

      3. missing or extra X chromosome in a female child _____

   c. What is the estimated incidence of gross chromosomal abnormalities in newborn babies?   (p. 96)

   d. Place the words *chromosome* and *gene* in the proper location on the following diagram.   (p. 96)

   1. _____   2. _____

e. Answer true or false to the following questions: (pp. 96-97)

   1. The risk of Down's Syndrome raises with the age of the father. TRUE OR FALSE

   2. Chromosomal irregularities have been found in schizophrenics. TRUE OR FALSE

   3. Females are less vulnerable to genetic defects than males.   TRUE OR FALSE

   4. Genes can affect behavior only indirectly.   TRUE OR FALSE

   5. The genetic influences on abnormal behavior mainly involve
      dominant and recessive genes.   TRUE OR FALSE

   6. Most pathogenic genetic influences operate polygenically.   TRUE OR FALSE

f. Most of the information we have concerning the role of faulty genes is obtained through the family history method. Explain how this method works. (p. 98)

g. How likely is it that a person with an identical twin who is schizophrenic will develop that disease? (p. 98)

h. Which is the *most likely* outcome in a genetically affected person, occurrence or nonoccurrence of the disorder? (p. 98)

6. Constitutional liabilities
  a. Two constitutional factors are bodily physique and physical attractivenss. Respond to the following questions about these factors: (p. 99)

   1. Describe the link, if any, between muscular physique and criminality.

   2. Is the frequency of mental disorder higher among unattractive people?

  b. Respond to the following questions regarding the research of Snyder, Tanke, and Berscheid (1977). (p. 99)

   1. What did these researchers do?

2. What results did they obtain?

3. What does this study suggest about the impact of constitutional factors?

c. How many babies are born with mental or physical handicaps per 100 live births? Although up to one-third of these defects are genetic, the cause of the defect is unknown in half or more of the cases. (p. 100)

d. Low birth weight (prematurity) is the most common birth difficulty associated with later mental disorders. What are the major factors known to place a fetus at high risk for prematurity? (p. 100)

e. An infant's sensitivity to stimuli, temperament, and activity level are examples of primary reaction tendencies. Respond to these questions related to this concept. (p. 101)

1. Recent research has indicated that certain cognitive, affective, and behavioral differences between men and women appear early in life. Summarize Pervin's (1978) conclusions on this matter.

2. Chess and her colleagues (1965) found that 7-10% of babies were "difficult." What is a "difficult baby" and how might such behavior increase vulnerability to maltreatment?

3. What happens if there is a poor fit between environment and a child's temperament?

f. Childhood disturbance is often followed by adult disturbance, though the specific problems in childhood are poor predictors of the nature of later adult adjustment difficulties. Is this statement an accurate summary of the authors' opinion? (p. 102)

7. Brain dysfunction
a. Excluding the 25% of mental retardates who acquire brain damage before birth or in childhood, how likely is organic brain pathology to be a factor in psychological

disturbances among younger people?   (p. 102)

b. At least 17% of persons above the age of 65 have significant brain damage, but only
_____ percent of persons above the age of 60 have psychiatric problems attributed
to organic pathology.   (p. 102)

c. Neurotransmitters are chemicals secreted in the presynaptic cleft of neurons. If there
is an appropriately coded receptor in the postsynaptic neuron (in other words, one that
is sensitive to that particular neurotransmitter substance), <u>the neurotransmitter
will cause either an increased or a decreased likelihood that the neuron will fire</u>.
Is the underlined portion TRUE OR FALSE?   (p. 102)

8.   Physical deprivation
     a. Describe what happens when subjects are deprived of sleep for 72-98 hours.
                                                                       (p. 103)

     b. Refer to the study by Keys (1950) using 32 conscientious objectors as subjects.

        1.   What was done?   (pp. 103-104)

        2.   What were the results?   (p. 104)

     c. Refer to the work of researchers such as Winick (1976) on malnutrition.

        1. What has been learned by autopsies about the impact of malnutrition during
           the first year of life on the physical development of the brain?   (pp. 104-105)

        2.   Are these effects permanent?   (p. 105)

        3.   In areas of the United States where most families live in poverty , what are the
             estimates of the extent of childhood malnutrition according to the U.S. Public Health
             Service?   (p. 105)

     d. Describe the results of understimulation on children such as may occur among children
        who are institutionalized at a young age.   (p. 105)

e. Describe the impact on health of overstimulation in adults such as may occur during periods of high life stress.   (p. 105)

9.   Self-perception and cognition
     a. Our "cognitive map" is the rules or assumptions that govern how we see the world. New information may be distorted in order to fit the rules. This process is called _____.   Alternately, in a process called _____ the rules may be changed as a result of the conflicting input. In fact, the self can be seen as a set of rules for processing information and for selecting behavior. If one's rules for processing differ from others, then one's perceived reality will differ. In fact,   Vallacher and associates have concluded, we look "through" the rules of the self--rarely "at" them.   (pp. 106-107)

     b. Mischel (1973) has observed several learning-based differences among young children that become apparent very early in development. Such learned differences make some children far better prepared than others for further learning and personal growth. These differences will endure through childhood and into the adult years where they continue to shape later learning. Describe how children may differ in:
                                                                              (p. 107)

          1.   Competence

          2.   Processing of information

          3.   Expectations

          4.   Experiences they seek

          5.   Coping with impulses

c.   The following chart summarizes the psychological requirements for healthy
      development. Briefly describe each requirement: (pp. 108-110)

Psychological Requirement	Description	Example
understanding, order, predictability		attempts by primitive people to describe the origin of fire
adequacy, competence, security		preference for jobs with security
love, belonging, approval		need for human contact increases as death approaches
self-esteem, worth, identity		undergoing sex change operations
values, meaning, hope		prisoners of war who lost hope and died
personal growth and fulfillment		wondering "Who am I?"

10. The self and motivation
    a.   White (1959) introduced the concept of _____ motivation to
          describe the seemingly universal need to overcome obstacles and to have effects on the
          world, even at the expense of biological satisfactions. This is an example of a
          psychological motive. The authors suggest that psychologists have underestimated the
          power of motives that relate to our psychological selves as opposed to our biological
          heritage.   (p. 110)

    b.   The following figure illustrates what Maslow has named the _____
          of needs. The central point of this figure is the following: The authors' statements about
          the power of psychological motives assumes that basic biological survival needs have
          been met. Where biological jeopardy exists, as it did in Nazi concentration camps,
          biological motives may assume preeminence that overwhelms considerations of

self-enhancement. In fact, biological needs may become so urgent that people regress from whatever level of civilized humanity that had previously been reached.

(pp. 110-111)

c. Brunner (1957) observed that our cognitive categories or "schema" are strongly influenced by current motive states. When motivation is very strong, considerable misinterpretation of consensual reality may occur. In addition, motives have both conscious and _____ aspects, so we may not always be aware of our reasons for doing things. (p. 111)

d. Some people are primarily concerned with love and relations with others with material possessions and power. These essential elements of an individual's life-style are referred to as his/her _____. When goals are far beyond an individual's capacity, we speak of an unrealistically high _____. Are motive patterns constant over time? (p. 111)

11. Early deprivation or trauma
    a. Describe the consequences of parental deprivation from each of the following theoretical viewpoints: (pp. 112-113)

       1. Freud (psychoanalysis): The consequences of parental deprivation are. . .

2. Sullivan (object-relations): The consequences of parental deprivation are. .

3. Skinner (behaviorism): The consequences of parental deprivation are. . .

4. Rogers (humanism): The consequences of parental deprivation are. . .

b. Respond to the following questions regarding the research of Provence and Lipton (1962) which focused on the effects of institutionalization.   (p. 113)

1. Which two groups of infants were compared in this study?

2. How did the two groups differ at one year of age?

c. Refer to other studies on institutionalization (such as Beres and Obers, 1950):
                                                            (p. 113)
1. What has been learned about the long-range effects of early parental deprivation?

2. What is a common syndrome found by Beres and Obers (1950) among children who were institutionalized before the age of one year?

d. Refer to the study of child abandonment by Burnstein (1981).   (p. 113)

1. He concluded that abandoned children were characterized by excessive levels of _____, _____, and _____.

2. What is the long-range prognosis for children suffering early and prolonged parental deprivation?

3. To what extent can early deprivation be made up for by abundant love at a later time?

e. Are "polymatric" children and children placed in day care at an early age as well adjusted as "momomatric" children?   (p. 113)

f. Which of the following groups of children represent the largest number of cases of severe parental deprivation?   (pp. 113-114)

    1. Children separated from parents

    2. Children cared for at home by their parents

g. Regardless of its specific nature or intensity, parental rejection has been associated with a specific pattern of development in victimized children. Describe the characteristics of adults who were rejected or severely abused as children according to: (p. 114)

    1. Pringle (1965)

    2. Yates (1981)

h. Why do parents reject and abuse their children?   (pp. 114-115)

i. Complete the following list of the three reasons the authors give to explain why psychic traumas in infancy or early childhood are especially damaging.   (p. 115)

    1. Conditioned responses are readily established in situations characterized by strong emotions

    2. Traumas result in emotional conditioning rather than cognitive learning

3.
j. Under what circumstances may traumatic events in childhood fail to have negative
    consequences?   (p. 115)

12. Inadequate parenting
    a. The parent-child relationship is bidirectional. How is the child's own temperament
        and personality an important determinant of the quality of the parent-child
        relationship?   (p. 116)

    b. Fill in the missing data in the following summary chart of faulty parent-child
        relationships.   (pp. 114-121)

Undesirable Condition	Effect on Child's Personality that May Increase Vulnerability to Abnormal Behavior
rejection (p. 114)	
	submissiveness, lack of self-reliance, dependence, low self-evaluation, some dulling of intellectual striving (pp. 116-117)
unrealistic demands (pp. 117-118)	
overpermissiveness/ indulgence (p. 118)	
overpermissiveness/lack of discipline (p. 119)	

fear, hatred of parent, little initiative
or spontaneity, lack of friendly feelings
toward others (p. 119)

inconsistent discipline (p. 119)

tendency toward confusion, lack of
integrated frame of reference, unclear
self-identity, lack of initiative, self-
devaluation (p. 120)

undesirable parental models
(p. 121)

c. Parents may overprotect children to gain satisfactions of needs not met through their
adult contacts. What kind of personal behaviors demonstrate "overprotectiveness"?
(pp. 116-117)

d. How does an overly indulged child act?   (p. 118)

e. How is a child subjected to overly severe punishment, high moral standards, and
severe restrictions likely to grow up?   (p. 119)

f. How does the child subjected to *physical*, as opposed to verbal, discipline often turn out? (p. 119)

g. Do children always (or often) grow up to show the undesirable behavior of their parents, according to studies such as Kadushin (1967)? (p. 121)

13. Pathogenic family structures
   a. Complete the descriptions of the following five pathogenic family structures by explaining how each may contribute to the causes of abnormal behavior: (pp. 122-124)

   1. The discordant family: One or both parents are not gaining satisfaction....

   2. The disturbed family: One or both parents behave grossly eccentric...

   3. The disrupted family: The family is incomplete...

   4. The inadequate family: The family is unable to cope...

   5. The antisocial family: The family has values not shared by...

b. It is estimated that at any one time over _____ percent of the population that has ever been married is divorced or separated according to Bloom, Asher, and White (1978).   (p. 123)

c. What have Bloom, et al., (1978) concluded about the impact of family disruption on development of mental disorders?   (p. 124)

d. How can absence of a father affect the development of girls according to Hetherington (1973)?   (p. 124)

e. Is there a small but significant tendency for adult depression scores to be higher among persons who were separated at an early age for whatever reason from either parent?   (p. 124)

f. How can the long-range effects of family disruption on children be minimized?   (p. 124)

14. Maladaptive peer relationships
    a. Fill in the missing information is the following list which summarizes the results of research on the functions of popularity, status invariance, and rejection in producing maladaptive behavior in adulthood: (pp. 126-127)

        1. Popularity: The most consistent personality characteristics associated with popularity are being seen as friendly and _____.

        2. Status invariance: The child's status within the peer group tends to become stable by the _____ grade. Stars remain stars and rejects remain rejects.

        3. Rejection-inducing behavior: Children who are most likely to be rejected have the following behaviors and characteristics:

    b. Peer social problems in childhood have been linked to a whole variety of breakdowns including schizophrenia, anxiety disorders, crime, and greater than average use of mental health services.   TRUE OR FALSE (p. 126)

15. Sociocultural environment
Certain social roles people can learn to adopt such as low masculinity have been linked with maladaptive behavior and vulnerability to disorder for either biological sex. An example of research that supports this conclusion is Baucom's (1983) study of high feminine sex-typed women. How did the high feminine sex-typed women in this study act? Baucom likens this behavior to learned helplessness and has suggested it is a causal factor for depression.   (p. 128)

16. Pathogenic societal influences
a. Explain the following statement: "An inverse correlation exists between social class and the prevalence of abnormal behavior."   (p. 129)

b. Schizophrenia is more frequent in the lowest social class. There are two alternate explanations for this relationship. Complete the following description of each explanation.   (p. 129)

1. Social drift: Schizophrenia is more common in the lowest social class because some persons may drift to ...

2. Social stress: Persons of lower socioeconomic class undoubtedly encounter more stressors in their lives and have fewer resources for dealing with them. Hence, the increased tendency for schizophrenia may be at least partly due to...

c. How did Zimbardo (1975) demonstrate that the role of prison guard is a "disorder engendering social role"?   (p. 130)

d. The authors suggest that predjudice and discrimination might be one of the factors that

explains the fact that women seek psychotherapy more frequently than men. Explain.
(p. 131)

    e. What happens to the rates of mental illness, suicide, and crime during periods of extensive unemployment? (p. 131)

17. Unresolved issues on causation
    a. What is the major impediment in our efforts to better understand the cause-effect relationships in abnormal behavior? (p. 132)

    b. Even "hard" scientists like physicists are recognizing the limitations of the experimental method which seeks the one cause that leads invariably to the observed effect.   TRUE OR FALSE
(p. 133)

(18.)   Season of birth--a puzzling vulnerability factor
In what months are the birth dates of schizophrenics disproportionately concentrated?
(p. 93)

(19.)   Predisposing causes of depressive reactions to rape
Describe the relationship between post-rape symptomatology and: (p. 95)
    a. Level of trauma during rape

    b. Post-rape level of support

    c. Level of prior functioning

(20).   Separation from parents as a traumatic experience
    a. Describe the three stages children two through five years of age go through when separated from their parents. (p. 116)

        1.

        2.

        3

    b.   At what age is a child most vulnerable to long-term separation or loss? (p. 116)

CHAPTER QUIZ

1.   The expression "the straw that broke the camel's back" could refer to the _____
     cause of abnormal behavior.   (p. 92)

    a. primary   c. precipitating
    b. predisposing   d. reinforcing

2.   In the diathesis-stress model of abnormal behavior, diathesis refers to _____
     causes.   (p. 94)

    a. precipitating   c. primary
    b. predisposing   d. reinforcing

3.   An example of a disorder caused by autosomal abnormalities is: (p. 96)

    a. Huntington's chorea.   c. .Klinefelter's syndrome.
    b. Down's syndrome.   d. Turner's syndrome.

4.   Most forms of mental disorder that are due mainly to faulty genes can be explained in terms
     of: (p. 98)

    a. dominant genes.   c. sex chromosomes.
    b. recessive genes.   d. polygenic inheritance.

5.   When a person has an inherited predisposition to a disease, the most likely outcome is
     that the individual will: (p. 98)

    a. develop the disorder.
    b. experience more stress than others.
    c. experience more stressors than others.
    d. not develop the disorder.

6.   About what percent of babies born in the United States have congenital defects?
                                                        (p. 99)

    a. 1   c. 5
    b. 3   d. 7

7.   Primary reaction tendencies are: (p. 101)

a. relatively enduring for one's lifespan.
b. exclusively caused by genetic factors.
c. exclusively caused by prenatal environment.
d. incorrectly called constitutional.

8. Thomas, Chess and Birch found that "dissonant stress" develops when: (p. 101)

a. a baby's temperament changes in a short time.
b. a poor "fit" exists between a child's temperament and environmental demands.
c. parents of difficult children were difficult babies themselves.
d. twins have different temperaments.

9. Studies of the effects of prolonged malnutrition in children concluded all of the following
   except their: (p. 104)

a. brain growth was stunted.
b. physical development was impaired.
c. regard for their parents decreased.
d. resistance to disease was lowered.

10. The self is both a set of rules for processing information and the _____
    of those rules.   (p. 106)

a. breaker   c. maker
b. evaluator   d. product

11. All of the psychological strivings listed by humanists may be considered routes to:
                                                     (p. 110)
a. love.   c. security.
b. meaning.   d. self-actualization.

12. Spoiled, selfish, and inconsiderate children are most likely to have had a background of
    parental: (p. 118)

a. inconsistency.
b. unrealistic moral standards.
c. overprotectiveness.
d. overindulgence.

13. A family in which one or both parents is not gaining satisfaction is called a(an)
    _____ family.   (pp. 122-123)

a. discordant   c. disturbed

b. disrupted

d. inadequate

14. The startling differences that Margaret Mead found between the Arapesh and Mundugumor
tribes of New Guinea were probably caused by: (p. 128)

a. genetic influences.
b. mental abnormalities.

c. religious beliefs.
d. social forces.

15. Which of the following probably accounts in part for the fact that more women than men
present themselves for treatment of emotional disorders?   (p. 131)

a. hormonal imbalances associated with menstruation
b. the passive, dependent roles traditionally assigned to women
c. the tendency of men to overprotect women from special stressors
d. the tendency of women to be more right-brain dominant

5

Stress and Adjustment Disorders

OVERVIEW

The chapter begins with a detailed discussion of stress, a topic of increasing concern as modern life becomes more and more pressured. An understanding of the potential sources of stress, the functional equivalence of biological, psychological, and sociocultural sources of stress, and the general strategies for coping with stressful demands is probably the single most relevant topic to the average person that is presented in this text.

The reactions of individuals to war, concentration camps, and civilian disasters are described and can be viewed as case studies of human functioning under levels of severe stress. The chapter describes the coping techniques used by individuals in these situations and the symptoms that appear as coping techniques fail to eliminate the stress. It will seem unbelievable when reading about some of the incidents that there were *any* people who could cope without developing severely abnormal behavior. The practical implications of this chapter are seen in applications such as attempts to prepare people who will face stressful situations, such as surgery, to cope more effectively.

LEARNING OBJECTIVES

1. List, describe, and illustrate three categories of stressors which make demands on us.

2. Describe and illustrate three factors which influence the severity of stress.

3. Differentiate between *chronic* and *acute* life stressors and indicate one way these have been measured.

4. Differentiate between *task-oriented* and *defense-oriented* reactions to stress and describe five ego-defense mechanisms that are examples of the latter.

5. Describe two major effects of severe stress and explain biological, psychological, and sociocultural decompensation.

6. Describe some adjustment disorders which are reactions to unemployment, bereavement, divorce, and forced relocation.

7. List three stages of the "disaster syndrome" and explain the causes and treatment of chronic or delayed posttraumatic stress that may develop in the last stage.

8. Summarize the statistics on combat exhaustion and psychiatric discharges in World Wars I and II, the Korean War , and cite three reasons why these traumatic reactions were markedly   decreased in the Vietnam War.

9. List and illustrate some of the clinical symptoms of combat stress and describe some of the biological, psychosocial, and sociocultural factors responsible for this disorder.

10. Explain how the principles of immediacy, proximity, and expectancy were used to treat combat exhaustion in the Korean and Vietnam Wars and describe several long-term effects of the trauma of military combat.

11. Describe the "DDD Syndrome" manifested by POW's during the Korean War and list two factors that influenced the severity of the reactions of Vietnam POW's to their confinement.

12. Describe some of the reactions of concentration camp survivors and explain why the validity of many of these reports is questionable.

13. Summarize Janis' research on psychologically preparing patients to undergo dangerous surgery and describe a three stage type of stress innoculation used by cognitive-behavioral therapists.

14. Describe ways in which the post-traumatic stress syndrome has been used in both criminal and civil court cases.

15. State the legal precedent that has been established thus far for a "stress defense" and give some illustrations which show that considerable room for interpretation still exists.

TERMS YOU SHOULD KNOW

stress (p. 138)

stressor (p. 138)

eustress (p. 138)

distress (p. 138)

frustration (pp. 138-139)

conflict (p. 139)

approach-avoidance conflicts (p. 139)

double-approach conflicts (p. 139)

double-avoidance conflicts (p. 139)

pressures (p. 140)

stress tolerance (p. 142)

chronic (p. 143)

acute (p. 143)

crisis (p. 143)

life events scales (p. 145)

task-oriented (p. 145)

defense-oriented (pp. 145-146)

denial of reality (p. 146)

repression (p. 146)

emotional insulation (p. 147)

intellectualization (isolation) (p. 147)

regression (p. 147)

decompensation (pp. 147-148)

general adaptation syndrome (p. 149)

alarm reaction (p. 149)

stage of resistance (p. 149)

vigilance (p. 150)

recompensation (p. 150)

adjustment disorders (p. 151)

post-traumatic stress disorder (p. 151)

acute (p. 151)

chronic (p. 151)

delayed onset (p. 151)

uncomplicated bereavement (p. 154)

disaster syndrome (p. 157)

shock stage (p. 157)

suggestible stage (p. 157)

recovery stage (p. 157)

panic (p. 162)

combat exhaustion (p. 164)

startle reactions (p. 165)

immediacy (p. 170)

proximity (p. 170)

expectancy (p. 170)

duty-expectant attitude (p. 170)

doing role (p. 170)

sick role (p. 170)

Debility, Dependency, and Dread ("DDD") (p. 175)

reentry problem (p. 176)

CONCEPTS TO MASTER

1.   Adjustive demands and stress
     a. Adjustive demands, also known as _____, create effects
         within an organism that are known as stress.   (p. 138)

b. The following is a list of types of stressors. Match each type with the example that correctly illustrates it: (pp. 138-141)

Type of Stressor

1. frustration

2. approach-avoidance conflict

3. double-avoidance conflict

4. double-approach conflict

5. pressure

Example

a. A "mixed blessing dilemma" in which some positive and negative features must be accepted, no matter what the decision such as a black judge who is offered a membership in a discriminatory club.

b. A plus-plus conflict, choosing between two desirable alternatives such as deciding between a trip to Las Vegas or Reno

c. Finals week with a part-time job, studying, and social obligations.

d. Finding out that the women's basketball team must travel four to a room, but the men's team has only two per room.

e. A minus-minus conflict, choosing between two undesirable alternatives such as being given the choice to go on a diet or die.

2. Factors influencing the severity of stress
   a. How is the severity of stress gauged or measured? (p. 141)

   b. On what factors does the actual degree of disruption depend? (p. 141)

      1. At the biological level

      2. At the psychological level

c. The nature of the stressor is known to influence the degree of disruption that occurs. Indicate how each of the following factors about a stressor may relate to the degree of disruption that may result. (p. 141)

1. The importance of the stressor to the individual's life

2. The length of time the stressor operates

3. The number of stressors operative at any time

d. The severity of disruption experienced is also related to the individual's perception of the stressor, stress tolerance, and external resources and support. Indicate whether severe or minimal disruption may be expected under the following circumstances: (p. 141)

1. New adjustive demands that have not been anticipated by the individual and for which no ready-made coping patterns are available.

2. Adjustive demands placed upon a person with marginal previous adjustment.

3. Adjustive demands confronted by a person with a supportive spouse, close extended family, and strong religious traditions.

3. Individual stressor patterns over time
   a. Why are "crises" especially stressful? (p. 143)

   b. The authors estimate that a crisis occurs in the life of the average person once every _____. (p. 144)

   c. How can the outcome of a crisis affect a person's subsequent adjustment? (p. 144)

d. Life events scales are a method to measure the number of life changes currently active in a person's life. Research on life events has been extensive but the method has been severely criticized by Monroe. Indicate his views on the limitations of life events measurement. (p. 145)

4. General principles of reactions to stress
   Place the following reactions to stress in the appropriate space to indicate the level at which they operate: (p. 145)

   1. learned coping patterns
   2. immunological defenses against disease
   3. group resources such as religious organizations
   4. self-defenses
   5. damage-repair mechanisms
   6. support from family and friends

Levels of Coping	Reactions to Stress
1. biological level	1. 2.
2. psychological-interpersonal level	1. 2.
3. sociocultural level	1. 2.

5. Defense-oriented reaction patterns
   a. Two types of defense mechanisms are described in the text. What are they? (p. 146)
      1. Psychological damage repair mechanisms such as crying and repetitive talking

      2. _____ mechanisms which function to relieve anxiety

   b. In what three ways do defense mechanisms protect the individual from internal and external threats? (p. 146)

      1.

2.

3.

c. Place the following ego defense mechanisms in the appropriate blanks: denial of
    reality, repression, emotional insulation, intellectualization, regression.
                                                                          (pp. 146-147)

Ego defense mechanism	Example
_____	An American hostage in Iran thinks, "This isn't happening to me."
_____	After a young woman dies people tell her husband, "Well, she lived a full life."
_____	An unemployed person becomes apathetic and resigned.
_____	A child who has just gotten a new brother says, "Feed me like a baby, Mom."
_____	A soldier cannot remember any details of the battle in which his friend was killed.

d. Defense mechanisms are learned, automatic, habitual reactions designed to deal with
    inner hurt and anxiety. As such they serve useful self-protective functions. However,
    when they become the predominant way of coping with stress, they are considered
    maladaptive. In what way are defense mechanisms maladaptive?   (p. 147)

6. Decompensation under excessive stress
    a. Stress is a fact of life. However, stress can be damaging. Describe how severe stress:
                                                                          (p. 148)

        1. Lowers adaptive efficiency

2. Lowers resistance to other stressors

3. Causes wear and tear on the organism

b. Davidson and Baum (in press) studied the effects of stress over a 5-year period among residents at Three Mile Island and in a control community. Describe their findings.
(p. 148)

c. Personality decompensation under extreme stress appears to follow a course resembling biological decompensation, which consists of three stages: alarm and mobilization, resistance, exhaustion and disintegration.
Provide the missing information in the chart below that describes the behavior of the individual during each stage.
(pp. 149-150)

Stage	Behavior of Organism
alarm and mobilization	
	use of task-oriented and defense-oriented coping. Indications of strain appear and the individual may become rigid and cling to ineffective coping patterns.
stage of exhaustion	

d. The authors note the signs of sociocultural decompensation. Are any of these signs detected in present day American life?
(p. 150)

7. Psychological disorders and stress
    a. The DSM-III-R provides for the rating of current stress on Axis IV. In addition, it contains two relevant diagnostic categories: adjustment disorder and posttraumatic stress disorder. Both of these disorders occur in response to identifiable stressors. What is the key difference between them? (pp. 150-151)

    b. There are several subclasses of adjustment disorder that are defined by the predominant symptom. Give examples of these subclasses. (p. 151)

    c. In posttraumatic stress disorder the stressor is _____, or outside the realm of typical experience. (p. 151)

    d. Give specific examples of symptoms for each of the general symptom categories that typify posttraumatic stress disorder. (p. 151)

        1. Persistent reexperiencing of the traumatic event. Example:

        2. Individual avoids stimuli associated with the trauma. Example:

        3. Persistent symptoms of increased arousal. Example:

    e. Explain the difference among the following forms of posttraumatic stress disorder. (p. 151)

        1. Acute posttraumatic stress disorder

        2. Delayed onset posttraumatic stress disorder

        3. Chronic posttraumatic stress disorder

8. Adjustment disorders: reactions to difficult life stressors
    a. Describe the negative impact of chronic unemployment. (p. 154)

b. Janis (1969) provides a description of the process of uncomplicated bereavement. Provide the missing information in his observations. (p. 154)

The first reaction to death of a loved one is _____. Then feelings of _____overwhelm us, sometimes punctuated by brief periods of _____. This phase ends by the time of the funeral. The next two or three weeks are characterized by _____ _____. After a month or two the most acute symptoms begin to subside, but there may still be_____.

c. Many factors make a divorce or separation unpleasant and stressful for everyone concerned. List some of these factors. (pp. 155-156)

d. Describe the trauma associated with being forced to flee your homeland. (p. 157)

9. Reactions to catastrophic events
   a. Over half of the survivors of the disastrous Cocoanut Grove nightclub fire required treatment for psychological shock. All of the survivors of the collison of two jet planes on Santa Cruz de Tenerife Island suffered from serious emotional problems. A "disaster syndrome" has been observed among victims that has been divided into three stages. Fill in the following chart with the behavior that is typical of each stage. (p. 157)

Stage	Behavior Observed
shock stage	
suggestible stage	
recovery stage	

   b. If a person who underwent a terrifying experience were to exhibit symptoms that endured for weeks, months, or even years, posttraumatic stress reaction would be diagnosed. Complete the following information regarding the symptoms of posttraumatic stress disorder: (pp. 157-160)

1. anxiety, commonly associated with

   _____

2. tension often accompanied by _____

3. repetitive nightmares which reproduce the trauma either _____
   or _____

4. impaired concentration and memory

5. depression

c. The intensity of the trauma reaction seems to depend on the suddenness of the disaster. Explain the function served by the symptoms caused by stress during each stage of reaction.   (pp. 161-162)

   1. Shock stage symptoms: stunned, dazed, numbed. These symptoms appear to protect....

   2. Stage of suggestibility : symptoms result from.....

   3. Stage of recovery symptoms: recurrent nightmares and need to talk about the disaster. These symptoms appear to be mechanisms for...

   The anxiety that often accompanies the recovery stage appears to stem from the realization that...

d. Contrary to popular opinion, panic is not common following a civilian disaster. Panic, defined as acute fear and flight, occurs only under certain specific circumstances including: (p. 162)

e. What type of treatment is usually sufficient to lead to rapid alleviation of the symptoms of posttraumatic stress?   (p. 162)

f.   There is disagreement over the percentage of disaster victims who require treatment. Kingston and Rosser (1974) estimated that _____ percent required treatment. Parker (1974) found that _____ percent of the victims showed symptoms of disorder.   (p. 162)

10. Traumatic reactions to military combat

a.   According to the government figures presented in your text, the percent of soldiers who suffered combat exhaustion decreased in each successive war from World War II to Vietnam. According to government claims, _____ percent of soldiers experienced combat exhaustion in Vietnam.   (pp. 164-165)

b.   What are the reasons given to account for the decreases in the number of soldiers who experienced combat exhaustion in Vietnam?   (p. 165)

c.   The clinical picture in combat exhaustion differs among the services. Common symptoms among combat troops have been dejection, weariness, hypersensitivity, sleep disturbances, and tremors. How does the clinical picture differ among air corps personnel?   (p. 165)

d.   Laufer, Brett, and Gallops (1985) surveyed 251 Vietnam veterans who varied in combat exposure. Having participated in abusive violence was found to be correlated with the following symptoms: (p. 165)

e.   What are usually the first symptoms of combat exhaustion?   (p. 165)

f.   The common core of all combat reactions is overwhelming _____ which is less severe among wounded soldiers compared to nonwounded soldiers. Why is this true?   (p. 166)

g.   Biological factors that may increase the likelihood of combat exhaustion are severe climatic conditions, malnutrition, and disease which lower a soldier's physical resistance to stressors. Do constitutional differences in vigor, temperament, and sensitivity also figure into the prediction of vulnerability to combat exhaustion?   (p. 167)

h.   The psychosocial factors that may contribute to the overall stress load of soldiers are fear and anxiety, strangeness and unpredictability, the necessity of killing, length of combat duty and personal characteristics. Respond to the following questions about these psychosocial factors: (pp. 168-169)

1. The recurrent nightmares experienced as part of combat exhaustion may serve a purpose. What is it?

2. Sometimes soldiers are in a stupor or have amnesia. What purpose would these symptoms serve?

3. Is it true that some people find it psychologically impossible to kill another person?

4. What did Merbaum and Hefez (1976) find about the role of previous psychological adjustment in determining a soldier's vulnerability to combat exhaustion?

i. General sociocultural factors that play an important part in determining an individual's adjustment to combat include clarity and acceptability of war goals, identification of the soldier with his/her unit, *esprit de corps* (in other words, cohesiveness and morale), and quality of leadership. Respond to the following questions about sociocultural factors and combat exhaustion: (pp.169- 170)

1. What would be the purpose of teaching military officers to foster group identification among soldiers?

2. What is the result of fostering hatred of the enemy among soldiers?

j. In most cases, combat exhaustion can be quickly treated by warm food, sedation to promote sleep, and brief therapy. The lessons learned in World War II about effective treatment procedures were : Immediacy, proximity, and expectancy. Complete the following explanations of each of these treatment concepts:
(p. 170)

a. Immediacy:

b. Proximity:

c. Expectancy: This term refers to both a duty expectant attitude and to the emphasis of a doing role as opposed to a sick role.

k. There are residual, or long-lasting, effects of stress . Complete this list of the six
    most common feelings Shatan (1978) found in his study of veterans being treated for
    posttraumatic stress: (p. 171)

    1. Guilt feelings

    2.

    3.

    4.

    5.

    6. Mistrust of others and doubts about whether one really loves those people close to
        him or her

l. Complete the following summary statement about the results of studies such as that by
    DeFazio, Rustin, and Diamond (1975) and Penk (1982) that have compared the
    present adjustment of combat and noncombat veterans: (p. 173)

    The adjustment problems of combat veterans may be seen more in their personal
    relationships than in their _____.

m. Refer to Rosenbeck's (1986) study of the "continuing legacy " of Vietnam.
    Describe what he did and what he found in this study.   (p. 173)

11. Reactions of prisoners of war and concentration camp survivors
    a. Describe the meaning of the terms that make up the expression "DDD syndrome" which
        was seen in POWs during the Korean war?   (p. 175)

        1. Debility:

2. Dependency:

3. Dread:

b. Ursano and colleagues (1981) conducted an evaluation of 325 air force officers who had been prisoners of war in North Vietnam. Describe their findings regarding:

(p. 175)

1.   Frequency of psychiatric diagnoses

2.   Effect of length of imprisonment

c. What is the "re-entry" problem?   (p. 176)

d. The following is a summary of the residual damage found among survivors of Nazi concentration camps and POWs.   Why is it problematic to conclude that survivors of concentration camps carry serious psychological scars as several studies (e.g. Krystal, 1968) have suggested?   (p. 176)

1.   Elevated illness and death rates: Returning POWs from World War II compared to non-POWs had nine times the death rate from T.B and twice as many deaths from cancer, heart disease, and suicide.

2.   Long-term adjustment problems: Psychological scars so deep that they may be transmitted to the survivor's children.

12. Prevention of stress disorders
    a. Janis (1958) studied students before and after surgery. Respond to the following questions about his work: (p. 178)

1.   What did he learn about the relationship of preoperative fear and postoperative adjustment?

2.   How does Janis explain the importance of the "work of worrying" to postoperative adjustment?

b. Meichenbaum and Cameron (1983) have developed a cognitive-behavioral approach which is called "stress-innoculation training" to prepare individuals for stressful events. Describe the methods employed during each of the phases on the following chart: (p. 178)

Phase	Techniques
first	
second	
third	

13. Unresolved issues
    How is the posttraumatic syndrome being used in civil court cases involving compensation and personal injury? (p. 179)

(14.) Measuring life stress
    a. What is an "LCU"? (p. 149)

    b. What happens if a person accumulates more than 300 LCUs in one year? (p. 149)

(15.) Mt. St. Helen's and the Disaster Syndrome
    a. Dohrenwend and Egri (1981) are among those researchers who find clear evidence of mental disorders among individuals who experienced a severe stress but who were normal prior to the disaster. This evidence has been critized by psychologists such as Depue and Monroe (1986) who claim that.... (p. 159)

    b. In response to the above criticism, describe the epidemiological study of the persons victimized by the eruption of Mt. St. Helens (Shore, Tatum, & Vollmer, 1986). (p. 159)

(16.)   Aftereffects of rape
   a.   Discuss how each of the following variables are thought to affect a woman's response
        to rape: (p. 160)

        1.   Relationship to the offender

        2.   Age

        3.   Marital status

   b.   Describe the coping behavior of the rape victim during the following phases of
        response to rape: (p. 160)

        1.   Anticipatory phase

        2.   Impact phase

        3.   Posttraumatic recoil phase

        4.   Reconstitution phase

   c.   What features of the victim determine the severity of postrape aftereffects?
                                                                                   (p. 160)

(17.)   Counseling for disaster workers
         Following a plane crash in San Diego, many police officers, but few relatives of victims,
         sought counseling services. What reasons accounted for the high usage of counseling by
         police officers, a group usually resistant to psychological intervention?   (p. 163)

(18.)   Residual effects of combat exhaustion among outpatients at a VA clinic
         Describe the residual symptoms among combat veterans who experienced combat
         exhaustion compared to combat veterans who did not experience combat exhaustion.
                                                                              (p. 172)

(19.)   Failure to readjust after captivity: a case of diathesis or stress?
    a.   Selkin and Loya (1979) conducted a "psychological autopsy." What kind of
         information is needed for this type of inquiry?   (p. 177)

    b.   What were the psychologists' conclusions regarding the cause of Jerry L's suicide?
                                                                              (p. 177)

    c.   How were their conclusions similar to the reasons the police officer in San Diego
         sought counseling during the air crash clean-up?   (p. 177)

CHAPTER QUIZ

1. Which of the following terms refers to an adjustive demand on a person?   (p. 138)

    a. distress   c. stress
    b. eustress   d. stressor

2. Working at a job that was unfulfilling would probably lead to feelings of: (pp. 138-139)

    a. conflict.   c. pressure.
    b. frustration.   d. defensiveness.

3. A person wants to accept a party invitation because he is very social but is concerned
    because there will be a lot of drinking and he is a member of the AA (Alcoholics Anonymous).
    He is experiencing a(an):   (pp. 138-139)

    a. mixed blessing dilemma.   c. double-avoidance conflict.
    b. approach-avoidance conflict.   d. double-approach conflict.

4. In which of the following levels of reaction to stress are one's learned coping skills?
                                                                              (p. 145)
    a. biological   c. psychological
    b. political   d. sociocultural

5. Which of the following defense-oriented behaviors is of the damage-repair type?

(p. 146)

    a. denying   c. mourning
    b. intellectualizing   d. repressing

6. An unhappily married woman is asked at the maternity ward to give her name. She is unable momentarily to remember her married name but can give her maiden name. Her behavior might reveal the defense mechanism of: (p. 146)

    a. denial of reality.   c. regression.
    b. repression.   d. emotional insulation.

7. When coping resources are already mobilized against one stressor, they are:(p. 148)

    a. made stronger for coping with others.
    b. not available for coping with others.
    c. shifted immediately to the new stressors.
    d. unaffected by additional stressors.

8. In studying the effects of the nuclear incident at Three Mile Island, Davidson and Baum found even five years later a higher incidence (when compared to a control community) of all of the following except: (p. 148)

    a. elevated blood pressure.
    b. elevated levels of urinary norepinephrine.
    c. major depression.
    d. posttraumatic stress disorder.

9. The alarm and mobilization stage of personality decompensation under excessive stress is characterized by: (pp. 149-150)

    a. emotional arousal, increased tension, alertness.
    b. exaggerated and inappropriate defense measures.
    c. lowering of integration.
    d. rigidity as the individual clings to accustomed defenses.

10. During bereavement, semi-dazed behavior punctuated by attacks of irritability and anger are most typical: (p. 154)

    a. for several days immediately after the loss.
    b. for 2-3 weeks after the funeral.
    c. for 1-2 months after returning to work.
    d. up to one year after the loss.

11. In a study of 251 Vietnam veterans in 1985, Laufer, Brett, and Gallops concluded that the most severe psychopathology developed in those who: (p. 165)

    a. participated in abusive violence in combat.
    b. suffered debilitating physical injuries.
    c. were exposed to abusive violence in combat.
    d. were exposed to combat.

12. Which of the following biological causes of combat stress do we know the most about?
                                                                                   (p. 167)
    a. constitutional differences in sensitivity
    b. differences in temperament
    c. differences in vigor
    d. the conditions of battle that tax a soldier's stamina

13. In a 1975 study of Vietnam veterans who were making a satisfactory readjustment to civilian life, DeFazio, Rustin, and Diamond found that the most frequently reported symptom was: (p. 173)

    a. difficulties with emotional closeness.
    b. frequent nightmares.
    c. many fears.
    d. worries about employment.

14. The "DDD" syndrome exhibited by POWs during the Korean war stood for: (p. 175)

    a. debility, dependency and dread.
    b. decadence, disease and departure.
    c. decide, delay and death.
    d. decline, decay and demise.

15. Inmates of concentration camps in World War II showed greater use of which of the following ego-defense mechanisms?   (p. 175)

    a. denial and emotional isolation
    b. projection and intellectualization
    c. rationalization and overcompensation
    d. regression and repression

6

Anxiety-Based Disorders (Neuroses)

OVERVIEW

This chapter covers several behavior patterns that had, in the past, been called *neuroses.* Although treated as separate disorders in the DSM-III-R, many psychologists believe that many of these disorders are similar in that they are driven by anxiety. These disorders are usually of mild to moderate intensity and seem to be related to faulty learning of anxiety-avoidance methods. In most cases, the disorders are episodic in nature with dramatic symptoms occurring only during periods of high stress. However, in between flare-ups of symptoms, these individuals are less happy and less effective than they could be if they learned more appropriate coping behavior. Individuals with these disorders respond well to psychotherapy or behavior therapy and rarely require hospitalization. The chapter contains a detailed description of the clinical picture, causal pattern, and treatment of anxiety, somatoform, and dissociative disorders.

LEARNING OBJECTIVES

1. Describe the principal manifestation of anxiety disorders and summarize their relative occurrence among men and women.

2. Describe the symptoms of panic disorders and agoraphobia and explain why they are considered together.

3. List and define several simple phobias and describe the major manifestations of phobias as a class.

4. Summarize the major manifestations of obsessive-compulsive disorders and explain why they are considered maladaptive.

5. Compare and contrast symptoms of a generalized anxiety disorder and a panic disorder. Explain why the former is sometimes difficult to distinguish from a personality disorder.

6. Describe the major manifestations of somatoform disorders and explain why your text does not describe dysmorphic somatoform disorders in this section.

7. Describe the major manifestations of somatoform disorders and distinguish it from hypochondriasis.

8. Describe the major manifestations of hypochondriasis and explain why it may be viewed as a certain type of interpersonal communication.

9. Characterize an idiopathic pain disorder and explain why patients with this disorder often become physically disabled.

10. Describe the major manifestations of a conversion disorder and describe some sensory, motor, and visceral symptoms that often appear.

11. Compare the psychological functions of conversion disorders and dissociative disorders and explain why the text's coverage of the latter is brief.

12. List and describe four types of psychogenic amnesia and explain why fugue is considered in the same section.

13. Describe the symptoms of multiple personality and explain why some may be considered genuine and others fraudulent.

14. Describe the symptoms of a depersonalization disorder and distinguish it from feelings of depersonalization that sometimes occur with personality deterioration.

15. Define *neurotic style* and give two reasons for discussing it here rather than with "personality disorders."

16. Describe three related characteristics of persons adopting a neurotic style and explain how three types of inhibition may be involved.

17. Explain why people with neurotic styles often have difficulties interacting with others and show how mutually neurotic couples may get along quite well.

18. Explain and illustrate how biological, psychosocial and sociocultural factors cause and maintain anxiety-based disorders.

19. Describe some biological and psychological therapeutic approaches that have been successful in treating anxiety-based disorders.

20. Explain why your authors are only "loosely committed" to the anxiety-defense model for explaining anxiety-based disorders.

21. Explain why your authors are surprised that anxiety-based disorders don't cure themselves and indicate their speculation about the reason.

TERMS YOU SHOULD KNOW

neurosis (p. 183)

anxiety (p. 183)

anxiety disorder (p. 184)

agoraphobia (p. 185)

phobia (p. 186)

simple phobia (p. 186)

social phobia (p. 188)

obsession (p. 189)

compulsion (p. 189)

obsessive-compulsive disorder (p. 189)

generalized anxiety disorder (p. 192)

soma (p. 197)

functional (p. 197)

somatization disorder (p. 197)

hypochondriasis (pp. 197-198)

idiopathic pain disorder (p. 199)

hysteria (p. 199)

conversion disorder (pp. 199-200)

anesthesia (p. 200)

analgesia (p. 200)

paresthesia (p. 200)

astasia-abasia (p. 201)

aphonia (p. 201)

mutism (p. 201)

belle indifference (p. 201)

malingering (p. 202)

mass hysteria (p. 203)

dissociative disorder (p. 203)

amnesia (pp. 203-204)

psychogenic amnesia (pp. 203-204)

multiple personality (p. 206)

coconscious personality (p. 206)

depersonalization (p. 208)

neurotic style (p. 209)

aggression/assertion inhibition (pp. 210-211)

responsibility/independence inhibition (p 211)

compliance/submission inhibition (p. 211)

intimacy/trust inhibition (pp. 211-212)

anxiety-defense (p. 213)

meta-analysis (p. 216)

electrosleep (p. 216)

biofeedback-induced muscle relaxation (p. 216)

individual psychotherapy (p. 216)

behavior therapy (p. 216)

guided exposure (p. 217)

cognitive mediation (p. 218)

multimodal therapy (p. 219)

repetition compulsion (p. 220)

CONCEPTS TO MASTER

1. Introduction
    a. What was the original meaning of the term *neurosis* as introduced by Englishman
        William Cullen?   (p. 183)

    b. Later, Freud suggested that neurosis stemmed from intrapsychic conflicts. Complete the
        missing words in Frued's definition. Neurosis is the outcome of an inner
        _____ involving an unbearable _____ and
        prohibitions against its expression.   (p. 187)

    c. Freud's overall views on the nature of neurosis have come under attack as too
        theoretical.   In what way is his work too theoretical?   (p. 184)

    d. The DSM-III-R classification is theoretically neutral and abandons the use of the term
        neurosis. In its place are three general classes of symptoms. List these classes.
                                                                                 (p. 184)
        1.

        2.

        3.

e. The authors of the text have chosen to retain the term neurosis. In part, their decision is based on their hesitancy to reject automatically anything psychodynamic. In addition are lingering doubts in their mind that ..... (p. 184)

2. Anxiety disorders
a. Anxiety disorders are those in which unrealistic, intense, irrational fear is the principal symptom. Anxiety disorders are relatively common. According to the results of the New Haven-Baltimore-St. Louis Epidemiologic Catchment Area program, one form of anxiety disorder was the most common psychiatric disturbance among women and the second most common among men. Which form of anxiety disorder was it? (p. 184)

b. Anxiety disorders, which include panic, phobic, and obsessive-compulsive disorders, are thought to affect _____ million persons in the entire U.S. population. (p. 184)

3. Panic disorder and agoraphobia
a. Panic disorder is characterized by the occurrence of one or more unexpected _____ not triggered by an actual or threatened harm by another person. (p. 184)

b. To qualify for the diagnosis of panic disorder, an individual must have four panic attacks during a four-week period. Although a panic attack typically subsides within a few minutes, they are very frightening. The symptoms of panic attack include ... (pp. 184-185)

4. Other phobic disorders
a. A phobia is a persistent fear of some specific object or situation that presents no actual danger to the person or in which the danger is _____ _____. In the DSM-III-R , the label applied to these symptoms is *simple phobia*. (p. 186)

b. What types of symptoms can phobic individuals show in addition to their phobias? (p. 187)

c. Regardless of how they begin, phobias are reinforced in two ways. First, they are reinforced by the reduction in anxiety that occurs each time the individual avoids the feared situation. Second, phobias may be maintained by *secondary gains* which are .... (p. 187)

d. Over the years, some phobias remain fairly circumscribed, while others have a tendency to _____. (p. 188)

e. A *social phobia* is typified by "stage fright." List the two criteria for the diagnosis of social phobia. (p. 188)

1.

2.

5. Obsessive-compulsive disorder
a. What is the incidence of obsessive-compulsive disorder according to the Epidemiologic Catchment Area study? (p. 189)

b. What content is particularly common for obsessive thoughts to involve?
(p. 189)

c. The performance of the compulsive act or series of acts usually brings a feeling of reduced tension and satisfaction. What happens if a person with obsessive-compulsive disorder is prevented from performing the compulsive act? (p. 190)

d. Why is obsessive-compulsive behavior considered maladaptive? (p. 190)

e. A large proportion of obsessive-compulsive individuals are found to be unusually preoccupied with issues of _____ . (p. 190)

6. Generalized anxiety disorder
a. Generalized anxiety disorders are characterized by chronic, unrealistic, excessive worry of at least six months duration that does not appear to stem from any particular cause. This type of anxiety is referred to as _____ anxiety.
(p. 192)

b. Complete the following list of the symptoms characteristic of individuals suffering from generalized anxiety disorder. (pp. 192-193)

1. Strained posture, overeaction to sudden noise, nervous movements

2. Oversensitive in personal relationships and feel inadequate and depressed

3.   Physical symptoms including...
4.   No matter how well things seem to be going,...

7.   Somataform disorders
    a.   Sincere somatic symptoms that are thought to represent an anxiety-based neurotic pattern and for which no organic basis can be found are referred to as
_____.   (p. 197)
    b.   Complete the following list of the four distinct somatoform patterns covered in the text:

        1.   Somatization disorder

        2.   Hypochondriasis

        3.

        4.

8.   Somatization disorder
    a.   This disorder is characterized by multiple complaints of physical ailments over a long period, beginning before age _____ that cannot be attributed to physical disorder, illness, or injury.   (p. 197)

    b.   There are 35 symptoms that qualify as possible indicators of somatization disorder. To qualify, the symptoms must have been severe enough to require one of three courses of action. Complete this list of qualifications for a symptom to be considered:
                                                                            (p. 197)
        1.   Contacting a physician

        2.   Using medication

        3.

9.   Hypochondriasis
    a.   A hypochondriac's visit to the doctor has been humorously called an "organ recital." Describe the characteristic behavior of such individuals.   (p. 197)

    b.   Describe the typical attitude toward their illnesses among hypochondriacal patients.
                                                                            (p. 198)

c.   The authors believe that hypochondriasis can be viewed as an interpersonal strategy which results when an individual has learned to view illness as way to obtain special consisderation and avoid responsibility.   Complete the following statements typical of hypochoncriacal adults: (p. 199)

   1.   I *deserve* your attention and concern

   2.

10. Idiopathic pain disorder
   a.   Idiopathic pain disorder is characterized by severe pain anywhere in the body, except headaches, lasting at least six months for which no physical basis can be found. Even without an organic basis, many pschogenic pain sufferers eventually end up truly disabled. How does this result occur?   (p. 199)

   b.   Sometimes psychogenic pain sufferers have a mild injury or physical problem to which they trace their pain. How do the authors of the text view such organic causes?   (p. 199)

11. Conversion disorder
   a.   Freud used the term conversion hysteria because he believed that the symptoms were an expression of repressed sexual energy that was converted into a bodily disturbance. This view is no longer accepted. Rather, the physical symptoms are now viewed as serving a defensive function, enabling the individual to _____
_____without having to
_____.   (pp. 199-200)

   b.   Compared to the higher incidences in the past, how frequent are conversion disorders today?   (p. 200)

   c.   Why are these disorders decreasing in frequency?   (p. 200)

   d.   Ironside and Batchelor (1945) studied hysterical visual symptoms among airmen in World War II. Persons with hysterical deafness really cannot hear or see.

TRUE OR FALSE (pp. 200-201)
e. Hysterical motor symptoms such as paralysis are usually confined to a single limb.

TRUE OR FALSE (p. 201)

f. Mutism is the most common conversion disorder of speech.

TRUE OR FALSE (p. 201)

g. The authors discuss four ways in which conversion symptoms differ from actual physical illnesses. Complete the following list of the differences: (pp. 201-202)

1. *La belle indifference*, which is...

2. Failure of the hysterical dysfunction to conform to the symptoms of known diseases

3.

4.

h. How can you distinguish a person with conversion symptoms from a *malingerer*, that is a person who is consciously faking an illness? (pp. 202-203)

i. Place the following events in the development of a conversion disorder in the proper causal sequence: Under continued stress, the symptoms of illness appear; A desire to escape an unpleasant situation; A wish to be sick to avoid the situation. (p. 203)

1. _____

2. _____

3. _____

j. What determines the particular symptoms the person prone to conversion disorder will develop? (p. 203)

k. Can a conversion reaction occur after an accident in which the victim hopes to obtain compensation? (p. 203)

12. Dissociative disorders
   a. Dissociative disorders, like somatoform disorders, are ways of avoiding stress while gratifying _____ in a manner that permits the person to deny

personal _____ for his or her behavior.(p. 203)
   b.   The dissociative disorders consist of four different patterns. What are they?

(p. 203)

   1.   Psychogenic amnesia

   2.   Fugue states

   3.

   4.

13. Psychogenic amnesia and fugue
   a.   Amnesia is partial or total inability to recall or identify past experience. If it is due to
        brain disorder, the amnesia usually involves an actual failure of retention. In such
        cases, the memories are truly lost. In _____amnesia,
        the forgotten material is still there beneath the level of consciousness and can be
        recalled under hypnosis or narcosis.   (pp. 203-204)

   b.   Label the following descriptions of four forms of psychogenic amnesia using the
        following terms: localized amnesia, selective amnesia, generalized amnesia,
        continuous amnesia.   (p. 204)

Forms of Psychogenic Amnesia   **Definition**

_____   In this form of amnesia,the individual remembers
                                     nothing that happened during a specific
                                     period--usually the first few hours following
                                     some traumatic event.

_____   In this form of amnesia, the individual forgets
                                     some but not all of what happened during a given
                                     period.

_____   In this form of amnesia, an individual cannot
                                     recall events beyond a certain point in the past.

_____   In this form of amnesia, the individual forgets
                                     his or her entire life history.

   c.   Psychogenic amnesia is highly selective. What type of material is most likely to be
        forgotten?   (p. 204)

   d.   How is the pattern in psychogenic amnesia like that in conversion reaction?

(p. 204)

e   Kiersch (1962) found the _____ percent of amnesia cases among military
personnel were due to deliberate suppression of memories.   (p. 204)

f.   How do the authors of the text describe the personalities of people who experience
psychogenic amnesia?   (p. 205)

14. Multiple personality
a.   Multiple personality is rare. Only about 100 cases have been described but oddly, the
prevalence of this disorder seems to be increasing. Multiple personality is a
dissociative reaction, usually due to stress, in which the individual manifests two
usually dramatically different _____.   (p. 206)

b.   Describe the various types of relationships that may exist between the different
personalities in an individual who exhibits multiple personalities.   (p. 206)

c.   We all have many conflicting and warring tendencies and frequently do things that
suprise ourselves and others. How are "deep-seated conflicts between contradictory
impulses and beliefs" involved as a causal factor in multiple personality?
(p. 206)

15. Depersonalization disorder
In mild forms, depersonalization, or the loss of the sense of self, is a common
experience and no cause for alarm.   In individuals who experience depersonalized
states, functioning in between episodes is usually normal except for anxiety and fear of
_____.   (p. 208)

16. Is there a "neurotic style"?
a.   Abondonment of the concept of neurosis may be premature because it has research and
clinical support and remains a useful way for conceptualizing many behaviors. There
has never been a precise equivalent to the concept of neurotic style in the formal DSM
categories. These styles are symptomless ways of coping with _____.
(p 209)

b.   Even though neurotic styles are symptomless, the authors have included them in the chapter because many individuals who seek the services of mental health practitioners are more troubled by their unsatisfactory _____ than by specific clinical symptoms.   (p. 209)

17. The role of inhibition in neurotic styles
    a. Neurotic styles have three characteristics. Complete the following list:(p. 210)

        1. Behavioral deficits: behaviors that would be expected to be adaptive do not occur.

        2. A tendency to behave with inflexibility and in an exaggerated manner.

        3.

    b. Complete the following chart that summarizes four inhibition patterns common to neurotic styles that can be seen in our own culture: (pp. 210-212)

Inhibited Behavior System	Description	Neurotic Symptoms
aggression/assertion inhibition		hypertension, compulsive behavior
responsibility-independence inhibition		agoraphobia
	individuals deny impulses to comply or submit	defiance, noncompliance, dangerous risk taking
	individuals experience unusual anxiety over forming close attachments	

18. Interpersonal aspects of neurotic styles
    a. Individuals who adopt neurotic styles can create not only frustration and misery for themselves but also serious problems for persons with whom they interact. Describe the relationships typical among neurotic individuals.   (p. 212)

    b. How can interpersonal relationships be affected if the two individuals have complementary neurotic styles?   (p. 212)

19. Development and maintenance of neurotic behaviors
  a. Pollin et al. (1969) studies the concordance rates of neurotic behavior among identical and fraternal twins in the military. (p. 213)

     1. What did they find?

     2. Did they conclude that their results supported genetic causation of neurosis?

  b. The following are possible biological causes of neurosis. Check those areas that appear promising avenues of research. (p. 213)

     1. Sex

     2. Age

     3. Glandular functioning

     4. Ease of conditioning of the anxiety response

  c. What model of the etiology of neuroses does the following diagram illustrate?(p. 213)

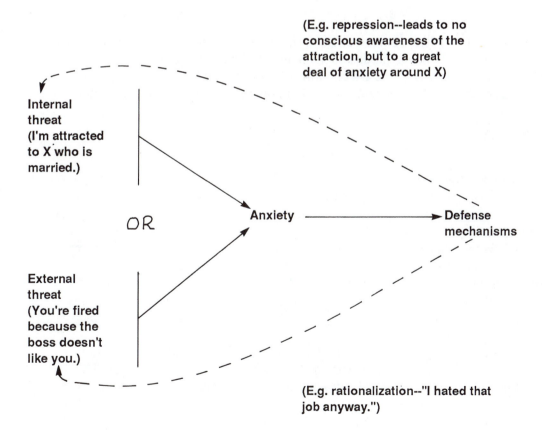

d. In addition to the anxiety-defense model of neurotic behavior that is illustrated above, there are three other general psychological causes of neurotic behavior listed by the authors. Complete the following description of how these causes contribute to the development of neurotic behavior.   (pp. 213-215)

1. Faulty learning: Irrational fears could be learned by simple conditioning, observational learning, and modeling. Ost and Hugdahl (1981) found that among 106 adult phobic patients questioned about the origin of their fears, 58% cited.....

2. Blocked personal growth: Lack of meaning and blocked personal growth often appear to stem from...

3. Pathogenic interpersonal relationships: Parents who overprotect or indulge their children may prevent them from...

e. That cultural factors influence neurotic behavior is demonstrated by the lack of such behavior among some native groups such as the aborigines of the Australian western desert. In our own society, there are differences in neurotic behavior across social classes. Describe the neurotic behaviors found relatively more frequently among:
                                                                                            (p. 215)

1. Upper-class persons

2. Lower-class persons

20. Treatment and outcomes
    a. How much better off is the average neurotic who has received psychotherapy compared to neurotics who haven't received treatment according to the Andrews & Harvey's (1981) meta-analysis of 81 controlled studies?   (p. 215)

    b. Approximately _____ percent of neurotic patients obtain symptom relief from drugs.   However, for many persons, drugs merely mask the symptoms. How is this viewed as detrimental to patients by the authors of the text?   (p. 216)

c. All individual psychotherapy with neurotic individuals aims to develop self-understanding, a realistic frame of reference, a satisfying pattern of values, and the development of effective techniques for coping with adjustive demands. Achievement of these objectives by psychotherapy faces a number of stumbling blocks. Complete the following list of obstacles: (p. 216)

1. Establishing a relationship in which the neurotic person feels safe enough to...

2. Provide opportunities for learning new...

3. Helping transfer what has been learned in therapy to...

4. Changing conditions in real life that may be...

d. Two behavioral therapies for neurotic behavior are controlled exposure and cognitive mediation. While cognitive therapies usually focus more on modifying _____ and pure behavior therapy usually focuses more on the removal of _____ , the outcomes of these two forms of therapy are often comparable.   (p. 219)

e. Indicate the percentage of neurotic persons who: (pp. 219-220)
    _____ percent benefit from psychotherapy for neurotic behavior.
    _____ percent decompensate into psychosis.

21. Unresolved issues
    a. What do the authors suggest has to happen before the controversy surrounding the concept of neurosis will be resolved?   (p. 220)

    b. Freud attributed the persistence of neurotic behavior to "repetition compulsion." What is an alternative explanation?   (p. 220)

(22.) Cognitive and motor behavior patterns in obsessive-compulsive disorders
    Give an example of each of the following forms of obsessive-compuslive symptoms:
    a. Ruminations   (p. 191)

    b. Cognitive ritual

    c. Motor ritual

    d. Compulsive avoidance

(23). Symptoms of generalized anxiety disorder
    Give two examples for each major class of symptoms of generalized anxiety disorder.
    a. Motor tension   (p. 196)

    b. Autonomic hyperactivity

(24.) Frequency of symptoms in 100 cases of generalized anxiety disorder
    List three symptoms that occured in more than 80% of cases.   (p. 196)
    a.

    b.

    c.

(25.) Qualifying symptoms for the diagnosis of somatization disorder
    Below are listed the organ systems in which symptoms may qualify for diagnosis of
    somatization disorder. Give an example of a symptom for each system.   (p. 198)
    a. Gastrointestinal

    b. Pain

    c. Cardiopulmonary

    d. Conversion or pseudoneurological

    e. Psychosexual

    f. Female reproductive

(26.)   Conversion reactions in student naval aviators
    a.   What did Mucha and Reinhart (1970) do?   (p. 202)

    b.   What were the background characteristics of their subjects?   (p. 202)

   c. What three factors did these researchers emphasize to account for the development of conversion symptoms among these subjects? (p. 202)

   1.

   2.

   3.

(27.) Treatment of obsessive-compulsive disorder with exposure and response-prevention
Steketee and Foa (1985) describe the treatment of obsessive-compulsive disorder as consisting of two phases: exposure treatment and response prevention. Describe what the therapist did during each phase. (p. 218)

   a. Exposure treatment

   b. Response prevention

CHAPTER QUIZ

1. In 1985, the National Institute of Mental Health estimated that between _____ percent of the adult population of the United States suffers from some anxiety-based disorder. (p. 183)

   a. 2 and 7   c. 16 and 24
   b. 8 and 15   d. 25 and 32

2. All phobic behaviors are reinforced by: (p. 187)

   a. increased self-esteem.   c. repetition.
   b. reduction in anxiety.   d. sympathy from others.

3. An irresistible impulse is called a(an): (p. 189)

   a. compulsion.   c. hallucination.
   b. delusion.   d. obsession.

4. A large proportion of obsessive-compulsive individuals have been concerned about issues of _____ long before their symptoms appeared. (p. 190)

   a. cleanliness   c. death
   b. control   d. suicide

5. Generalized anxiety disorder differs from other neurotic patterns in its: (p. 192)

    a. degree of disability.   c. lack of sleep disturbances.
    b. lack of avoidance mechanisms.   d. level of anxiety.

6. Which of the following is characterized by a multiplicity of physical compliants not restricted to any coherent symptom pattern and unrealistic fears of disease?   (p. 197)

    a. somataform disorder   c. psychogenic pain disorder
    b. hypochondriasis   d. conversion reaction

7. A hidden message in the compliants of the hypochondriacal adult is: (p. 199)

    a. "I am terribly anxious about dying."
    b. "I can do things as well as you even though I'm sick."
    c. "I deserve your attention and concern."
    d. "You make me sick."

8. Aphonia is: (p. 201)

    a. inability to speak.   c. a grotesque, disorganized walk.
    b. ability to talk only in a whisper.   d. pseudopregnancy.

9. Belle indifference would be expected in cases of: (p. 201)

    a. malingering.   c. conversion disorder.
    b. hypochondriases.   d. psychogenic pain disorder.

10. All of the following are part of a chain of events in the development of a conversion disorder except: (p. 203)

    a. a conscious plan to use illness as an escape.
    b. a desire to escape from an unpleasant situation.
    c. a fleeting wish to be sick in order to avoid the situation.
    d. the appearance of the symptoms of some physical ailment.

11. Dissociative disorders are methods in which individuals avoid stress by: (p. 203)

    a. escaping from their core personalities.
    b. projecting blame for their "sins" on others.
    c. separating themselves from significant others.
    d. withdrawing from stressful situations.

12. In _____ amnesia, the individual forgets his/her entire life history.

(pp. 203-204)

   a. localized   c. generalized
   b. selective   d. continuous

13. If two neurotics form a relationship on the basis of complimentary patterns and one
    partner experiences effective therapy, the outcome is usually: (p. 212)

   a. a reduction in the anxiety of the other partner.
   b. disruption of the relationship.
   c. strengthening of the relationship.
   d. termination of the neurotic patterns of both partners.

14. The biological factors involved in the development of neurotic behavior: (p. 213)

   a. clearly include differences in temperament.
   b. have been identified as glandular in nature.
   c. have not been delineated.
   d. include genetic predispositions.

15. A meta-analysis done by Andrews and Harvey revealed that the average neurotic client
    who had received treatment was more functional than nearly _____ percent of
    comparable disordered, untreated control clients.   (p. 215)

   a. 40   c. 80
   b. 60   d. 90

7

Personality Disorders

OVERVIEW

In this chapter several specific disorders of personality are discussed. With these disorders we encounter, for the first time, behavior that is not episodic and that, generally, is not exacerbated by stress. Rather, the personality disorders represent ingrained "life-styles" or characteristic patterns that are maladaptive of meeting the individual's needs. Often, the person with a personality disorder ends up imposing on other people's rights in order to obtain his or her goals. Chapter 7 includes descriptions of the various types of personality disorders, their causal patterns, and their treatment.

LEARNING OBJECTIVES

1. Define *personality disorder* and explain four special problems that may cause misdiagnoses in this category.

2. Describe six clinical features that all personality disorders seem to have in common.

3. List and describe the general characteristics of three clusters of personality disorders and note two additional disorders that appear in DSM-III-R.

4. Describe and differentiate among the following personality disorders in Cluster I: paranoid, schizoid, and schizotypal.

5. Describe and differentiate among the following personality disorders in Cluster II: histrionic, narcissistic, antisocial, and borderline.

6. Describe and differentiate among the following personality disorders in Cluster III: avoidant, dependent, compulsive, and passive-aggressive.

7. Describe and differentiate between the following personality disorders which appear in DSM-III-R: self-defeating and sadistic.

8. Explain why we know comparatively little about the causal factors in personality disorders

and summarize what we do know about the biological, psychological, and sociocultural factors that seem implicated.

9. List several reasons why personality disorders are especially resistant to therapy and describe Mulvey's treatment strategy for persons who are already too dependent.

10. Describe four criteria that must be met before an individual is diagnosed as an antisocial personality, according to DSM-III.

11. List and describe five characteristics that are typical of antisocial personalities in general.

12. List and explain several biological, family, and sociocultural factors that may cause the development of an antisocial personality.

13. Explain why most individuals with antisocial personalities seldom come to the attention of mental hospitals and clinics and evaluate the success of traditional psychotherapy in treating this disorder.

14. List and describe three steps which Bandura recommends to modify antisocial behavior of individuals with antisocial personalities.

15. List three conclusions which Vaillant reached about the effective treatment of individuals with antisocial personalities.

16. Identify and explain two major problems that make Axis II diagnoses quite unreliable and describe two solutions offered by the authors.

TERMS YOU SHOULD KNOW

personality (p.223)

personality disorder or character disorder (p. 233 and p. 225)

learned coping patterns (p. 226)

paranoid personality (p. 227)

schizoid personality (pp. 227-228)

schizotypal personality (p. 228)

histrionic personality (p. 229)

CONCEPTS TO MASTER

1. Introduction
   a. Healthy adjustment throughout life is primarily a matter of flexibly adapting to
      _____ at each life stage.   (p. 223)

   b. Tension and defense mechanisms are important in understanding adjustment disorders
      and neurotic disorders. Personality disorders, however, typically do not stem from
      reactions to stress nor from defenses against anxiety. Rather, they stem largely from
      immature and distorted _____ which results in
      individuals with persistently maladaptive ways of _____,
      _____, and relating to the world around them.   (p. 223)

   c. The actual prevalence of personality disorders is unknown since many individuals
      never come in contact with mental health agencies or the criminal justice system.

However, estimates available from the NIMH epidemiological study suggest that the prevalence of antisocial personality is approximately _____ percent.

(p. 224)

2. Personality disorders
    a. Respond true or false to the following statements about personality disorders.
        People with personality disorders: (p. 225)

        1. Live aberrant lives.   TRUE OR FALSE

        2. Suffer unduly from anxiety and depression.   TRUE OR FALSE

        3. Cause as much difficulty for others as for themselves. TRUE OR FALSE

        4. Experience significant occupational or social impairment. TRUE OR FALSE

        5. Show a continuous pattern of behavior since adolescence. TRUE OR FALSE

        6. Are extremely resistant to modification.   TRUE OR FALSE

    b. Misdiagnoses occur within the categories of personality disorders more often than in any other section of DSM-III. The authors suggest four problems that lead to unreliability of diagnoses of personality disorders. Complete this list of the problems.

        (pp. 225-226)

        1. Because there is little research on personality disorders, they are not as sharply defined as other diagnostic categories and we have no clear set of criteria for diagnosing them.

        2. The diagnostic categories are not mutually _____.

        3. The features of personality disorder are _____.

        4. Personality disorders are defined by _____ rather than by clearly observed behaviors.

    c. Millon (1981) finds very little to agree with in the DSM-III approach to diagnosis of personality disorders. He proposes instead that personality disorders be categorized according to individual differences in learned coping patterns. Eight coping patterns have been established by combining three dimensions: nature (positive or negative); source (self versus others) and _____ (active versus passive).   (p. 226)

3. Clinical features of personality disorders
Persons with personality disorders have several features in common. Describe the characteristic behavior of personality disordered people in each of the following general areas: (p. 226)
a. Personal relationships

b. Duration of difficulties

c. Life outcomes

d. Flexibility to behave differently in new situations

e. Motivation for change through psychotherapy

4. Types of personality disorders
a. List the personality disorders that belong to each cluster: (p. 227)

1. Cluster I: odd or eccentric individuals

2. Cluster II: dramatic, emotional individuals

3. Cluster III: anxious, fearful individuals

b. Fill in the clinical description in the following personality disorders:

Personality Disorder	**Clinical Description**
paranoid (p. 227)	suspicious, hypersensitive, rigid, envious, and argumentative
schizoid (p. 228)	
schizotypal (p. 228-229)	seclusive, oversensitive, and eccentric; frequently see chance events as related to themselves. Oddities of thought, perception, and speech.
histroinic (p. 229)	
narcissistic (pp. 229-230)	exaggerated sense of self importance; do not seek therapy because they view themselves as nearly perfect
borderline (p. 230)	
avoidant (p. 231)	hypersensitive to rejection and apprehensive of any sign of social ridicule
dependent (p. 232)	
compulsive (p. 232)	excessively concerned with rules, order, efficiency, and insistence that everyone do things their way; unable to express warm feelings
passive-aggressive (p. 244)	
self-defeating (p. 234)	avoids pleasurable experiences and persistently involved in punishing relationships; discourages

others from helping them to get out of the relationships (But: does this category misplace blame for abusive relationships on the victim instead of the perpetrator?)

sadistic (p. 234)

5. Causal factors in personality disorder
   a. Research on the causal factors of personality disorders is difficult for two reasons. Complete the following list of reasons why research is difficult. (pp. 234-235)

   1. Those who come to attention already have a fullblown disorder. Thus only _____study is possible.

   2. Personality traits are dimensional. It is hard to identify the point at which a normal range characteristic, like attention to detail, becomes a personality disorder such as compulsive personality disorder.

   b. Respond true or false to the following statements about the causes of personality disorders: (p. 235)

   1. Theories that link physique or constitutional reaction tendencies to the development of personality disorders are hypothetical, that is, are not supported by evidence.
      TRUE OR FALSE

   2. Suggestions that early learning contributes to personality disorders are speculative and inferential. TRUE OR FALSE

   3. The incidence of personality disorders has increased in recent years leading the authors to speculate that our present high value on instant solutions is leading more people to develop self-centered, irresponsible life-styles. TRUE OR FALSE

6. Treatment and outcome
   a. Persons with personality disorders are usually considered to be resistant to therapy. Why is this so? (p. 235)

b. Under what circumstances do persons with personality disorders generally get involved with psychotherapy?   (p. 235)

c. How do the difficulties personality disordered people have with personal relationships, acting out, and avoiding problems affect the course of psychotherapeutic treatments?
                                                                              (p. 236)

d. Can group psychotherapy be more effective with personality disorders than individual psychotherapy?   (p. 236)

e. Leeman and Mulvey (1973) describe a four step treatment strategy for individual outpatient therapy with the dependent person. Complete the following listing of treatment components: (p. 236)

    1. Inform the patient that therapy will be brief

    2. Make it clear that the therapist will not assume responsibility for the patient's life

    3. Keep therapy sessions focused on...

    4. Place demands on the patient to change...

7. Antisocial (psychopathic) personality
    a. The prevalence of antisocial personality in United States men is approximately _____ percent according to recent large epidemiological surveys. Among women, the prevalence is approximately _____ percent.   (p. 237)

    b. What is the typical age of onset for antisocial personality among men and among women?
                                                                              (p. 237)

8. Clinical picture in antisocial personality
   a. The DSM-III classification of antisocial personality involves the following criteria.
                                                                    (p. 238)
      1. At least three instances of deviant behavior such as theft before age _____.

      2. Four behavior problems such as _____ since age 15 and no period of 5 years without problems.

      3. No remission since age 15 except when _____.

      4. No mental disorder that could cause the symptoms.

   b. Fill in the missing information on the following chart that summarizes the personality characteristics of antisocial persons: (pp. 238-239)

Area of Functioning	Behavior Typical of the Antisocial Person
conscience development	
feelings of anxiety and guilt	act out tension rather than to worry: apparent lack of anxiety and guilt combined with an appearance of sincerity allows them to avoid suspicion
inpulse control	
frustration tolerance	seldom forgo immediate pleasure for future gains, live in the present, unable to endure routine jobs or accept responsibility

ability to accept authority

profit from experience   despite difficulties and the punishment they receive,
                                          they continue to behave as if the rules do not apply to
                                          them

interpersonal and sexual
    relationships

ability to manipulate
others

9. Causal factors in antisocial personality
    a. The authors cite the following three biological factors as possible causes of
        antisocial personality disorder. Respond to the following question regarding these
        factors.

        1. Deficient emotional arousal
            Many investigators--e.g., Lykken (1957), Eysenck (1950), Hare (1970)--
            have found that antisocial individuals seem to lack normal fear and anxiety
            reactions. What appears to happen in the development of antisocial persons as
            a result of their lack of anxiety and fear?   (p. 241)

            Schmauk (1970) found that antisocial persons can learn to avoid punishment
            only if the punishment is meaningful to them. Which of the following punishments
            did he find was effective with antisocial persons: physical punishment (electric
            shock), social punishment ("that was a very dumb thing to do"), or loss of
            money?   (p. 241)

Describe Valliant's view regarding antisocial individuals' handling of anxiety.
(p. 241)

2. Stimulation seeking
   Hare (1968) reported that antisocial individuals were deficient in autonomic variability. What do such individuals do to attempt to compensate for this deficit according to Quay (1965)? (p. 242)

3. Cognitive functioning deficits
   Gorenstein (1982) suggested that antisocial individuals have deficits in cognitive processes such as attention to detail that could reflect brain dysfunction. On what grounds has Hare (1984) disputed these results? (p. 242)

4. Genetic influences
   What does sociobiological theory, as demonstrated in the work of MacMillan and Kofoed (1984) suggest about the purpose of antisocial behavior? (p. 242)

b. The authors state that three types of family relationships may be causally related to antisocial personality. Respond to the following questions regarding these factors.

1. Early parental loss and emotional deprivation
   Although the loss of a parent during childhood was more common among antisocial subjects than normal controls, the authors of the text conclude that this factor can only be a partial or interactive cause of antisocial personality. What has Hare (1970) suggested about the circumstances under which parental loss can be problematic? (p. 243)

2. Parental rejection and inconsistency
   McCord and McCord (1964) concluded that severe _____ by parents was a primary cause of antisocial personality. Buss (1966), on the other hand, states that the following two parental patterns account for development of antisocial personality. Why must caution be exercised in using parental rejection and inconsistency as a basic explanation of antisocial personality? (p. 243)

    a. Parents who are cold and distant toward the child and allow no warm or close relationship to develop.

    b. Parents who are inconsistent in supplying affection, rewards, and punishments.

3. Faulty parental models

    Hare (1970) has concluded that one important factor in the development of antisocial behavior is modeling of another antisocial person, often the father. Describe the parental behavior seen by Greenacre (1945) in his study of antisocial persons from middle-class families. (pp. 243-244)

c. The authors also highlight the role of sociocultural factors in the causation of antisocial personality.

    1. What factors in our urban ghettos may foster the development of antisocial behavior in youngsters who grow up in such areas? (p. 244)

    2. Are there cultural groups among whom antisocial behavior is virtually unknown? (p. 245)

10. Treatment and outcomes

    a. In general, traditional psychotherapeutic approaches have not proven very effective in altering the personality problems of psychopaths. Among the factors inherent in the psychopathic individual's personality that make the prognosis for psychotherapy very poor are the inability to _____, to fantasize, and to learn from _____. (p. 245)

    b. Perhaps the most promising therapeutic approach is _____ therapy. (p. 245)

    c. Bandura (1969) has suggested a treatment program to modify antisocial behavior through the application of learning principles. Briefly summarize the three components of this treatment: (p. 245)

1.

2.

3.

d. Is psychotherapy with antisocial persons usually successful when attempted on an outpatient basis? (p. 245)

e. Is one-to-one, as opposed to group, therapy usually effective? (p. 246)

f. Why do many antisocial persons seem to improve after age 40? (p. 246)

11. Unresolved issues
   a. Axis II diagnoses (the personality disorders) are more unreliable than diagnoses made for Axis I (mental disorders). The authors of the text suggest the following two reasons for the   unreliability: (p. 246)

      1. No attempt is made in the DSM-III-R to quantify the traits or to provide a means of grading the degree to which a trait is present.

      2. The DSM-III-R is not based on mutually _____ criteria. Many of the traits are correlated with other traits and may also be seen as symptoms of various mental disorders.

   b. What do the authors of the text suggest to resolve the difficulties with Axis II? (p. 247)

(12.) Wanted: everyday psychopaths
      Describe Widom's (1977) approach to recruiting research participants and the type of people who volunteered. (p. 237)

CHAPTER QUIZ

1. Personality disorders are: (p. 223)

    a. reactions to stress.
    b. intrapsychic disturbances.
    c. episodic in nature.
    d. maladaptive ways of perceiving, thinking, and relating.

2. According to a recent NIMH epidemiological study, the prevalence of antisocial personality disorder is about _____ percent of our population.   (p. 224)

    a. 3   c. 23
    b. 13   d. 33

3. Personality disorders are coded on Axis _____ of DSM-III-R.   (p. 225)

    a. I   c. III
    b. II   d. IV

4. Millon suggests that personality disorders be categorized by individual differences in:
                                                                      (p. 226)
    a. anxiety level.   c. etiology.
    b. coping patterns.   d. motivation.

5. Which of the following belongs in the cluster of personality disorders characterized by anxiety?   (p. 227)

    a. avoidant   c. schizoid
    b. schizotypal   d. paranoid

6. Individuals with this personality disorder typically show oddities of thought, perception or speech: (p. 228)

    a. schizoid.   c. histrionic.
    b. schizotypal.   d. antisocial.

7. David, the 29-year-old "great procrastinator," is an example of _____ personality disorder.   (p. 233)

    a. passive-aggressive   c. narcissistic
    b. avoidant   d. borderline

8. Establishing the causal factors of personality disorders hasn't progressed very far for all the following reasons except: (pp. 234-235)

   a. the behaviors of interest blend into the normal range.
   b. affected individuals do not seek professional help.
   c. the personality disorders weren't recognized before 1952.
   d. only retrospective studies have been possible so far.

9. Research indicates that there may be a constitutional basis for _____ personality disorder. (p. 235)

   a. antisocial
   b. obsessive
   c. histrionic
   d. schizoid

10. In a recent epidemiological study, Robins and his colleagues found that the prevalence of antisocial personality disorder is: (p. 237)

   a. about equal for males and females.
   b. higher for females than for males.
   c. higher for males than for females.
   d. higher in prepubertal females than in prepubertal males.

11. Research evidence indicates that a primary reaction tendency typically found in psychopathic individuals is: (p. 241)

   a. deficient emotional arousal.
   b. hyperactive reflexivity.
   c. over-sensitivity to noxious stimuli.
   d. phlegmatic temperament.

12. With respect to the relationship of anxiety to antisocial personalities, Vaillant believes they: (p. 241)

   a. convert it into bodily complaints.
   b. don't have it and therefore don't have to avoid it.
   c. either conceal it or escape it.
   d. replace it with anger.

13. While a number of early studies linked antisocial personality formation with losing a parent at an early age, Hare suggested that the key factor was the: (p. 243)

    a. age at which the loss occurred.
    b. emotional family disturbance before the parent left.
    c. length of the marriage before the loss.
    d. sex of the parent who left.

14. According to Hare, there is a high incidence of psychopathic fathers in families that produce psychopathic children. He reasons that this is caused by: (p. 244)

    a. genetic factors passed from father to children.
    b. the children modeling their father's behavior.
    c. the children's reaction to harsh discipline.
    d. the father's reinforcement of his children's long-term gains.

15. Vaillant believes that antisocial individuals can be effectively treated only: (p. 245)

    a. as a part of family therapy.
    b. by outpatient psychotherapy.
    c. in a one-to-one therapeutic relationship.
    d. in controlled situations.

8

Psychological Factors and Physical Illness

OVERVIEW

Emotional factors occupy a central position in our understanding of physical disease. The chapter presents the view that all physical disease is related to stress to some degree. At one end of the continuum are diseases, such as viral meningitis, that are primarily due to the invasion of body cells by a potent virus. However, the degree of stress a person is experiencing influences the efficiency with which the individual resists the virus and how rapidly he or she recovers. At the other end of the continuum are diseases such as peptic ulcers, that mainly represent the direct results of psychological overload. This type of disease would not be seen in an individual unless high levels of stress were present.

Chapter 8 first discusses the interrelationship of health, attitudes, life style, and coping resources. Then, the functioning of the autonomic nervous system and the immune system are described. Finally, specific data on the clinical picture and treatment of diseases such as coronary heart disease, essential hypertension, anorexia/bulimia, and peptic ulcers are presented.

LEARNING OBJECTIVES

1. Give several examples of the close relationship between psychological factors and health.

2. Explain how excessive arousal of the autonomic nervous system may cause actual tissue damage.

3. List and describe the two main divisions of the immune system and explain the functions of each of their component parts.

4. Summarize the meager research findings that point to some psychosocial effects on the immune system and describe some future directions such investigations may take.

5. List several aspects of the way we live that may produce severe physical problems and explain why conclusive proof of these allegations is difficult to obtain.

6. Describe three clinical manifestations of coronary heart disease (CHD) and summarize the evidence linking it to the type A personality.

7. Describe anorexia and bulimia, explain some of the psychosocial factors which may be responsible for these disorders, and list some of the serious physical conditions that often result.

8. Define *essential hypertension*, list some physical diseases that it causes, and explain McClelland's variation of the suppressed-rage hypothesis about the cause of essential hypertension.

9. Describe the symptoms of peptic ulcers and explain how dependency conflicts have been implicated as causal factors.

10. Differentiate between the physical causes of migraine and simple tension headaches and summarize the research findings about psychosocial factors that may cause these dysfunctions.

11. Describe the sequence of events that appear to characterize the development of most psychogenic illness.

12. List and explain three types of biological factors that determine the adequacy of one's response to stressors.

13. List and explain three classes of psychosocial factors which may cause and/or maintain physical diseases.

14. Summarize the research results that show a link between sociocultural factors, physical disease and other physical and mental problems.

15. Describe the use of drugs and Morita therapy in treating psychogenic diseases.

16. List and describe three types of psychosocial measures that have been used to treat psychogenic diseases.

17. Explain why psychogenic illnesses must be treated by a combination of medical and psychological measures and describe how such combinations have been used to treat anorexia nervosa.

18. Indicate the major objectives of sociocultural efforts to reduce psychogenic diseases and describe the five-pronged North Karelia Project and some of its early results.

19. Describe three major problems that remain unresolved in our understanding of psychological influences on the physical body.

TERMS YOU SHOULD KNOW

behavioral medicine (p. 249)

psychogenic (p. 249)

health psychology (p. 249)

etiology (p. 250)

host resistance (p. 250)

disease mechanisms (p. 250)

patient decision-making (p. 250)

compliance (p. 250)

intervention (p. 250)

psychophysiologic disorders (p. 250)

apathy deaths (p. 251)

type A (p. 251 and p. 258)

placebo effect (p. 252)

flight or fight pattern (p. 252)

diseases of civilization (p. 252)

autonomic nervous system arousal (p. 252)

immune system (p. 253)

serum (p. 253)

white blood cells or lymphocytes (p. 253)

B-cells or humoral immune functioning (p. 253 and p. 254)

T-cells or cellular immune functioning (p. 253)

macrophages (p. 253)

natural killer cells (p. 253)

humoral branch (of the immune system) (p. 253)

cellular branch (of the immune system) (p. 253)

antigen (p. 253)

anaphylactic shock (p. 253)

antibodies or immunoglobulin substances (p. 254)

helpers (p. 255)

suppressors (p. 255)

cytotoxic or effector cells (p. 255)

psychoneuroimmunology (p. 255)

hypothalamus-pituitary-adrenocortical (HPA) axis (p. 256)

adrenocortical hormones (steroids) (p. 256)

immunosuppression (p. 256)

habits or habit patterns (p. 257)

coronary heart disease (CHD) (p. 258)

angina pectoris (p. 258)

myocardial infarction (p. 258)

type A behavior pattern (p. 258)

type B behavior pattern (pp. 258-259)

Framingham Heart Study (p. 260)

anorexia nervosa (p. 261)

bulimia (p. 262)

essential hypertension (p. 265)

suppressed rage hypothesis (p. 266)

peptic ulcer (p. 266)

pepsinogen (p. 267)

migraine headache (pp. 267-268)

aura (p. 268)

simple tension headaches (p. 268)

organ specificity (p. 269)

stomach reactor (p. 270)

corticovisceral control mechanisms (p. 270)

broken heart syndrome (p. 272)

secondary gains (p 272)

acupuncture (p. 274)

Morita therapy (p. 274)

biofeedback (p. 275)

North Karelia Project (p. 277)

CONCEPTS TO MASTER

1. Introduction
   a. Although an illness may be primarily physical or primarily psychological, it is always a disorder of the whole person, not just of the lungs or the psyche. The interdisciplinary approach to treatment of physical disorders is known as _____. Psychologists who are interested in psychological factors that induce or maintain disease specialize in _____

which includes research on etiology, host resistance, disease mechanisms, patient
decision-making, compliance, and intervention. (p. 249)

b. How are illnesses that are definitely or probably influenced by psychological factors
categorized in DSM-III-R? (p. 250)

2. Health, attitudes, and coping resources
a. Why do many surgeons refuse to operate unless the patient has a reasonably optimistic
attitude about the outcome? (p. 251)

b. What has been learned by researchers such as Rahe (1974) and Payne (1975)
about the likelihood of illness under increasing levels of stress? (p. 251)

c. What difference might it make if a cancer patient, for example, believed in his or her
doctor, had faith in the treatment, and had an overall positive mental outlook compared
to a patient who had lost hope? (pp. 251-252)

3. Autonomic excess and tissue damage
Describe how autonomic nervous system arousal, adaptive among lower animals, leads to
diseases of civilization among human beings. (p. 252)

4. Psychosocial factors and the immune system
a. The huge number of times that one's nose must be blown during a cold is an example of
the "adaptiveness without intelligence" of the body's defensive resources. Explain.
(p. 253)

b. The _____ system is responsible for maintaining bodily health in
an intrusion of foreign substances such as bacteria, viruses, and tumors. The primary
components of this system are the blood, thymus, bone marrow, spleen, and lymph

nodes. The blood _____, made up of large protein molecules and water, is the medium by which the body transports its defenses.   (p. 253)

c.   The organism has been invaded by an antigen--that is a substance recognized as foreign. Once this foreign substance has been detected, the immune system begins its work to protect the body.   Fill in the missing types of T-cells and the chart below and then respond to the following questions about the immune system: (pp. 254-255)

1.   What is anaphylactic shock?

2.   Where does the destruction occur of cells that bear antigens?

3.   What is the specific job of each type of T-cell?

IMMUNE SYSTEM

White Blood Cells

Humoral Functions   **Cellular Functions**

   B-cells   **T-cells**

   formed in bone marrow   develop in thymus

   produce antibodies   secrete substances toxic to cells

                                                  there are three types of T-cells:

                                                  _____

                                                  _____

                                                  _____

d.   The AIDS virus invades the T-cells and reduces their performance. What happens as a result?   (p. 255)

e. Many stressors such as marathon running, sleep deprivation, and exams have been shown to reduce white blood cell production which would affect immunity.   Until recently, researchers were convinced that the HPA axis was the pathway by which stress affected immune response. However, recent research has turned up a number of competing paths. There may even be direct neural control of the secretion of immunologic agents as suggested by evidence that immunosuppression can be _____ and therefore may be a learned response to previously neutral stimuli.   (p. 256)

5. Life-style as an added factor in health maintenance
    a. What three habits under personal control are thought to play a major role in three of the leading causes of death. List these three causes of death.   (p. 257)

        1.

        2.

        3.

    b. The data between habits and disease is correlational. Why can't these data be considered conclusive proof?   (p. 257)

6. Coronary heart disease and the "type A" behavior pattern
    a. Coronary heart disease (CHD) is the nation's number one killer. It is a potentially lethal blockage of the arteries supplying blood to the heart muscle (called the myocardium). The clinical picture of CHD includes (a) _____, which is severe chest pain and signals that insufficient blood is getting to the heart muscle; (b) _____ , which is complete blockage of a section of the blood supply to the heart and leads to death of heart muscle tissue; and (c) disturbance of electrical conduction in the myocardium resulting in interruption or stoppage of pumping action leading to sudden death.   (p. 258)

    b. The Type A behavior pattern as conceptualized by Friedman and Rosenman is characterized by excessive competitive drive, time urgency, hostility, accelerated speech and motor activity. Type B behavior is the absence of Type A characteristics. Respond true or false to the following questions about Type A and Type B behavior.
                                                                              (pp. 258-259)
                    Type A Behavior and Coronary Heart Disease (CHD)

        1. The most popular way to measure Type A behavior is the Jenkins Activity Survey.
                                                                              TRUE OR FALSE

2. The alternative approaches to measuring Type A behavior are highly correlated which suggests widespread agreement on the definition of this concept.

   TRUE OR FALSE

3. Not all components of Type A behavior are equally correlated with CHD. The hyper-aggressivity/hostility component of the pattern is most correlated with artery deterioration.

   TRUE OR FALSE

4. The Western Collaborative Group Study typed people for A-B type and followed their health for over 8 years. The strong virtue of this study is that it was retrospective.

   TRUE OR FALSE

5. In the WCGS, Type A personalities were approximately twice as likely as Type B personalities to have developed CHD by the end of the study.

   TRUE OR FALSE

6. The Framingham Heart Study is a prospective study that has been ongoing for more than 40 years. It has demonstrated that the Type A-CHD correlation holds for women as well as for men.

   TRUE OR FALSE

7. Some aspect of the Type A behavior pattern, most likely hostility, contributes to the development of potentially lethal CHD.

   TRUE OR FALSE

7. The anorexic/bulimic syndrome

   a. Anorexia nervosa and bulimia are coded as Eating Disorders of Adolescence and Adulthood in DSM-III-R. In fact, both syndromes are rare before adolescence and after age _____ . They occur 20 times more frequently in women than men. Anorexia is considered difficult to treat and dangerous, the death rate approaches _____ percent. (p. 261)

   b. The central features of anorexia are: (pp. 261-262)

      1. Intense fear of _____ and the irrational belief that one is fat

      2. Weight loss of more than _____ percent of original body weight

      3. Refusal to maintain weight within the lower limits of normal

      4. Often cessation of _____

      5. Marked overactivity

      6. Brief binges of eating and self-induced _____ or purging may be seen

c. Anorexic girls often describe their mothers in unflattering terms as excessively dominant, intrusive, and overbearing. Why must we be cautious in interpreting these reports? (p. 262)

d. Describe the life stage at which anorexia begins and the behavior out of which it develops. (p. 262)

e. Bulimia nervosa involves recurrent episodes of seemingly uncontrollable _____ with full awareness of the abnormality of this eating pattern. Boskin-White & White have described a common core of psychological attributes of bulimic girls including perfectionism, obsessive concern with _____ and _____, low self-esteem, social withdrawal, and excessive preoccupation with pleasing others. (p. 262)

f. The estimated frequency of bulimia among women of college age is _____ percent. (pp. 263-264)

g. Fallon and Rozin (1985) used figure drawings as stimuli to be judged by men and women. Compare men's and women's perceptions of the ideal woman's figure. (p. 264)

h. Most anorexics and bulimics come from socioeconomically advantaged homes. Researches consider that both anorexics and bulimics are dealing with similar problems but that the typical _____ is at a more advanced stage of identity development. The establishment of independent selfhood and mature _____ remains a difficult hurdle for both groups of women. (p. 264)

8. Essential hypertension
   a. What changes in blood distribution take place when an individual is subjected to stress? (p. 265)

   b. Under what circumstances does high blood pressure become chronic? (p. 265)

c. About _____ percent of Americans suffer from hypertension. Hypertension is the primary cause of more than 60,000 deaths each year and a major predisposing factor in another million deaths a year from strokes and heart disease.   (p. 265)

What is the incidence among Blacks as compared to Whites?

d. Why are so many people unaware that they have hypertension?   (pp. 265-266)

e. Obvious organic causes can be ruled out in approximately _____ percent of hypertension cases.   (p. 266)

f. The "suppressed rage" hypothesis of hypertension suggests that hypertensives often must keep their anger to themselves and outwardly appear submissive and controlled. McClelland (1979) has developed a variant of the suppressed rage hypothesis. Describe his ideas and the experimental data on which they are based.   (p. 266)

9. Peptic ulcers
a. How has the incidence of ulcers changed during the last century?   (p. 266)

b. The ulcer itself results from an excessive flow of the stomach's acid-containing digestive juices which eat away the lining of the stomach or upper intestine (duodenum). What types of emotional states may stimulate the flow of gastric juices?   (p. 267)

c. Respond to the following questions regarding the research of Weiner et al. (1957).   (p. 267)

1. Who were the subjects in this study, and how were they divided into two groups?

2. What did the researchers find?

3. Complete the following list of the three factors that all had to be present in order to "challenge the equilibrium" and produce an abnormally high ulcer risk?
    a.

    b.

    c. A special stressor such as basic training

10. Recurrent headaches
    a. More than 50 million Americans suffer from tension or migraine headaches. Among college students, approximately _____ percent reported headaches at least once or twice a week.   (p. 267)
    b. The typical migraine occurs in two phases. Complete the following description of the physiological changes associated with each stage of migraine headache.   (pp. 267-268)

        1. First Phase: Reduced blood flow to certain parts of the brain--may cause victims to experience an aura.

        2. Second Phase:

    c. Do stressors, such as frustrations, and excessive performance demands, cause cranial artery dilation in everyone or just among migraine sufferers?   (p. 268)

    d. Are the physiological changes that lead to tension headaches indisputedly different from the changes that lead to migraine headaches?   (p. 268)

    e. At what life period do headaches typically begin?   (p. 268)

    f. Do migraine sufferers differ from people who don't suffer from headaches in terms of psychological adjustment according to Andrasik et al. (1982)?   (p. 269)

11. Psychogenic physical disease: additional etiologic considerations

a. What is the "problem of organ specificity"?   (p. 269)

b. The *primary* causal factor that underlies all psychologic contribution to disease is
    _____.   (p. 269)

c. Place the following events in the development of psychogenic illness in
    their correct order:

    1. Responses of organ systems to arousal

    2. Failure of emotions to be dealt with adequately

    3. Arousal of negative emotions in response to stress

    _____   _____   _____

12. Biological factors
    The authors discuss three general biological causal factors: genetic causes, differences
    in autonomic reactivity/somatic weakness, and disruption of corticovisceral control
    mechanisms. Respond to the following questions regarding each causal factor:
    a. Genetic causes

        1. What results were found by Gregory and Rosen (1965) regarding the frequency of
            ulcers among members of the same family?   (p. 270)

        2. What kinds of twins did Liljefors and Rahe (1970) study? What are the
            implications of their findings?

    b. Autonomic reactivity/somatic weakness

        1. What is a "stomach reactor"?   (p. 270)

        2. How early would such a pattern of response be developed?   (p. 270)

        3. If a stomach reactor were to develop a psychogenic illness, which one
            would it likely be?   (p. 270)

4. What kinds of factors might lead an individual to develop a particular organ weakness? (p. 270)

c. Corticovisceral control disruption

1. Some individuals appear to have a deficiency in their hypothalamus that leads to overstimulation of the pituitary that subsequently leads to overstimulation of the adrenal gland and, untimately, to oversecretion of adrenocortical hormones. An excess of these hormones can cause an organism to function the majority of time as if it were under stress. The authors label this sequence of events an inadequate_____ control mechanism. (p. 270)

2. Deficient hypothalamic regulation could lead to deficient control of both the autonomic nervous system and the _____ of the endocrine system. (p. 270)

13. Psychosocial factors
Respond to the following questions regarding the three major psychosocial causes of psychophysiologic illness:
a. Personality characteristics/coping patterns

1. Dunbar (1943, 1954) thought that there were specific personality characteristics associated with particular psychophysiologic disorders. Recent research, such as Kidson's (1973) has cast doubt on this view. Describe Kidson's comparison of hypertensive patients' personalities to the personalities of a group of nonhypertensive people. (p. 271)

2. What has been learned in experimental situations where subjects are purposely frustrated and then permitted physical or fantasy aggression? (p. 271)

b.   Interpersonal relationships

    1.   How is the incidence of illness related to the following stressors:
        a. Marital problems, divorce (Bloom et al., 1978)   (p. 272)

        b. Bereavement (Parkes et al., 1969)   (p. 272)

    2.   What is the theory about the high rate of heart disease in industrialized
        societies described in the book, The Broken Heart?   (p. 272)

    3.   Explain how the overprotectiveness and tendency to reject the child that has
        been observed in asthmatic children's mothers could just as easily be viewed as
        both a *cause* of the child's asthma and an *effect* of the child's asthma.
                                                                        (pp. 272-273)

c.   Learning in the autonomic nervous system

    1.   It is now known that the autonomic responses can be learned involuntarily
        through _____ conditioning and voluntarily through
        _____ conditioning.   (p. 272)

    2.   Regardless of how a physical symptom may have been developed, it may be
        elicited by suggestion and maintained by the reinforcement provided by
        secondary gains. The ability of suggestion to elicit a physical symptom
        was demonstrated by Blecker (1968) among asthmatics. What did this experiment
        involve and how were the results interpreted?   (p. 272)

14. Sociocultural factors
    a.   How common are psychophysiologic illnesses among nonindustrialized peoples?
                                                                        (p. 273)

    b.   Are psychogenic illnesses more common among certain social classes in our own
        society?
                                                                        (p. 273)

15. Treatment and outcomes--biological measures
    The following are the biological treatments used for psychogenic illnesses. Briefly
    indicate what each treatment accomplishes.   (p. 274)
    a.   Mild tranquilizers--reduces emotional tension

    b.   Antidepressant medication

    c.   Acupuncture

    d.   Morita therapy--enhances sense of self-efficacy

16. Psychosocial measures
    a.   In the treatment of psychosocially medicated illness, one-to-one, verbally oriented
         psychotherapies including psychoanalysis have been relatively ineffective. On the other
         hand, _____ therapy has shown promising results.
                                                                            (p. 274)

    b.   On what assumption is behavior therapy for physical disorders based?
                                                                            (p. 275)

    c.   How successful are relaxation techniques in the treatment of migraine headaches and
         hypertension?   (p. 275)

    d.   How was the success of biofeedback related to the severity of illness in the case of
         asthmatic children studied by Davis et al. (1973)?   (p. 276)

    e.   Some investigators have cautioned about the bandwagon effect in regard to the use of
         biofeedback for psychogenic diseases. They have hypothesized that biofeedback may
         represent simply a more complex approach to teaching relaxation. A study by Blanchard
         et al. (1980) supports this conclusion. Describe that study.   (p. 276)

    f.   Some cognitive behavior therapists have worked to modify maladaptive behaviors such
         as rushing, impatience, and hostility--characteristics of Type A personalities. Others

such as Kobasa (1985) have been experimenting with methods to increase
_____which is defined as the ability to withstand stressful
circumstances and remain healthy in the face of them.   (p. 276)

17. Combined treatment measures
   a. What factors does Leon (1983) believe must be addressed in a comprehensive
       treatment program for anorexia?   (p. 277)

   b. Describe the treatment approach used by Lucas et al (1981) at the Mayo Clinic to meet
       the physiological and psychological needs of anorexic patients.   (p. 277)

       1. The treatment setting

       2. The techniques

       3. The format of treatment

18. Sociocultural measures
    The North Karelia Project was aimed at reducing atherosclerotic disease in an entire
    Finnish province. Describe the following aspects of the program: (p. 277)
    a. Overall goal

    b. Activities undertaken by project staff

    c. Early results

(19.) Star Wars in microcosm: the body's exquisitely organized defensive system
       Match the following components of the human immune system with the role each plays in
       the body's response to invasion by bacteria or virus.   (p. 254)

       Component   **Role in the Immune Response**

       1. phagocyte   a. A foreign, "nonself" substance

       2. helper T-cell   b. Cells that turn off the immune system

       3. cytotoxic T-cell   c. Responsible for producing antibodies

Psychological Factors
and Physical Illness
153

4. B-cell   d. Antigen/antibody complex combines with these to
                           stimulate secretion of histamine

5. antibodies   e. Cells that attempt to eat invading organisms; identifying
                           parts of the ingested invader remain imbedded in the the
                           membrane of this cell

6. macrophages   f. Makes contact with a foreign substance-containing
                           phagocyte using an antibody code to match the foreign
                           material

7. complements   g. These cells produce antibodies

8. supperssor T-cells h. Attack foreign invaders

9. antigen   i. Attach or bind to foreign material to render it vulnerable
                           to attack by macrophages

(20.)   Heart attack
   a. What is the cause of atherosclerosis?   (p. 259)

   b. List the warning signs of heart attack.   (p. 259)

       1.

       2.

       3.

       4.

(21.)   Biological clocks
        What is a "circadian cycle?"   (p. 271)

CHAPTER QUIZ

1. Health psychology deals with the diagnosis, treatment and prevention of: (p. 249)

   a. anxiety disorders.   c. stress disorders.
   b. physical disorders.   d. psychogenic physical disorders.

2. In behavioral medicine, a search for the predisposing causes of a disease is a problem of:
   (p. 250)

   a. ecology.   c. epidemiology.
   b. entymology.   d. etiology.

3. A patient who shows improvement after a trusted physician gives him an injection of sterile water is demonstrating: (p. 252)

   a. Hawthorne effect.   c. demand characteristics.
   b. placebo effect.   d. faith healing.

4. Early psychosomatic theorists Flanders Dunbar and Franz Alexander believed that chronic *internal* psychological sources of threat could damage the physical body because:
   (p. 252)

   a. anxious people seldom get proper nutrition.
   b. autonomic arousal could not be discharged.
   c. self-mutilation is a symptom of some disorders.
   d. suicide often results from psychological conflict.

5. The immune function is divided into two branches which are: (p. 253)

   a. blood-related and lymph-related.
   b. glandular and nervous.
   c. humoral and cellular.
   d. red cell-mediated and white cell-mediated.

6. B-cells produce antibodies which are involved chiefly with protection against the more common varieties of: (p. 254)

   a. bacterial infection.   c. cellular dysfunction.
   b. cancerous growth.   d. viral infection.

7. Effector-type T-cells: (p. 255)

   a. cause the thymus to produce more T-cells.
   b. destroy cells that bear antigens.

    c.   limit or terminate the production of antibodies.

    d.   signal B-cells to turn on antibody production.

8.   The fact that immunosuppression can be classically conditioned suggests that:

                                                    (p. 256)

    a.   immunological changes can affect mental states.

    b.   the HPA interpretation is correct.

    c.   the placebo effect is mediated by the pons.

    d.   there is direct neural control of imunological agents.

9.   Severe chest pain resulting from too little oxygenated blood being delivered to the heart muscle is called: (p. 258)

    a.   angina pectoris.   c.   myocardial infarction.

    b.   arhythmia.   d.   tachycardia.

10. According to Friedman and Rosenman, all of the following indications are involved in the Type A behavior pattern <u>except</u>:   (p. 258)

    a.   decelerated speech and motor activity.

    b.   excessive competitive drive with poorly defined goals.

    c.   hostility.

    d.   impatience or time urgency.

11. In the Framingham Heart Study, all of the following Type A groups showed a higher incidence of coronary heart disease (CHD) than their Type B counterparts <u>except</u>:   (p. 260)

    a.   blue collar men.   c.   white collar men.

    b.   blue collar women.   d.   white collar women.

12. The mortality rate for anorexia nervosa approaches _____ percent.   (p. 261)

    a.   3   c.   7

    b.   5   d.   9

13. Weiner's classic study of peptic ulcers involved monitoring the level of _____ among army draftees undergoing basic training.   (p. 267)

    a.   sex hormone   c.   white blood cells

    b.   glucocorticoids   d.   pepsinogen

14. Dilation of the cranial arteries is associated with: (pp. 267-268)

    a.   tension headaches.   c.   migraine headaches.
    b.   essential hypertension.   d.   asthma.

15. Sociocultural treatment of psychogenic diseases is targeted <u>most often</u> toward:

(p. 277)

    a.   encouraging diseased individuals to seek help.
    b.   obtaining social support after treatment.
    c.   preventing pathogenic life-style behaviors.
    d.   raising money for research.

9

Mood Disorders and Suicide

OVERVIEW

The disorders of mood--depression and mania--are discussed in this chapter. Depression is an extremely important topic, since it is the most common mood clinicians encounter among persons who seek psychological help. Depression is widespread among the normal population who do not seek professional help but who depend on family, friends, clergy, physicians, and even bartenders or hairdressers for support. This first half of the chapter begins with a differentiation of clinical depression from the normal depression many people experience. Then, the clinical picture of the several different levels of depression is described. The section concludes with a description of the causal pattern and treatment approaches to both depression and mania.

The second half of the chapter discusses suicide which is a risk with all depressed individuals. Well-known persons periodically capture the headlines by killing themselves at the height of success and in the midst of lives of luxury and recognition. Often, they do not seem, from the outside, to have a bad life or many insolvable problems. These deaths mystify and disturb most of us and raise questions about what makes life livable (or unlivable). This section presents information relevant to these questions, asking, for instance, whether all persons who commit suicide are mentally disordered. Data are also presented on the increasing problem of suicide among young people and college students. The section concludes with a discussion of some of the factors that characterize the person who is at high risk for suicide and a brief description of the procedures of suicide prevention.

LEARNING OBJECTIVES

1. List three hints about depression that may help us understand its normal and abnormal manifestations.

2. Describe several of the milder forms of normal depression and list three main psychological variables that are involved with normal forms of depression.

3. List the three principle dimensions customarily used to differentiate the mood disorders and describe the three main DSM-III-R categories for mild to moderate examples.

4. Describe the clinical manifestations of a major depression and summarize what research tells us about the disorder.

5. Describe the symptoms of a bipolar disorder and summarize what research tells us about it.

6. Describe the symptoms of a schizoaffective disorder and explain why this diagnosis may be controversial.

7. Describe three sets of biological factors that may be bases for mood disorders.

8. Describe five sets of psychosocial factors that are related to mood disorders.

9. Describe the relationship between certain sociocultural factors and the incidence of certain types of mood disorders.

10. Describe several biological and psychosocial therapies that have been successful in treating mood disorders.

11. Describe the type of people who commit suicide, list some of their motives for ending their lives, and explain how some sociocultural variables are important for understanding this result of depression.

12. Summarize what we know about why people commit suicide with reference to degree of intent, communication of intent, and suicide notes.

13. List five emphases that guide the approach of the crisis counselor who is talking to a person contemplating suicide and describe the long-range outcomes of crisis intervention.

14. Describe the "befriending" approach to people in high-risk groups and list three other methods of broadening the approach of suicide prevention programs.

15. Describe the ethical dilemma surrounding a person's right to end his or her own life and differentiate between cases which involve the terminally ill and those whose wish to die is based on temporary depression.

16. List and explain three problems concerning mood disorders that are still unresolved.

TERMS YOU SHOULD KNOW

mood disorder (formerly affective disorder) (p. 281)

mood congruent (p. 283)

mania (p 283)

depression (p. 283)

major depression (or unipolar disorder) (p. 283 and p. 289)

bipolar disorder (283 and p. 291)

normal depression (p. 284)

cyclothymia (pp. 285-286)

subsyndromal (p. 286)

dysthymia (p. 286)

adjustment disorder with depressed mood (p. 287)

depressive stupor (p. 289)

unipolar disorder (p. 289)

melancholic type (p. 289)

endogenous causation (p. 290)

cluster analysis (p. 290)

familial concordance (p. 290)

double depression (p. 290)

complete recovery (pp. 290-291)

manic-depressive psychosis (p. 291)

(bipolar disorder), "mixed" (p. 292)

schizoaffective disorder (p. 293)

adoption method of genetic research (p. 295)

neurotransmitters (p. 296)

seasonal affective disorder (SAD) (p. 297)
cortisol (p. 297)

dexamethasone (p. 297)

dexamethasone suppression test (DST) (p. 297)

response contingent positive reinforcement (RCPR) (p. 301)

learned helplessness (p. 301)

lithium carbonate (p. 304)

electroconvulsive therapy (ECT) (p. 305)

antidepressants (pp. 304-305)

electroconvulsive therapy (ECT) (p. 305)

cognitive-behavioral therapy (p. 305)

interpersonal therapy (p. 305)

group cohesiveness (p. 310)

"to be" group (p. 311)

"not to be" group (p. 311)

"to be or not to be" group (p. 311-312)

Samaritans (p. 316)

psychological autopsies (p. 316)

CONCEPTS TO MASTER

1. Introduction
    a. The mood disorders are so named because they involve states of persistent positive or negative emotion or _____ . When a mood change, because of

its extent, brings about behavior that seriously endangers the welfare of the person, the person is considered disordered. By contrast , schizophrenia and paranoia are *primarily* disorders of _____. (pp. 281-282)

b. The person who has a mood affective disorder may have disturbed thinking, but, in contrast to schizophrenics, the thinking is often mood congruent. This statement means that the thinking disorder is consistent with the predominant mood. For example, what type of mood would likely be associated by the persistent delusion that one's insides were rotted out and there were worms infesting the abdominal cavity? (pp. 282-283)

c. Record the appropriate incidence information for major depression.   (p. 283)

   1. _____ million Americans will be affected by major depression sometime during their life or _____ persons out of 100.

   2. The bulk of cases occur between ages _____.

   3. Females are affected considerably more often than males.

2. Mood disturbances and disorders
    Depression is unpleasant but it usually does not last very long and it seems to be self-limiting, turning off after a period or a certain intensive level has been reached. Depression in its mild form may even be viewed as adaptive because much of its "work" seems to involve self-exposure to _____, _____, and _____ that would normally be avoided. Thus, the capacity to experience depression may be a normal--even a desirable--state of affairs provided that it is maintained within certain limits. (p. 284)

3. Normal depression
    a. "Normal depression" is almost always related to the occurrence of
       _____. (p. 284)

    b. Grief is a psychological process one goes through following the death of a loved one. It can be thought of as a normal depression. Describe the following symptoms of grief: (p. 284)

       1. Turning-off on events

2. Fantasies

3. Capacity to enjoy the external world

c. Clayton (1982) suggests that the normal length of the grieving process is
    _____. After this, therapeutic intervention is called
    for.   (p. 284)

d. In early work, Blatt et al (1976) suggested that three psychological variables are
    involved in normal depression among college students. These variables are:
                                                                              (p. 284)
    1.

    2.

    3.

e. Later, Blatt and colleagues (1982) suggested that there may be two basic types of
    depression. The first type is organized around themes of dependency and the second type
    is organized around themes of self-criticism. _____, or
    the sense that events in the world are independent of one's own actions, is common to
    both types.   (p. 285)

4. Mild to moderate mood disorders
    a. The point on the severity continuum at which mood disturbance becomes a mood disorder
        is a matter of clinical _____.   (p. 285)

    b. Mood disorders are differentiated along three dimensions: severity, type, and duration.
        Place each of these terms in the proper blank next to the terms that describe each
        dimension.   (p. 285)

        1. _____   whether the disorder is acute, chronic,
                                              or intermittent

        2. _____   whether depressive, manic or mixed
                                              symptoms predominate

        3. _____   the number of dysfunctions in various
                                              areas of living and the relative degree of
                                              impairment in these areas

c. The three main mood disorders of mild to moderate severity recognized by DSM-III-R are cyclothymia, dysthymia, and adjustment disorder with depressed mood. Which of these describes: (pp. 285-287)

    1. Nondisabling cyclical mood alterations between depression and elation with no obvious precipitating circumstance and lengthy normal periods between episodes

    2. Nonpsychotic levels of depression lasting two years or more with no tendency toward hypomanic episodes

    3. Nonpsychotic level of depression developing within three months of an identifiable stressor

d. Few, if any, depressions occur in the absence of significant _____ and the distinction between the two, at clinical levels, has little justification. Even at the neurophysiological and neurochemical level there is an intrinsic relationship between them.   (p. 288)

e. There are no officially recognized _____ or _____ counterparts to dysthymia or adjustment disoder with depressed mood. The implicit assumption appears to be that all manialike behaviors must be part of a cyclothymic or bipolar disorder. However, most clinicians are familiar with persons who are chronically overactive, dominant, and excessively optimistic.   (p. 288)

5. Moderate to severe affective disorders
a. Major depression

    1. The diagnostic criteria for major depression involve merely more intense forms of the symptoms for dysthymia including sadness, fatigue, loss of interest, self-denunciation, and guilt. Delusions or hallucinations, if present, are mood congruent. There are two subcategories of major depression (a) single episode and (b) recurrent. Each of these subcategories may be labeled melancholic type if the patient complains of loss of interest or pleasure in almost all activities. Respond to the following questions regarding major depression: (pp. 288-290)
        a. To be diagnosed major depression, at least five symptoms must have been present all day and nearly every day during _____.

        b. The diagnosis cannot be made if the patient has ever experienced a manic episode. If the person has had such an episode, the current symptoms are viewed as a bipolar disorder. This is why major depression can also be known as _____.

    c.   The most severe form of major depression is _____.

    d.   Of people suffering from mood disorders, approximately _____ percent experience recurring episodes according to Coryell and Winokur (1982). Each episode lasts an average of _____ months. In between episodes the individual may behave essentially normally, but this point hasn't been fully resolved.

    e.   Approximately _____ percent of persons with major depression recover completely (have no episodes for five years).

    f.   A chronic, residual type of low-grade depression affects some _____ percent of persons who recover from major depression.

2.   There are several research techniques that have been used to study whether the present subcategories of depression are valid. Explain how each of the following methods has been used: (290)

    a.   Cluster analysis

    b.   Familial concordance

b.   Bipolar disorder

1.   Bipolar mood disorder is distinguished from major depression by at least one episode of mania. The features of the depressive form of bipolar disorder are clinically indistinguishable from those of major depression. The symptoms of mania and depression are compared in the following chart. Fill in the missing information. (p. 291)

Area of Behavior	Depression	Mania
activity level	loss of interest in activities	
mood	sad	euphoric
mental activity	diminished cognitive capacity	flight of ideas
verbal output	reduced	

self-esteem   self-denunciation and guilt

sleeping   hypersomnia or insomnia

2. Circle the correct words: Compared to patients with major depression, patients
    with bipolar disorder have their first episode at a (younger or older age) have
    (more or less) episodes in the course of their lifetimes, have episodes that tend to
    be (longer or shorter) in duration, and have a substantially (higher or lower)
    mortality rate from suicide and other unnatural causes.   (p. 290)

3. Mood disorders at all levels of severity are more prevalent among women than men
    by a ratio of almost two to one. What are some of the factors that increase women's
    risk of depression?   (p. 292)

c. Schizoaffective disorder
    These patients present a disorder of mood equal to anything seen in major depression but
    whose mental and cognitive processes are so deranged as to suggest the presence of
    schizophrenia. Respond to the following questions regarding schizoaffective disorder.
                                                                        (pp. 293-294)

    1. How are these patients unlike schizophrenics?

    2. Does a disorder really exist in which the symptoms of affective psychosis and
        schizophrenia are mixed?

6. Biological factors
    Three biological factors are thought to contribute to the development of affective
    disorders: hereditary predisposition, neurophysiological factors, and biochemical
    factors. Respond to the following questions regarding these factors:
    a. Hereditary predisposition

        1. The concordance rate for depression is much higher among identical than
            fraternal twins according to Kallman.   Also, Slater (1944) reported that
            _____ percent of close relatives of "manic-depressives" (old name for
            bipolar disorder) were also affected compared to a rate of _____ percent.
            These findings could suggest a genetic basis for bipolar disorder.   (pp. 294-295)

2. What have "adoption method" studies of bipolar disorder, such as those in Denmark by Wender et al. (1986) revealed about unipolar depression and suicide? (p. 295)

3. On what type of evidence is the "X-linkage hypothesis" of bipolar disorder based? (pp. 295-296)

4. Describe what has been learned from the study by Eagland et al. (1987) that traced cases of bipolar disorder among the Amish. (p. 296)

b. Biochemical factors

1. Many therapies for affective disorders, such as ECT, lithium, and antidepressants, affect the level of transmitter substances at the synapeses. What is the implication of this observation? (p. 296)

2. Research in the sixties and seventies focused on two substances including serotonin because it had been observed that antidepressant medications reduced their activity within the central nervous system. This led to a depletion theory for depression and an excess theory for mania.   What is the present status of research in this area? (pp. 296-297)

3. The authors of the text state that the evidence that affective disorders involve a biological mechanism is compelling. They further state that this conclusion rests on"three facts that are beyond reasonable dispute." Complete the following list of these three facts: (p. 297)
    a. A predisposition for depression may be genetically transmitted

    b.

    c.

c. Neurophysiologic and neuroendocrine factors

1. Some depressed persons show disturbances in their EEG (brain wave) sleep patterns and show a delay in onset of REM sleep. In addition, there is a growing

body of evidence that some mood disorders are to an extent under
_____ control and are sensitive to the amount of light
in the environment. These individuals are said to have SAD which stands for
_____.   (p. 297)

2. In 50-75% of depressed patients, the level of the hormone _____
    is elevated. Furthermore, a potent suppressor of plasma cortisol in normals,
    _____ fails to suppress among
    one-third to two-thirds of depressed persons. These findings have given rise to
    the widespread use of the DST test. DST stands for the _____
    _____.Those people whose DST
    test indicates that they are not suppressing cortisol may be the group sometimes
    referred to as having an endogeneous or melancholic form of depression.   There
    is considerable evidence that nonsuppression is correlated with clinical
    severity and retarded response to _____.
                                                                   (p. 298)

3. However, several reviewers including Zimmerman et al. (1986) have
    questioned the the utility of the DST. Why do they suggest that the DST may not
    be clinically useful?   (p. 298)

7. Psychosocial factors
    The authors of the text present five categories of psychosocial factors that may
    influence the development of affective disorders: stress, personality characteristics,
    feelings of helplessness/loss of hope, defenses against stress, and interpersonal effects.
    Respond to the following questions regarding these categories.
    a.   Stress

        1. How might stress affect the biochemistry of the brain, according to Barchas
            et al. (1967)?   (p. 298)

        2. Beck (1967) has listed six events that he believes are the most frequent
            aversive experiences occurring in the lives of people who become depressed.
            What are the first three of these?   (p. 298)
            a.

            b.

            c.

3. Paykel(1982) suggested that _____
were most strongly associated with the emergence of depressive states.

(p. 298)

4. What were more important than loss events in determining the onset of depression among older persons according to Phifer & Murrell (1986)?

(p. 298)

5. A very rigorous study conducted by Billings et al. (1983) compared 409 matched pairs of normal people and "unipolar" depressive people. Describe the results of this study. (p. 300)

b. Predisposing personality characteristics

1. What does a "negative cognitive set" consist of? (p. 300)

2. The evidence strongly suggests that early parental loss through death or permanent separation leaves a long-lasting vulnerability to
_____. (p. 300)

3. How have the personality characteristics of adults who later suffer manic episodes been described? (p. 301)

4. How have the personality characteristics of adults who later suffer depressive episodes been described? (p. 301)

c. Feelings of helplessness/loss of hope
There are two explanations of depression that are based on learning theory.
Briefly explain each one: (p. 301)

1. "Learned helplessness"--Seligman (1973 and 1975)

2. Insufficient reinforcers (RCPR)--Lazarus, Lewinsohn (1968 and 1974)

    d.   Defenses against stress

        1.   How can mania be viewed as a defense against stress?   (p. 301)

        2.   How can depression be viewed as a defense against stress?   (p. 302)

        3.   How do the authors of the text suggest that aberrant biological mechanisms interact with psychological defenses in the causation of depression?
                                                                          (p. 302)

    e.   Interpersonal effects of mood disorders

        1.   Mania and depression have been viewed by some theorists as "social roles." If they are roles, what is the goal of: (pp. 302-303)
           a.   The "manic role"

           b.   The "depressed role"

        2.   Depression has also been viewed as an attempt to communicate. What is the depressed person often trying to communicate?   (p. 303)

8.   General sociocultural factors
    a.   How does the frequency of affective disorders differ in industrialized versus non-industrialized countries?   (p. 303)

b. When depressive disorders occur in nonindustrialized societies, describe the symptom picture compared to depression in our own society.   (p. 304)

c. How does the depression rate vary with marital status?   (p. 304)

9. Treatment and outcomes
   a. Is medication necessary for the treatment of mild depression?   (p. 304)

   b. In which cases is treatment with lithium most successful?   (pp. 304-305)

   c. Why is electroconvulsive therapy often used in addition to antidepressant drugs on patients who present a serious suicide risk?   (p. 305)

   d. In the best of circumstances, the treatment of depression is not confined to drugs or ECT alone but is combined with _____.

                                               (p. 305)

   e. Beck's (1977) cognitive-behavioral therapeutic approach to depression is a relatively brief treatment that focuses on here-and-now problems rather than remote issues. The Beck approach has amassed an impressive record of success even when compared with drug treatment. Describe the Beck approach .   (p. 305)

   f. What was the verdict regarding psychotherapy with depression according to the carefully designed, multi-site study sponsored by the National Institute of Mental Health?   (p. 305)

g. Other behavioral techniques applied in the treatment of depression include training in progressive goal attainment, decision-making, self-reinforcement, social skills, and relaxation. Even without formal therapy, however, the great majority of depressed patients recover from a given episode within less than _____.
At the same time, the mortality rate for depressed patients appears to be about _____ as high as that for the general population because of the increased risk of suicide.   (p. 306)

10. Suicide
Fill in the missing information in the following questions about the risk of suicide:
                                                                                                                      (pp. 306-307)

a. The vast majority of those who commit suicide do so during the _____ phase of depression.

b. The risk of suicide is significant in depressed persons. The risk of suicide is just _____ percent during the year a depressive episode occurs but rises to _____ percent over the entire lifetime of an individual who experiences recurrent episodes.

c. Experts agree that the actual number of suicides is probably _____ times as high as the official number.

11. Clinical picture and causal pattern
a. Respond to the following questions about relative suicide rates by circling the group which has a relatively higher suicide rate.   (p. 307-308)

    1. Men or women

    2. Persons between 45-65 or persons between 24-44 years of age

    3. Widows or widowers

    4. Community college students or students at large universities

    5. Female physicians and psychologists or women in the general population

b. In recent years, disproportionate increases have occurred in the suicide rates among certain groups. The greatest increases have been among _____ year olds where the rate has tripled.   (p. 307)

c. Complete the following list of high risk groups for suicide:

1. Depressed persons

2. White elderly persons

3. Alcoholics

4.

5.

6.

7. Members of some Native American tribes

8. Certain professionals such as physicians, dentists, lawyers, and psychologists

d. The same factors that are linked to the onset of depression are correlated with suicidal behavior. What are some of these factors? (p. 308)

e. Suicide rates vary considerably from one society to another. _____ has the world's highest rate (33 cases per 100, 000). Countries with low rates (9 cases per 100,000) include Greece, Italy, Israel, the Netherlands, Portugal, and Norway. Among some groups, such as the _____ of western Australia, the rate is zero. (p. 309)

f. How may religious attitudes influence suicide rates? (p. 309)

g. Briefly explain Durkheim's thoughts regarding the relationship of group cohesiveness and suicide. (pp. 310-311)

h. What have reserachers such as Havighurst (1969) suggested about the relationship between suicide rates and murder rates in a country? (p. 311)

12. Suicidal ambivalence
   a. Farberow and Litman (1970) have developed the following classification of suicidal
      intent. Although of little practical clinical value, it is very richly descriptive. Place
      the following labels on the diagram to indicate the relative frequency of each type of
      suicidal person: "to be," "not to be," "to be or not to be." (p. 311)

1. _____

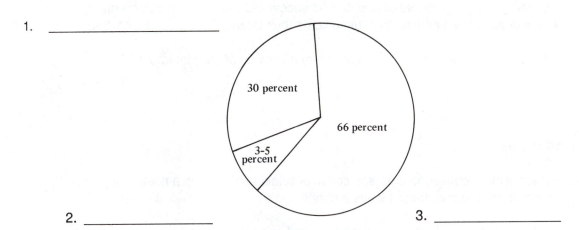

2. _____   3. _____

   b. Fill in the missing information in the chart below that summarizes Farberow and
      Litman's (1970) inferences and observations about suicidal behavior. (pp. 311-312)

Group	Feelings About Death	Method of Suicide Selected
"to be" group	do not wish to die	
"not to be" group		
"to be or not to be" group		tend to choose methods that are moderately slow acting to allow for the possibility of intervention

c.   Communication of suicidal intent

   1.   Which of the following patterns of communication is most common according to Rudestam's (1971) study: no communication of suicidal intent, direct communication of suicidal intent, or indirect communication of suicidal intent?

(p. 313)

   2.   Overall, _____ percent of people who successfully committed suicide made a direct or an indirect attempt to communicate their intent.   (p. 313)

   3.   Give common examples of "indirect" communications of suicidal intent.

(p. 313)

d.   Suicide notes

   1.   Which is more common: a person commits suicide and leaves a note, or a person commits suicide and doesn't leave a note?   (p. 313)

   2.   Fill in the missing information on the following chart that summarizes the frequency and content of different types of suicide notes.   (pp. 313-314)

Type of Note	Frequency	Content
positive emotional content	51 percent	expresses affection, gratitude, concern for others
negative emotional content		
neutral emotional content		
mixed emotional content		

   3.   Why does Shneidman (1973) find suicide notes disappointing?   (p. 314)

13. Suicide prevention
   a. Less than one-third of suicidal people seek help. Why don't many suicidal persons voluntarily seek help?   (p. 314)

   b. The primary objective of crisis intervention therapy is to help the individual with an immediate life crisis. When persons contemplating suicide are willing to discuss their problems at a suicide prevention center, it is often possible to avert an actual suicide attempt. The primary objective is to help individuals regain their ability to cope with their immediate problems. Emphasis is placed in five areas. Complete the following list: (p. 315)

      1. Maintain contact with the person for one-six contacts

      2.

      3.

      4.

      5. Help the person see that the present distress will not be permanent

   c. Why is a person who has made a previous suicide attempt at a particularly high risk for suicide?   (p. 315)

   d. Farberow (1974) states that two types of people come to a suicide prevention center.
                                                                              (p. 315)
      1. Describe the larger group (60-65 percent of persons coming to a suicide prevention center), and indicate the treatment they should receive.

      2. Describe the smaller group (35-40 percent), and indicate the treatment they should receive.

   e. Farberow & Litman (1970) reported that the suicide rate was 6% among persons at high risk for suicide, compared to less than 2% for the 8,000 persons who used the Los Angeles Suicide Prevention Service. A problem with suicide prevention is that the majority of people seen do not follow up their initial call with additional help. What did Sawyer, Sudack, and Hall (1974) find in their study of 53 persons who committed suicide even after contact with a suicide prevention center? (p. 316)

    f.   Describe some of the measures that suicide prevention centers can adopt to:

(p. 316)

        1.   Focus on high risk groups

        2.   Broaden the scope of their programs

    g.   Why do many professionals believe that the term *suicide intervention* is preferable to the term suicide prevention? (pp. 316-317)

(14.)   Varieties of depression according to DSM-III-R
           Match the following diagnoses with the appropriate clinical features: (p. 281)

Diagnosis

Main features

1. major depression

    a. Person is having a major depressive episode; previously had manic episode.

2. bipolar disorder, depressed

    b. Person has been bothered for two years by a chronic but mild depressed mood.

3. dysthymia

    c. Person is having a major depressive episode and has had just one previous episode that was also depressive.

4. cyclothymia, depressed

    d. Person is depressed after being divorced three months ago.

5. adjustment disorder with depressed mood

    e. Person has suffered for the last two years with subclinical episodes of depression.

(15.)   Stressors preceding severe depression
         Name the four major stressors found to precede the onset of depression by both Paykel
         et al. (1973 and Leff et al. (1970).   (p. 299)
         a.

         b.

         c.

         d.

(16.)   Warning signs for student suicide   (p. 309)
     a. List some of the signs that indicate a student may be suicidal.

     b. Do students commit suicide becaues they are doing poorly in school?

     c. Is the breakup of a romance more likely to cause suicide in women than in men?

(17.)   Native American tragedy: the young men of Wind River
         Describe the problems that beset many Native American tribal societies and the impact
         especially on their young males which could account for this tragedy.   (p. 310)

(18.)   Lethality scale for assessment of suicide potentiality
         Fill in the missing information in the following table that summarizes indicators of
         greater probability of suicide.   (p. 312)

Category	Suicide More Probable If:
age and sex	individual is male and individual is over 50

symptoms

stress

acute versus chronic aspects

suicidal plan

resources

prior suicidal behavior

medical status

communication aspects

reaction of significant others

(19.)   A "right " to suicide?
         Do people in the U.S. generally have a right to die, or is aiding and abetting another
         person's suicide a felony that carries severe penalities?   (p. 317)

CHAPTER QUIZ

1. Psychologists conclude that a person is disordered when a mood change: (p. 281)

    a. endangers the welfare of the affected person.
    b. is sudden and can't be accounted for.
    c. lasts longer than a week.
    d. seems inappropriate for the situation.

2. A disorder which involves mood swings between subclinical levels of depression and mania is: (pp. 285-286)

   a. bipolar disorder.
   b. manic depression.

   c. cyclothymic disorder.
   d. dysthymic disorder.

3. Bipolar mood disorder is distinguished from major depression by: (p. 291)

   a. at least one episode of mania.
   b. disturbance of circadian rhythms.
   c. evidence of earlier cyclothymia.
   d. evidence of earlier dysthymia.

4. All of the following are symptoms of the manic phase of bipolar mood disorder except: (p. 291)

   a. deflated self-esteem.
   b. euphoria.

   c. high levels of verbal output.
   d. notable increase in activity.

5. The prevalence of mood disorders among women is: (p. 292)

   a. one-third that of men.
   b. half that of men.

   c. twice that of men.
   d. three times that of men.

6. In a study of genetic factors in bipolar mood disorders in the Amish, Egeland found that the disorder was transmitted on the _____ chromosome. (p. 296)

   a. eleventh
   b. twelfth

   c. X
   d. Y

7. All of the following have been suggested as biological causes of bipolar affective disorder except: (pp. 294-297)

   a. inhibition/excitation imbalance.
   b. X-linked genetic abnormality.
   c. levels of biogenic amines.
   d. acetylcholine depletion.

8. Learned helplessness refers to the depressed patient's perception that: (p. 301)

   a. accustomed reinforcement is no longer forthcoming.
   b. there is no way to cope with the stress.
   c. reinforcement is inadequate.
   d. the world is a negative place.

9. Behaviorists such as Lazarus, Lewinsohn and Ferster assert that depression results when: (p. 301)

    a. angry responses are inhibited by aversive conditioning.
    b. conditioned grief responses are reactivated.
    c. negative reinforcers overwhelm positive reinforcers.
    d. response contingent positive reinforcement is not available.

10. Jaco found that the incidence of psychotic mood disorder was: (p. 304)

    a. higher among the divorced than among the married.
    b. higher in rural than in urban areas.
    c. higher in the lower socioeconomic classes.
    d. less evenly distributed than schizophrenia in the population.

11. While lithium therapy is highly effective in the treatment of manic psychoses, it is believed that it is effective in treating depression only when: (p. 305)

    a. electroconvulsive therapy has failed.
    b. the disorder is bipolar in nature.
    c. the disorder is melancholic in nature.
    d. used in tandem with psychedelic drugs.

12. Which of the following treatments has proven most effective? (p. 305)

    a. antidepressant drug treatment
    b. Beck's cognitive-behavioral approach
    c. Klerman and Weissman's interpersonal therapy
    d. all of the above are equally effective

13. Most hospitalized manic and depressed patients can now be discharged within _____ days. (p. 306)

    a. 10   c. 40
    b. 30   d. 60

14. While the overall national suicide rate has increased slightly but consistently in recent years, disproportionate increases have occurred among: (p. 307)

    a. females and the elderly.   c. males and the elderly.
    b. females and the young.   d. males and the young.

15. In Rudestam's study of suicides in Stockholm and Los Angeles, _____ percent of the victims had made direct or indirect verbal threats of their intent. (p. 313)

    a. 20   c. 60

    b. 40   d. 80

10

The Schizophrenias and Delusional (Paranoid) Disorders

OVERVIEW

The most severe derangement of human behavior possible may be seen in some cases of schizophrenia. Thus, this condition fascinates many people, including psychologists. Because schizophrenia involves disorders in thought, perception, affect, motor behavior, and social relationships, researchers have hoped that study of schizophrenics--where the processes have broken down-- might lead to better understanding of unimpaired psychological functioning.

Several different types of schizophrenia are described in Chapter 10 and then the causal factors of the whole group are discussed. There are many different studies described, since the causes of schizophrenia have been more thoroughly researched than many of the other conditions studied so far. Finally, the treatment of schizophrenia--mainly with drugs--is described and evaluated. The chapter concludes with a short discussion of delusional disorders.

LEARNING OBJECTIVES

1. List several general symptoms that characterize the schizophrenias and explain how this label came to be used instead of dementia praecox.

2. Briefly summarize the case study of the Genain quads and explain why their schizophrenic breakdowns were probably due to both heredity and environment.

3. Distinguish between *process* and *reactive schizophrenia*, list some near-synonyms for each, and explain what is meant by paranoid and nonparanoid.

4. Describe nine clinical criteria that are used in the diagnosis of the schizophrenias.

5. Give several reasons for the difficulty in defining schizophrenic behavior and describe some suggested solutions to this dilemma.

6. Describe four types of schizophrenia that have been identified and list three additional schizophrenic patterns that appear in DSM-III-R.

7. Summarize the evidence from four types of research on the genetic basis for schizophrenia and explain the conclusions your authors have reached.

8. Explain why researchers believe that some biochemical factors may cause schizophrenia and describe the rise and demise of the dopamine hypothesis.

9. Summarize the results of research on neurological factors that may cause schizophrenia and explain why these findings are difficult to interpret.

10. Summarize the results of research on neuroanatomical factors that may underlie the schizophrenias and explain your authors' evaluation of these conclusions.

11. Evaluate the evidence that early psychic trauma may increase a person's vulnerability to the schizophrenias.

12. Describe five aspects of schizophrenic families that have been studied and explain why pathogenic family interactions cannot be the sole cause of this disorder.

13. Explain why learning a deficient self structure and/or an exaggerated use of ego-defense mechanisms may be contributing causes of the schizophrenias.

14. Evaluate Laing's hypothesis that schizophrenia may be a social role and explain how this may be related to the insanity defense used in some criminal cases.

15. Summarize the results of research concerning the connection between excessive stress and decompensation and explain how expressed emotion (EE) of a schizophrenic's family members may be pathogenic.

16. Summarize the results of research concerning the possibility that some general sociocultural factors may contribute to the development of schizophrenia.

17. Summarize the success of biological and psychosocial interventions in the treatment of the schizophrenias and list six research-supported conclusions about these dysfunctions.

18. List and describe six types of delusional (paranoid) disorders that appear in DSM-III-R and explain why formal diagnoses of these kinds of abnormal behavior are rare.

19. Describe the clinical symptoms that characterize delusional (paranoid) disorders and evaluate the popular belief that paranoid individuals are dangerous.

20. Differentiate *paranoia* from *paranoid schizophrenia* and describe three major factors which may be involved in the development of delusional (paranoid) disorders.

21. Explain how behavioral therapy may be used successfully in the early stages of a delusional

disorder and give some reasons for the resistance to treatment of the well-established delusional system.

22. Describe several major issues surrounding the schizophrenias and delusional disorders that remain unresolved and note the authors' thoughts about some possible solutions.

TERMS YOU SHOULD KNOW

the schizophrenias (p. 322)

dementia praecox (p. 322)

process schizophrenia, poor premorbid schizophrenia , or chronic schizophrenia (equivalent terms) (p. 326)

reactive schizophrenia, good premorbid schizophrenia, or acute schizophrenia (equivalent terms) (pp. 326-327)

negative symptom schizophrenia (p. 327)

positive symptom schizophrenia (p. 327)

cognitive slippage (pp. 327-328)

breakdown in perceptual filtering (p. 329)

hallucinations (p. 329)

anhedonia (p. 329)

blunting (of affect) (p. 329)

cosmic or oceanic feelings (p. 329)

autism (p. 329)

undifferentiated type (of schizophrenia) (p. 331)

catatonic type (of schizophrenia) (p. 334)

catatonic stupor (p. 335)
echopraxia (p. 335)

pseudomutuality (p. 350)

double bind (p. 350)

amorphous style (of thinking) (p. 350)

fragmented style (of thinking) (p. 350)

mask of insanity (pp. 352-353)

expressed emotion (EE) (p. 353)

major tranquilizers (p. 356)

paranoia (p. 357)

jealous type (of delusional disorder) (p. 357)

erotomanic type (of delusional disorder) (p. 357)

somatic type (of delusional disorder) (p. 357)

grandiose type (of delusional disorder) (p. 357)

ideas of persecution (p. 358)

delusions of grandeur (p. 358)

overconceptualize (p. 361)

paranoid illumination (p. 362)

paranoid pseudocommunity (pp. 362-363)

(folie a deux) (p. 358)

CONCEPTS TO MASTER

1. Introduction
    a. In what sense are schizophrenia and delusional disorders the opposite of the mood disorders? (p. 321)

b. Currently, are delusional disorders considered manifestations of schizophrenia or as distinct from schizophrenia? (p. 322)

2. The schizophrenias
   a. The schizophrenias are a group of _____ disorders characterized by gross distortions of _____; withdrawal from _____; and disorganization and fragmentation of perception, thought, and emotion. (p. 322)

   b. The original term for the schizophrenias was *dementia praecox*. In light of on our current views, the term *dementia praecox* is misleading because schizophrenia becomes apparent during adolescence or adulthood, not during childhood; and because there is no convincing evidence that schizophrenia leads to permanent mental deterioration. Later, Bleuler introduced the term schizophrenia which means split mind. He did not mean "split personality" by this term. What did he mean? (p. 322)

   c. Respond true or false to the following statements about schizophrenia: (pp. 322-323)

      1. Schizophrenia is a unitary process; all forms of schizophrenia represent different manifestations of the same disease. TRUE OR FALSE

      2. Schizophrenia is unknown in native or aborginal groups. TRUE OR FALSE

   d. In the United States the six-month prevalence rate of schizophrenia is _____ percent of the population aged 18 or older. (p. 323)

   e. About _____ percent of new admissions to state and county mental hospitals are diagnosed as schizophrenic. Because schozophrenic individuals often require prolonged or repeated hospitalization, they usually constitute about _____ of the patient population in U.S. mental hospitals. (p. 323)

   f. The median age (the age that has exactly half the cases below it and half the cases above it) of first admission to a psychiatric hospital with a diagnosis of schizophrenia is _____ years old. (p. 323)

g. Complete the following list of reasons why schizophrenia is considered the most serious of all psychotic disorders. (p. 323)

   1. The schizophrenic disorders are complex.

   2. The schizophrenic disorders have a high rate of incidence during the productive years of life.

   3. The schizophrenic disorders have a tendency to ....

3. A case study
   Why is it impossible to determine how much of the Genain's schizophrenia was due to heredity and how much was due to environment? (p. 326)

4. Clinical picture in schizophrenia
   a. One of the major distinctions among the schizophrenias is the differentiation of process and reactive forms. The following diagram represents the process-reactive continuum. Place an *H* where Hester Genain would fall on the distribution. (She was the quadruplet who was never as well off as her sisters and moved in imperceptible steps toward serious deterioration.) Place an *M* where Myra Genain would fall. (She was the least disturbed quadruplet before her breakdown and was able to regain effective control of her life afterwards.) (pp. 326-327)

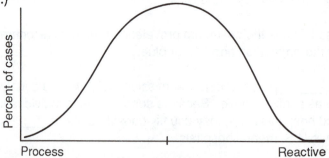

   b. A second distinction among the schizophrenias is between paranoid and nonparanoid symptom patterns. In general, paranoid schizophrenic individuals tend to be more _____ than process. However, there is a substantial number of people originally diagnosed as having paranoid forms of schizophrenic disorder who later are diagnosed as nonparanoid forms of schizophrenia. (p. 327)

c.   The DSM-III-R presents criteria characteristic of the schizophrenic disorders,
     although all of them would not be seen in every case. These characteristics are listed in
     the following chart.   Fill in the empty spaces by writing a short description of the
     characteristic or providing a clinical example chosen from the text to illustrate
     the characteristic as appropriate.   (pp. 327-329)

Characteristics of Schizophrenia

Characteristic	Brief Description	Clinical Example
disorganization of a previous level of functioning	there is impairment in routine areas of daily functioning	Patient stops taking baths and wearing clean clothes.
disturbance of language and communication		Patient says, "I'm growing my father's hair."
disturbance in content of thought	many types of delusions may be seen	
disturbance in perception	breakdown in perceptual filtering occurs; hallucinations may be seen	
disturbance in affect	inappropriate affect	Patient laughs uproariously upon receipt of news of a parent's death.
	anhedonia	Patient can't recall the last time he or she was happy.
confused sense of self		Patient feels he or she

is tied up to universal
powers.

disturbed volition   a disruption of goal-directed
activity occurs

disturbed relationship
with external world
(autism)

Young person develops a
fantasy world and spends
most of the day conversing
with imaginary people.

disturbed motor
behavior

Patient exhibits excited
hyperactivity, apparent
clumsiness, stupor, rigid
posturing, ritualistic
mannerisms, and bizarre
grimacing.

5. Problems in defining schizophrenia behavior
   a. Are the authors convinced that the DSM-III and DSM-III-R criteria for diagnoses of
      schozphrenia have substantially improved validity?   (p. 330)

   b. Although the DSM-III and III-R clearly differentiate between schizophrenias and mood
      disorders, it is not clear whether these disorders are distinct clinically. What is clear
      is that with revision of diagnostic criteria have come drastic changes in the numbers of
      persons who are diagnosed as mood disordered compared to the numbers of persons who
      are diagnosed as schizophrenic. In a study by Winters, Weintraub, and Neale (1981),
      only about half of 68 patients diagnosed as schizophrenic under DSM-II rules still
      qualified as schizophrenic under DSM-III rules. What is the disconcerting conclusion of
      this study and one by Harrow et al. (1985) regarding the schizophrenics of the
      1980s?   (p. 330)

   c. What did Endicott et al. (1985) conclude about the ability of DSM-III schizophrenic
      diagnoses to predict clinical statue 6 to 25 months following admission? (p. 331)

   d. Sarbin and Mancuso (1980) state that schizophrenia is a moral verdict. Explain their view. (p. 331)

e. Bellak (1979) states that schizophrenia is the "common pathway" of severe adaptive breakdown. What does he mean? (p. 331)

f. Indicate whether the following statements are true or false. (p. 331)

1. All symptoms of schizophrenia occur in every case.   TRUE OR FALSE

2. There are universally accepted signs of the presence of schizophrenia.   TRUE OR FALSE

3. The symptom picture in schizophrenia may change over time.   TRUE OR FALSE

4. Most schizophrenics fade in or out of reality.   TRUE OR FALSE

5. Acute schizophrenia may clear up rapidly or progress to a chronic condition.   TRUE OR FALSE

6. Types of schizophrenia
   a. Match the following types of schizophrenia with the appropriate definition:
   (pp. 331-340)

   1. undifferentiated type   a. Those persons who are in remission following a schizophrenic episode and show only mild signs of schizophrenia.

   2. paranoid type   b. A form of schizophrenia that occurs at an early age and includes blunting,

   inappropriate mannerisms, and bizarre behavior.

   3. catatonic type   c. A person in whom symptoms of schizophrenia have existed for six months or less.

4. disorganized type

    d. A person who shows absurd, illogical, changeable delusions and, frequently, hallucinations.

5. residual type

    e. A form of schizophrenia in which all the primary indications of schizophrenia are seen in a rapidly changing pattern.

6. schizoaffective disorder

    f. A person who shows some schizophrenic signs as well as obvious depression or elation.

7. schizophreniform disorder

    g. A type of schizophrenia characterized by alternating periods of extreme excitement and extreme withdrawal.

b. What has happened to the relative frequency of paranoid schizophrenia and un-differentiated schizophrenia over the last several years?   (p. 337)

c. Under what circumstances might a paranoid schizophrenic become violent?
                                                                                   (p. 338)

d. At the present time, all new cases of schizophrenia would first receive a diagnoses of
_____ until the symptoms have been established for six
months. After six months if symptoms persist, a formal schizophrenic diagnosis can be
applied.   (p. 340)

7. Biological factors in schizophrenia
    The authors of the text consider four general categories of biological causes of schizophrenia: heredity, biochemical factors, neurological factors, and neuroanatomical factors. Respond to the following questions regarding these causes:

    a. Heredity
        There are four types of experimental designs that have been used to study the heredity of schizophrenia: twin studies, children reared apart from schizophrenic parents, family studies, and studies of high-risk children.

        1. Twin Studies
            a. Two large and well-controlled twin studies were conducted by Gottesman and Shields (1972) and Cohen et al. (1972). Using a sample of armed forces

personnel, Cohen et al. found that the concordance rate for schizophrenia among identical twins was 23.5% compared to 5.3% among fraternal (nonidentical) twins. Using a sample more representative of the general population, Gottesman and Shields (1972) found rates of _____percent for identical twins and _____ percent for fraternal twins.   (p. 341)

b. If schizophrenia were exclusively a genetic disorder, what concordance rate for identical twins would be found?   (p. 341)

c. Twin studies cannot prove a genetic transmission of predisposition. Why not?
                                                                        (p. 341)

2. Children reared apart from their schizophrenic parents (adoption strategy)
    a. What did Heston (1966) do, and what were his major findings?   (pp. 341-342)

    b. What did Heston (1966) conclude?   (pp. 341-342)

    c. While the authors of the text conclude that the adoption studies have provided the strongest evidence yet obtained for the genetic transmission of a vulnerability   to schizophrenia, the work has not gone unchallenged. What unusual findings were reported by Benjamin (1976) which challenge assumptions about genetic effects?   (p. 342)

    d. What criticisms of the adoption method have been offered by Sarbin and Mancuso (1980)?   (p. 342)

3. Family studies
    a. Describe the results of Rieder's (1973) study of children raised by their own schizophrenic parents.   (p. 342)

    b. Kringlen (1978) found that _____ percent of children born to schizophrenic parents develop psychosis as adults, whereas _____ percent develop entirely normally.   (pp. 342-343)

4. High risk children

    a.   How well have studies of high risk children paid off?   (p. 343)

    b.   Refer to the Israeli-NIMH High-Risk Study and answer the following questions about it:

       1. Who were the index groups?

       2. In which group (Kibbutzim raised or home raised) did the majority of cases of schizophrenia occur?

    c.   Summarize the authors' overall conclusion regarding a genetic basis for schizophrenia based on evidence from high risk research, family studies, twin studies and adoption methods.   (p. 343)

b. Biochemical factors

    1.   Match the following columns: (pp. 343-344)

Hypothesis	**Proposed Mechanism**
1. dopamine hypothesis	a. Hallucinations and other thought disturbance is caused by a chemical synthesized within the body.
2. endogenous hallucinogen hypothesis	b. Person has excess dopamine activity, too many receptors, or the receptors are supersensitive.

    2.   The dopamine hypothesis has the most support but recent research on dopamine-blocking drugs for schizophrenia have raised questions. Discuss this research.   (p. 344)

c. Neurological factors
    Neurophysiological distrubances that could be related to schizophrenia include an
    imbalance in excitatory and inhibitory processes and inappropriate autonomic arousal.

    1. Describe some of the deficiencies in normal attention and information processing
        that have been observed in schizophrenics and even in some of their close relatives.
        (p. 344)

    2. Considerable evidence suggests that schizophrenic persons process information in a
        way that is both abnormal and relatively specific to schizophrenic disorder. Magaro
        (1980,1981) concluded that schizophrenics are unable to...   (p. 345)

    3. Sarbin and Mancuso (1980) argue that such findings are "guaranteed in advance."
        by the simple process of labeling a person a schizophrenic. In fact, these
        "neurophysiological deficits" are more simply viewed as _____
        attention shortcomings because the patients don't care about the research.
        (p. 345)

        If the deficiencies do exist, what factors might have caused them?   (p. 370)

d. Neuroanatomical factors
    The frequency of obstetrical complications in the histories of persons who later become
    schizophrenic is markedly above the general population. Such observations have led to
    speculation about the anatomical intactness of the schizophrenic brain.
    1. In some cases of schizophrenia, particularly those of chronic course, there is an
        abnormal enlargement of the brain's ventricles. Enlarged ventricles imply a
        decrement in _____.   (pp. 345-346)

    2. According to the authors of the text, can the evidence regarding the biological
        causal factors of schizophrenia be dismissed in a summary fashion?
        (p. 346)

8. Psychosocial factors in schizophrenia
    The authors consider five psychosocial causes of schizophrenia: early psychic trauma and

increased vulnerability , pathogenic parent-child and family interactions, faulty learning and coping, social role problems, and excessive stress and decompensation.

a.   Early psychic trauma

1.   What do the authors of the text conclude regarding the importance of early psychic traumas (child abuse, separations, divorce, death, etc.) as causal factors in schizophrenia?   (p. 347)

2.   Why does Meehl (1978) believe that it may be very difficult to trace schizophrenia to particular life events?   (pp. 347-348)

b.   Pathogenic parent child and family interactions
The authors discuss five topics in this section: schizophrenogenic mothers and fathers, destructive marital interactions. pseudo-mutuality and role inflexibility, faulty communication and undermining personal authenticity. Respond to the following questions about these forms of pathogenic interactions:

1.   Schizophrenogenic mothers and fathers
a.   How have some studies described the mothers of schizophrenics?   (p. 348)

b.   The concept of schizophrenogenic mother was largely abandoned in the 1970s but made a partial comeback in the work of Roff and Knight (1981), particularily as applied to the mothers of male schizophrenics? Describe this study.   (p. 348)

c.   Roff and Knight (1981) found that this mother-son pattern can be especially damaging if the father is also _____ and _____.   (pp. 348-349)

d.   Describe what has been learned about fathers of schizophrenics in studies conducted by Lidz and colleagues (1965).   (p. 349)

e.   What have several researchers (e.g., Liem, 1974) noted about the impact of schizophrenic children's behavior on their parents?   (p. 349)

2. Destructive marital interactions
   a. In a group of 14 families with schizophrenic offspring, Lidz and colleagues (1965) failed to find a single family that was reasonably well integrated. In 8 of the couples, there was a state of severe chronic discord where the continuation of the marriage was constantly threatened. This condition has been labeled _____. In the other six couples, a maladaptive equilibrium had been reached in which some family members collude to allow another member to behave abornmally. This condition is called
   _____. (pp. 349-350)

   b. Roff and Knight (1981) found that the presence of marital schism and skew among parents was predictive of _____.
   The effect was especially strong if parental separation or divorce occurred subsequent to marital disharmony. (p. 350)

3. Faulty communication
   a. Bateson (1959, 1960) coined the term double-bind to describe the conflicting and confusing nature of communications among members of schizophrenic families. Give an example of double-bind communication. (p. 350)

   b. Singer and Wynne (1963, 1965) have described amorphous and fragmented communication patterns in schizophrenic families. Describe each of these patterns. (p. 350)

   c. Under what circumstances is a schizophrenic's thinking most disturbed according to Bannister (1971)? (p. 350)

   d. In more recent work, Singer et al. (1978, 1979) have referred to high "communication defiance" in schizophrenic families. Were Goldstein and colleagues (1978) able to confirm a link between communication deviance and schizophrenia in their longitudinal study employing a variant of a high risk strategy? (p. 350)

4. Undermining personal authenticity

Describe actions by which some family members can undermine the selfhood of
other family members.   (p. 351)

c. Faulty Learning and coping
    The authors discuss two ways in which faulty learning may increase vulnerability to
    schizophrenic breakdown: faulty learning of the components of the self-structure and
    learning excessive use of ego-defense mechanisms.

    1. Deficient self-structure
        a. There are four components of the self-structure where deficiencies in past
            learning may be seen. A person with faulty learning might show: (1) grossly
            inaccurate reality assumptions, (2) confused self-identity and feelings of
            inadequacy, (3) immaturity that is seen in an overemphasis on being "good",
            and (4) lack of necessary life competencies and ineffective
            _____.   (p. 352)

        b. Lack of compentencies to handle sexual and hostile impulses combined with
            generally deficient social skills usually leads to ...   (p. 352)

    2. Excessive ego-defense mechanisms
        a. It is not surprising that individuals who feel inadequate come to rely
            excessively on ego-defense mechanisms. These defense mechanisms often
            include _____ elements that have great potential for
            secondary gain because they serve as excuses for the person's withdrawal and
            nonperformance.   (p. 352)
        b. The exaggerated use of the defense mechanisms of _____
            and _____ are particularly likely to
            predispose an individual to delusions and hallucinations.   (p. 352)

d. Social role problems
    Social role behavior has also been tied to the development and course of schizophrenic
    reactions.

    1. Laing has written extensively about social roles and schizophrenia. Complete the
        following statements about his views: (pp. 352-353)
        a. Laing maintains that in schizophrenia, a split arises between the false
            _____ self and the true _____self. Madness is an
            attempt to recover the sense of wholeness.

    b.   The "mask of insanity" is a social role. Behind this false self, the true
           _____ self remains.

  2. Support for Laing's views comes from research that demonstrated that the
      occurrence of schizophrenic symptoms depends to a remarkable extent on the
      _____ in which the individual is being observed.   For example, a
      demand for intimate exchange appears to exacerbate schizophrenic symptoms.
(p. 353)

  e. Excessive stress and decompensation
      There is evidence that there is a marked increase in the severity of life stress during
      the period prior to an actual schizophrenic breakdown. Relapse into schizophrenia
      following remission is often associated with a certain negative communication called
      expressed emotion (EE). Two components appear critical in the pathogenic effects of EE:
        a.   overinvolvement of the family with the patient and excessive criticism

        b.   familial communication _____.   (p. 353)

9. Treatment and outcomes
    a.   The chance that a schizophrenic patient admitted to a modern mental hospital
       and given chemotherapy will be discharged in a matter of weeks is _____
       percent. However, the chance a patient will be readmitted during the first year after
       release is high.   (p. 355)

    b.   The overall outcome of schizophrenia can be broken down into three groups. What
       percentage of schizophrenic patients fall into each of these groups?   (pp. 355-356)

      _____ percent   1.   Those patients who recover from the schizophrenia and
                                       remain symptom-free for five years.
      _____percent   2.   Those patients who show partial recovery with some
                                         residual symptoms.
      _____percent   3.   Those patients who remain largely or totally disabled
                                         for their entire life.

    c.   Do forms of psychological therapy exist that are useful in the treatment of
       schizophrenia?   (p. 356)

10. Delusional (Paranoid) Disorder
    a.   Paranoia is rarely seen in clinics, because these persons do not come for treatment.
       What types of people in the community are likely to be suffering from paranoia?
(p. 357)

b. DSM-III-R requires that diagnoses of delusional disorder be specified by type on the basis of the predominant theme of the delusions. Complete the following list of the types of delusions that may be seen. (p. 357)

Type of Delusion	Description
1. persecutory type	1. The belief that one is being subjected to bad treatment. Often leads to lawsuits to seek redress.
2. jealous type	2.
3.	3. The belief that a famous person is in love with you or desires a sexual relationship with you.
4. somatic type	
5.	

11. Clinical picture in delusional disorder
    a. Briefly describe the behavior of a person with delusional disorder.
    (pp. 357-358)
    b. Under what circumstances may paranoid individuals become dangerous? (p. 360)

12. Causal factors in delusional disorder
    a. Meissner (1978) regards feelings of frustration and brooding over fancied and real injustices to be an essential phase of personality development and a necessary component in the achievement of _____. (pp. 360-361)

    b. Magaro (1980, 1981) sees schizophrenic and paranoid processes as quite independent of one another and related to two different stages of information processes. While schizophrenia is seen as a disorder of _____, paranoia is regarded as a disorder of _____. (p. 361)

    c. Are biological factors thought to be an important cause of paranoia? (p. 361)

d. The family background typical of paranoid persons appears to be authoritarian and excessively dominating. Frequently, some family members practice _____ the thoughts of other family members. There is often an air of superiority that is a cover-up for an underlying lack of acceptance which creates the need for the child to prove superiority. (p. 361)

e. Many problems of paranoid people can be seen as problems of selfhood. The person seems unable to achieve distance from conflicts over issues of aggression, victimization, power, weakness, and humiliation. Describe the personal relationships of such a person. (p. 362)

f. The lives of paranoid individuals are full of failures at critical life tasks: marriage, work, family. What seems to be the cause of these difficulties? (p. 362)

g. Grunebaum and Perlman (1973) have pointed to the naivete of the preparanoid person in assessing the interpersonal world. Because such persons do not see people "for what they are," continual hurtful interactions occur. The ability to trust others realistically requires that the individual be able to tolerate.... (p. 362)

h. What is "paranoid illumination" and how does it lead to the establishment of a paranoid "pseudo-community"? (pp. 362-363)

13. Treatment and outcomes
    a. Describe a treatment package useful for patients in the early stages of paranoia. (p. 363)

    b. What type of treatment is effective once a paranoid person's delusional system is well established? (p. 363)

14. Unresolved issues
    a. The authors believe that the understanding of schizophrenia will only increase if there is a _____ which enables us to view these behavioral phenomena in a new and productive light. (p. 364)

b. Do the authors of the text feel that many schizophrenic individuals have benefited from advances made to date in the understanding and treatment of what is called schizophrenia?   YES OR NO   (p. 364)

c. Does the knowledge exist to better help persons diagnosed as schizophrenics according to the authors?   YES OR NO   (p. 364)

(15.)   DSM-III-R diagnostic criteria for schizophrenia
The diagnostic criteria for schizophrenia are very behaviorally specific regarding the symptoms that must be present; the decrements of life functioning that must occur; the absence of symptoms of affective disorder, organic disorder, autistic disorder; and the duration of symptoms for at least six months. Complete the following list of the symptoms that must be present to qualify for a diagnosis of schizophrenia:

Two of the following:
a. delusions

b. prominent hallucinations

c.

d.

e.

(16.)   Regression to primary thought processes in schizophrenia
    a. How does the regression seen in schizophrenia compare to a child's behavior?
                                                                                        (p. 330)

    b. What appears to be the purpose of the regression seen in schizophrenia?
                                                                                        (p. 330)

(17.)   Conditions associated with favorable outcomes in the treatment of schizophrenia
    a. What type of background factors have been associated with favorable outcomes in schizophrenia?   (p. 356)

    b. What did Hawk, Carpenter, and Strauss (1975) find in their comparison of treatment outcomes of acute (i.e. reactive) schizophrenics with other types of schizophrenics?
                                                                                        (p. 356)

(18.)   Folie a deux
        When folie a deux occurs, what is the most frequent relationship between the
        affected parties?   (p. 358)

(19.)   Sequence of events in paranoid mode of thinking
        Place the following stages in the development of paranoid thinking in their proper
        order: hostility, protective thinking, paranoid illumination, delusions, suspiciousness.
                                                                                 (p. 360)

        a. _____   b. _____

        c. _____   d. _____

        e. _____

CHAPTER QUIZ

1. In the United States the estimated incidence of schizophrenia is about _____ percent of
    the population.   (p. 322)

    a. one   c. five
    b. three   d. seven

2. The median age of onset for schizophrenia is: (p. 323)

    a. below 15.   c. over 45.
    b. around 30.   d. older in females than males.

3. Hester Genain was never as well off psychologically as her sisters and moved in
    imperceptible steps toward psychosis. She could be viewed as a(an) _____
    schizophrenic.   (p. 324)

    a. acute   c. process
    b. residual   d. reactive

4. A schizophrenic's statement that he is "growing his father's hair" is an example of:
                                                                            (pp. 327-328)

a. anhedonia.   c. echolalia.
b. autism.   d. cognitive slippage.

5. The new DSM-III-R criteria for the diagnosis of schizophrenia, according to the authors,
    have: (p. 330)

    a. certainly increased diagnostic validity.
    b. increased the number of patients diagnosed as schizophrenic.
    c. probably decreased both diagnostic reliability and validity.
    d. probably increased diagnostic reliability.

6. Sarbin and Mancuso insist that schizophrenia is a: (p. 331)

    a. final common pathway of severe adaptive breakdown.
    b. legal verdict.
    c. mood disorder with complications.
    d. myth.

7. The central feature of _____ schizophrenia is pronounced motor symptoms.
                                                                            (p. 334)
    a. undifferentiated   c. disorganized
    b. catatonic   d. paranoid

8. The results of twin studies of hereditary factors in the development of schizophrenia show:
                                                                            (p. 341)
    a. equal concordance rates for identical and fraternal twins.
    b. higher concordance rates for fraternal twins.
    c. higher concordance rates for identical twins.
    d. higher incidence of schizophrenia among twins than among others.

9. If schizophrenia were exclusively genetic, the concordance rate for identical twins would
    be _____ percent.   (p. 341)

    a. -1   c. 50
    b. +1   d. 100

10. Monitoring over time children born to schizophrenic mothers is the research strategy
    known as: (pp. 342-343)

    a. twin studies.   c. family studies.
    b. adoption studies.   d. high risk studies.

11. Which of the following findings contributed to the demise of the dopamine hypothesis about
    the cause of schizophrenia?   (p. 344)

a. Dopamine-blocking drugs also reduce psychotic symptoms for other disorders.
b. Dopamine-blocking drugs work almost immediately.
c. Dopamine-stimulating drugs are an antidote for the effects of LSD.
d. Dopamine-stimulating drugs cause hallucinations.

12. Since the brain normally occupies the skull fully, the enlarged ventricles of some schizophrenics imply a(an): (p. 345)

a. decreased pressure on the brain.
b. decrement in the brain mass.
c. increased amount of spinal fluid.
d. predisposition to hydrocephaly.

13. "You got all As. I suppose good grades are pretty easy to get nowadays." This is an example of: (p. 350)

a. pseudomutuality.
b. undermining personal authenticity.
c. double bind communication.
d. fragmented thought.

14. The exaggerated use of defense mechanisms such as _____ may predispose a person to develop hallucinations and delusions. (p. 352)
a. repression   c. projection
b. regression   d. isolation of effect

15. What proportion of schizophrenic patients remain symptom free for five years? (p. 355)

a. 10 percent   c. 50 percent
b. 30 percent   d. 60 percent

11

Substance-Use and Other Addictive Disorders

OVERVIEW

It has been estimated that a major proportion of America's health problems are due to self-injurious practices such as excessive drinking, smoking, and overeating. They are all considered forms of addiction, along with drug use and compulsive gambling. These problems are explored in Chapter 11.

A great deal of background information is presented to help document the extent of the various addictive behaviors and their costs to society. Treatment approaches that have been developed for each specific addiction are then described.

LEARNING OBJECTIVES

1. Define *alcoholic* according to the 1978 President's Commission on Mental Health and summarize the statistics on the number of alcoholics and alcohol-related problems in this country.

2. Describe three major physiological effects of alcohol and describe several symptoms experienced by individuals who are alcohol-dependent.

3. Describe some physical ailments that can result from alcoholism and explain how these may lead to interpersonal problems.

4. Describe four different types of alcoholic psychoses.

5. Describe the withdrawal symptoms experienced by alcoholics who try to quit and summarize the evidence for genetic factors predisposing some to become alcoholics.

6. List and describe three major psychosocial factors that may be partially responsible for the development of alcohol-dependence.

7. Describe several sociocultural factors which may influence one's becoming alcohol-dependent.

8. Describe several biological and psychosocial interventions that have been used to treat alcohol-dependent persons.

9. Summarize the research findings on the results of treatment and relapse prevention for alcohol-dependent persons.

10. Summarize the history of the use of opium and its derivatives over the last five thousand years.

11. Describe the major physical and psychosocial effects of ingesting morphine and heroin.

12. List and explain four major causal factors in the development of opiate-dependence.

13. Describe some psychosocial and biological treatments that have been used as therapy for opiate-dependent individuals and evaluate the success of using methadone hydrochloride.

14. Describe some of the effects of barbiturate abuse, list some of its causes, and summarize the dangers of withdrawal from this class of drugs.

15. Describe some causes and effects of amphetamine abuse and note some physical and psychological effects of withdrawal.

16. Describe some physical and psychological effects of ingesting cocaine and some symptoms that are experienced in withdrawal.

17. Describe the physical and psychological effects of using LSD and note the treatment used for the acute psychoses induced by its use.

18. Compare the effects of using mescaline and psilocybin with those of ingesting LSD.

19. Describe the physical and psychological effects of marijuana use and explain why it has been compared to heroin.

20. List five controversies that have arisen concerning the use of marijuana and summarize what we know about each.

21. Define *hyperobesity* and list some biological, psychosocial, and sociocultural factors that may underlie its development.

22. Describe and evaluate several biological and psychosocial interventions that have been used to treat hyperobesity.

23. Define *pathological* gambling and describe its symptoms.

24. Summarize what is known about the causes of and treatments for pathological gambling.

25. Describe and evaluate several non-abstinence methods that have been used to help alcoholics control their drinking.

TERMS YOU SHOULD KNOW

psychoactive (p. 367)

substance-induced organic mental disorder (p. 367)

toxicity (p. 367)

psychoactive substance abuse (p. 368)

psychoactive substance dependence (p. 368)

tolerance (p. 368)

withdrawal symptoms (p. 368)

alcoholic (p. 368)

problem drinker (p. 368)

blackouts (p. 371)

hangover (p. 371)

alcoholic psychoses (p. 373)

alcohol idiosyncratic intoxication (p. 373)

alcohol withdrawal delirium (p. 373)

chronic alcoholic hallucinosis (p. 374)

alcohol amnestic disorder (p. 375)

detoxification (p. 380)

Disulfiram (antabuse) (p. 381)

aversive conditioning (pp. 381-382)

emetine chloride (p. 382)

covert sensitization (p. 382)

Alcoholics Anonymous, Al-Anon, and Ala-Teen (p. 383)

honeymoon effect (p. 384)

relapse prevention (p. 385)

indulgent behaviors (pp. 384-385)

abstinence violation effect (p. 385)

opium (p. 388)

alkaloids (p. 388)

morphine (p. 388)

soldier's illness (p. 388)

analgesic (p. 388)

heroin (p. 388)

codeine (p. 388)

Harrison Act (p. 388)

snorting (p. 388)

skin popping (p. 388)

mainlining (p. 388)

rush (p. 388)

withdrawal symptoms (p. 388)

receptor sites (p. 390)

endorphins (p. 390)

total resocialization (p. 391)

methadone hydrochloride (p. 391)

barbiturates (or "downers") (p. 392)

silent abusers (p. 392)

potentiates (p. 392)

amphetamines (p. 393)

narcolepsy (p. 394)

Schedule II substances (p. 394)

amphetamine psychosis (p. 394)

cocaine (p. 394)

cocaine bug (p. 395)

crack or rock (p 396)

hallucinogens (p. 397)

model psychoses (p. 397)

LSD trip (p. 397)

bad trip (p. 397)

flashbacks (p. 397)

mescaline (p. 398)

psilocybin (p. 398)

marijuana (or cannibis sativa--also called "grass," reefers," or "joints") (p. 398)

hashish (p. 398)

THC (p. 399)

a-motivational syndrome (p. 400)

hyperobesity (p. 401)

adipose cells (p. 402)

developmental obesity (p. 402)

reactive obesity (p. 402)

externality hypothesis (p. 402)

TOPS (p. 403)

anorexigenic drugs (p. 404)

jejunoileal bypass operation (p. 404)

pathological or compulsive gambling (pp. 404-405)

Gamblers Anonymous (p. 407)

key informants (p. 407)

abstinence viewpoint (p. 409)

CONCEPTS TO MASTER

1. Introduction
   Fill in the missing blanks in the following schematic representation of the DSM-III
   classification of substance related disorders: (p. 367)

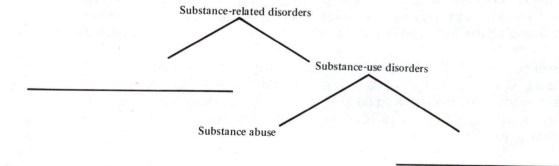

2. Alcohol abuse and dependence
   a. Alcoholism has varying definitions. The World Health Organization has a very broad definition that would include many people. The national Council on Alcoholism has a narrower definition and behaviorists have an even more restrictive definition. They conceptualize alcoholism as the very extreme point on the continuum of problem drinking. The authors of the text adopt the definition of the President's Commission on Mental Health. How does this group define alcoholism? (p. 368)

   b. Approximately _____ million Americans experience abusive use of alcohol, but only about _____ million currently receive treatment. (p. 368)

   c. Complete the following lists of some of the ways in which alcoholism harms the individual and is a drain on society: (pp. 368-369)

Individual harm	**Society harm**
1. Leads to a 12 year shorter lifespan	1. Causes problems for 4-6 other people
2. Is the third major cause of death	2. Linked to half of major auto accidents
3.	3.

   d. What is the ratio of male alcoholics to female alcoholics? (p. 369)

3. Clinical picture of alcohol abuse and dependence
   a. Alcohol is a depressant. Indicate how alcohol: (pp. 370-371)

      1. Affects higher brain centers

      2. Affects behavior

   b. If the percent of alcohol in the blood reaches _____percent a person is intoxicated. When the blood alcohol reaches .5% the individual passes out, and concentrations of blood alcohol above .55% usually cause death. (pp. 370-371)

   c. Polich et al. (1981) studied the symptoms of alcohol dependence among identified alcoholics. Underline the symptoms that were reported by more than one-quarter of the respondents: tremors, morning drinking, loss of control, blackouts, missed meals, continuous drinking. Almost two-thirds of the respondents had one or more of these symptoms. (p. 371)

   d. The liver works on assimilating alcohol into the system. How is it effected by large amounts of alcohol? (pp. 371-372)

e.   How can excessive intake of alcohol lead to malnutrition?   (p. 372)

f.   What did Golden et al. (1981) find about the left hemisphere of the brains of chronic alcoholics?   (p. 373)

g.   Four psychotic reactions are caused by alcohol: alcohol idiosyncratic intoxication, alcohol withdrawal delirium, chronic alcoholic hallucinosis, and alcohol amnestic disorder. Respond to the following question about these psychoses:
                                                                                        (pp. 373-375)

   1.   Idiosyncratic intoxication is a confused, disoriented state that follows even moderate amounts of alcohol. What individuals may have low tolerance for alcohol?

   2.   Alcohol withdrawal delirium is a form of psychosis that may occur following a long drinking bout or a physical disease or injury. Also, it may occur upon sudden withdrawal from alcohol. The symptoms include disorientation, acute fear, suggestibility, tremors and physical symptoms such as fever and rapid heartbeat. However, the most vivid symptom is hallucinations of small, fast moving animals including snakes, rats, and roaches. Are these symptoms serious? How long do these symptoms usually last?

   3.   In chronic alcoholic hallucinosis, the main symptoms are auditory hallucinations of voices, chain clanking, and the sharpening of knives that continue for several days or even weeks. Are these symptoms solely related to alcohol?

   4.   Alcoholic amnestic disorder is considered to be caused by vitamin B deficiency and other dietary inadequacies. It could be prevented by adding vitamin B to all alcoholic beverages. Describe the memory deficit that occurs in alcoholic amnestic disorder.

4.   Causes of alcohol abuse and dependence
   a.   Biological factors
        Investigators have theorized that some people are predisposed to become alcoholics by inherited unusual cravings for alcohol or tendencies toward loss of control. However, the evidence is inconclusive. Complete the following summary of the data base:

1. Cotton (1979) completed a review of 39 studies of families of alcoholics and nonalcoholics. He found that almost _____ of alcoholics had at least one parent with an alcohol problem. (pp. 375-376)

2. Cloninger et al. (1986) found strong evidence for the inheritance of alcoholism. They found the following rates of alcoholism: _____ percent among women with no alcoholic parents, _____ percent among women with one alcoholic parent, and _____ percent among women whose parents were both alcoholics. (p. 376)

3. Goodwin et al. (1974) found that both adopted (25% rate) and nonadopted (17% rate) sons of alcoholics had high rates of alcoholism. What did they conclude from these data? (p. 376)

4. Fenna et al. (1971) and Wolff (1972) suggested that a hypersensitive reaction to alcohol occurs among Oriental and Eskimo persons. However, Shafer (1978) has challenged this conclusion. State Shafer's criticisms. (pp. 376-377)

b. Psychosocial factors
The authors suggest that three psychosocial factors contribute to alcoholism: psychological vulnerability; stress, tension reduction and reinforcement; and marital/intimate relationships. Respond to the following questions regarding these factors.

1. Alcoholic Personality
   a. What do the authors of the text mean by the expression *alcoholic personality?* (p. 377)

   b. About 75-80% of the studies of alcoholic personalities have shown an association between alcoholism and _____ personality. (p. 377)

   c. Why is it difficult to determine if an alcoholic personality exists from interview with people who are alcoholics? (p. 377)

   d. What results have been obtained in prospective studies, such as Loper et al. (1973)? (pp. 377-378)

    e.   What are the general personality characteristics of alcoholics once their drinking has become well established?   (p. 378)

2.   Stress, tension reduction, and reinforcement
    a.   Schaefer (1971) has concluded that alcoholism is a conditioned response to anxiety. Describe how such a conditioned response would be maintained.
        (p. 378)

    b.   Some critics respond that alcoholism could not possibly be a conditioned response, since its consequences are so negative (e.g. passing out, vomiting, hangover, and arguments with spouse and employer). How does Bandura (1969) respond to these arguments?   (p. 378)

3.   Marital and other intimate relationships
    a.   Excessive drinking often begins during crisis periods in marital or other intimate personal relationships. Describe Curlee's (1969) study of the triggers of alcoholism among middle and upper class women.   (p. 378)

    b.   Siegler et al. (1968) have suggested that alcoholism is a family game with complimentary roles. Describe the roles played by the alcoholic and his/her spouse.   (p. 379)

    c.   How important is alcoholism as a cause of marital discord?   (p. 379)

c.   Sociocultural factors
    1.   Bales (1946) described three cultural factors that determined whether a specific group would have a high or low rate of alcoholism. What were these factors?
        a.   (p. 379)

        b.

        c.

2.   Alcoholism is a major problem among Eskimos in rural Alaska. Why does the United
     States Public Health Service believe this is so?   (p. 379)

3.   Place the following groups and countries under the heading that accurately
     represents their rate of alcoholism: United States, Moslem countries, France,
     Jews, Soviet Union, Mormons.   (p. 379)

High Rates of Alcoholism   Exceedingly Low Rates of Alcoholism

4.   Thus, it appears that religious sanctions and social customs can determine whether
     alcoholism is one of the modes of _____ used in a society.
                                                         (p. 379)

5.   Treatment and outcomes
     a.   A _____ approach to the treatment of drinking problems appears to be
          most effective. _____ treatment appears to be as effective as
          inpatient treatment. The objectives of treatment programs include physical
          rehabilitation, _____, and _____.
          _____.   (p. 380)

     b.   Why are drugs such as chlordiazepoxide (librium, a minor tranquilizer) used during
          the detoxification process?   (pp. 380-381)

     c.   Antabuse (disulfuram) is not considered a complete treatment for alcoholism.
          When might Antabuse be used?   (p.381)

     d.   Sometimes spouses and children of alcoholics are included in group therapy.
          Complete the list of reasons why this is done.   (p. 381)

          1.   The alcoholic is part of a unit. All members of the unit have the responsibility
               for the problem and its resolution.

          2.

3. Members of the family may unwillingly encourage an alcoholic to remain addicted.

e. Relapses are generally associated with a lack of _____ or with living in a stressful environment.   (p. 381)

f. There are several behavior approaches to treating alcoholism. One involves injecting an emetic (i.e. a drug that causes the person to become extremely nauseated and to vomit). What is the purpose of repeating this procedure over several days?
                                                                                    (pp. 381-382)

g. Emetic drugs and shock are not always used. Covert sensitization can be used instead. Describe this treatment.   (p. 382)

h. One of the most promising procedures for treating alcoholics is the cognitive-behavioral approach recommended by Marlatt (1985). Often referred to as a skills-training procedure, the program is aimed at younger problem drinkers who are considered to be at risk for developing more severe drinking problems on the basis of their family history of alcoholism or their current heavy consumption. The procedure has four components. Complete the following list: (p. 383)

1. Teaching facts about alcohol

2. Developing coping skills in situations where alcohol is typically abused

3.

4. Teaching stress management skills to deal with current stressors

i. Briefly describe how AA and Al-Anon family groups operate.   (p. 383)

j. Bandsma et al. (1980) suggested that AA had a high dropout rate. Why?   (p. 383)

k. Polich et al. (1981) studied the course of alcoholism after treatment. Fill in the percentages they reported among treated alcoholics with serious drinking:

(pp. 383-384)

_____ percent abstained for four years,
_____ percent showed alcohol-related problems,
_____ percent maintained alcohol dependency, and
_____ percent had alcohol-related adverse consequences.

l. Under what conditions is treatment for alcoholism likely to be most effective?

(p. 384)

m. Define the following components of a cognitive-behavioral approach to relapse prevention. (pp. 384-385)

1. Indulgent behaviors

2. Mini-decisions

3. Abstinence violation effect

6. Drug abuse and dependence
The psychoactive drugs most commonly associated with abuse and dependence in our society are: narcotics, sedatives, stimulants, antianxiety drugs, and hallucinogens.
Drug abuse and dependence may occur at any age but seem to be most common during _____. The most common action of all drugs-- even those which are medically prescribed--is their alteration of cell _____. The changes that drugs bring about are in a direction away from _____. Thus, drugs do not result in cells performing "better than ever." (p. 385).

7. Opium and its derivatives (narcotics)
a. How is heroin made from morphine? What did chemists originally think they were going to accomplish through this procedure? (p. 388)

b. What happened to the rate of heroin addiction during the 1960s? (p. 388)

c. What happens if a person takes heroin repeatedly for 30 days? (p. 388)

d. What is likely to happen if this person now stops taking the heroin abruptly?

(p. 389)

e. Is withdrawal from heroin dangerous and painful?   (p. 389)

f. What are the effects of heroin use during pregnancy?   (p. 389)

8. Causal factors in opiate abuse and dependence
    a. What is the single most common cause for heroin use given by addicts?   (p. 390)

    b. The authors present four causes for opiate addiction: neural bases for physiological
        addiction, relief of pain, psychopathology, and sociocultural factors (association with a
        drug subculture). Respond to the following questions regarding these causes:

(pp. 390-391)

        1. Neural bases
            a. There are two different types of receptor sites for narcotic drugs. What are
                they?   (p. 390)

                1.

                2.

            b. Explain the possible role of endorphins in drug addiction.   (p. 390)

        2. Relief of pain
            Do the authors place much value on an addict's statement that he/she became
            addicted to drugs during an illness?   (p. 391)

        3. Psychopathology
            What were the distinguishing features found among a large number of addicts
            studied by Gilbert and Lombardi (1967)?   (p. 391)

4. Sociocultural factors
What changes are seen in the young addict who has joined the drug subculture?
(p. 391)

9. Treatment and outcomes
a. How successful were English hospitals at curing addiction with group and individual counseling?
(p. 391)

b. Describe the research that Dole et al. (1968, 1969) did with methadone hydrochloride.
(p. 391)

c. Has psychotherapy been found to add significant benefit to that achieved through the use of methadone alone according to Rounsaville et al. (1986)? YES OR NO   (p. 391)

d. List the pros and cons of methadone maintenance programs:

Pros	Cons
1. Methodone is legal, safe	1.
2. The dose does not increase	2.
3. Patients can hold jobs	3.

10. The barbiturates (sedatives)
a. How can barbiturates cause death?   (p. 392)

b. What age group is most often found to be addicted to barbiturates?   (p. 392)

c. What happens after prolonged, excessive use of barbiturates?   (p. 392)

d. What type of feelings might lead a person to seek relief from barbiturates?
(p. 392)

e. Describe the typical symptoms of barbiturate withdrawal.   (p. 392)

f. How can these symptoms be minimized?   (pp. 392-393)

11. The amphetamines and cocaine (stimulants)
    a. What are the legitimate medical uses of amphetamines?   (p. 393)

    b. Are amphetamines addicting?   (p. 394)

    c. Does one build up tolerance to them?   (p. 394)

    d. What are the major physiological effects of taking amphetamines?   (p. 394)

    e. When does amphetamine psychosis occur?   (p. 394)

    f. How can amphetamine intoxication lead to acts of violence?   (p. 394)

    g. What happens when an established user of amphetamines abruptly stops taking the drug?   (p.394)

12 Cocaine
    a. What are the effects of taking cocaine?   (p. 395)

    b. What is the "cocaine bug"?   (p. 395)

    c. Does tolerance to cocaine develop?   (p. 395)

    d. Why is crack believed to be the most dangerous drug introduced to date?   (p. 396)

13. LSD and related drugs (hallucinogens)
    a.   Name four hallucinogenic drugs: (p. 397)

        1.

        2.

        3.

        4.

    b.   What effects does LSD have on sensory perception?   (p. 397)

    c.   Under what circumstances is LSD likely to lead to a bad trip as opposed to a good trip according to the research of Blacker (1968)?   (p. 397)
    d.   Does LSD usually induce psychosis in a person who only takes the drug once and who has previously been well adjusted?   (pp. 397-398)

    e.   Is there evidence that LSD enhances creativity?   (p. 398)

    f.   How difficult is it to treat dependence on LSD?   (p. 398)

14. Marijuana
    a.   What is the difference between marijuana and hashish?   (p. 398)

    b.   During the 1970s what proportion of teenagers and young adults experimented with marijuana?   (p. 398)

    c.   Describe the physical effects of marijuana: (pp. 398-399)

        1.   Psychological effects: pleasurable experiences seem to be enhanced but use may lead to unpleasant feelings if the drug is taken when unhappy or angry.

        2.   Short-range physiological effects: _____
        _____

d. How likely is marijuana to cause problems leading to hospitalization compared to alcohol and barbiturates? (p. 399)

e. Regarding the effects of marijuana:

    1. Does marijuana lead to physiological dependence? (p. 399)

    2. Does lead to psychological dependence? (p. 399)

f. Respond true or false to the following controversial statements regarding marijuana:
(pp. 400-401)

    1. There are important personality differences
between users and nonusers.   TRUE OR FALSE

    2. Marijuana has some adverse effects on physical
health.   TRUE OR FALSE

    3. Marijuana has beneficial medical uses.   TRUE OR FALSE

    4. Marijuana enhances creativity.   TRUE OR FALSE

    5. Marijuana does not effect driving or piloting skills.   TRUE OR FALSE

g. What are the arguments against legalization of marijuana use? (p. 401)

15. Extreme obesity
    a. The population of the United States is 220 million. How many of these people are over-weight according to Jeffrey and Katz (1977)? (p. 401)

    b. How does obesity put a person at greater risk for death? (p. 401)

16. Causes of persistent overeating
    a. Obesity in adults is related to the number and size of the adipose cells (fat cells) in the body. People who are obese have markedly _____ adipose cells that people of normal weight. (p. 402)

    b. How can overfeeding a child predispose him or her to obesity in adulthood?
(p. 402)

c. Although there is no conclusive research to support it, there is a psychodyanmic explanation of obesity. What is the psychodynamic explanation of obesity?

(p. 402)

d. What is the externality hypothesis of obesity and is it supported by research findings?

(pp. 402-403)

e. What is the behavioral explanation of obesity?   (p. 403)

f. It has been said that you can never be too rich or too thin. Is there in fact any evidence that weight is related to income or social class?   (p. 403)

17. Treatment of extreme obesity
  a. What is the average outcome of diets according to Stuart (1967)?   (p. 403)

  b. What type of treatment has been found to be most effective for obesity?   (p. 403)

  c. What do the authors of the text conclude about the effectiveness of the following methods of losing weight?   (pp. 403-404)

    1. TOPS and Weight Watchers

    2. Fasting or starvation diets

    3. Anorexigenic drugs

    4. Bypass operations

    5. Behavioral management methods

18. Pathological gambling
  a. In what ways can gambling be considered an addictive disorder?   (p. 405)

b. It is estimated that _____ percent of the population (over 100 million people) gambles in some form. However, only _____ get hooked on gambling.

(p. 406)

c. How can compulsive gambling be explained by the principle of intermittent reinforcement?

(p. 406)

d. How did Rosten (1961) characterize the compulsive gambler?

(p. 407)

e. What type of evidence suggests that gambling, alcoholism, and drug use may be related to common personality characteristics?

(p. 407)

f. Work by Aronoff (1987) has pinpointed Loatian refugees as very high risk group for compulsive gambling. What four factors are thought to account for the problem of gambling in this group of people?

(pp. 407-408)

1.

2.

3.

4.

19. Treatment and outcomes
    a. If a gambler joins a Gambler's Anonymous group, how likely is it that he/she will overcome the addiction to gambling?

(p. 408)

    b. List the treatment approaches used to assist compulsive gamblers at the Brecksville, Ohio Veteran's Administration Medical Center.

(p. 408)

20. Unresolved issues
    a. Sobell and Sobell (1973) claim that many alcoholics could learn to drink socially and did not have to abstain totally from alcohol. What evidence supports their view?

(pp. 409-410)

b.   Does AA accept the validity of the controlled drinking philosophy of treatment?

(p. 410)

(21.)   Some common misconceptions about alcohol and alcoholism   (p. 371)
a. Does alcohol help a person sleep more soundly?
YES OR NO

b. Does alcohol produce a true addiction in the same sense that heroin does?
YES OR NO

(22.)   Alcohol levels in the blood after drinks taken on an empty stomach by a 150-pound male
drinking for one hour   (p. 372)

The legal level of intoxication, .1% blood alcohol level, would be reached after a 150
pound man had drunk _____ bottles of beer in one hour.   It would require
_____ hours for the alcohol to leave the body before it was safe to drive.

(23.)   Early warning signs of drinking problems
When is frequent desire to drink a warning sign of drinking problems?   (p. 375)

(24.)   Fetal alcohol syndrome
How commonly are birth defects related to alcohol abuse?   (p. 376)

(25.) Psychoactive drugs commonly involved in drug abuse
Complete the following table that summarizes psychoactive drug abuse: (p. 387)

CLASSIFICATION	SAMPLE DRUG	EFFECT
sedatives	alcohol	reduce tension, blot out
stimulants		
	heroin	induce relaxation and reverie
psychedelics		induce changes in mood, mind expansion
antianxiety		

CHAPTER QUIZ

1. A person who shows tolerance for a drug or withdrawal symptoms when it is unavailable
    illustrates: (p. 368)

    a. psychoactive substance abuse.
    b. psychoactive substance dependence.
    c. psychoactive substance toxicity.
    d. psychoactive substance-induced organic mental disorders and syndromes.

2. The life of the average alcoholic is about _____ years shorter than that of the average
    citizen.   (p. 368)

    a. 3   c. 12
    b. 6   d. 18

3. A person who is considered intoxicated when the alcohol content of the bloodstream reaches
    _____ percent.   (p. 371)

    a. 0.1   c. 1.0
    b. 0.5   d. 1.5

4. Maynard is 75 and has been an alcoholic for 15 years. He has a lot of trouble remembering
    things that just happened. In order to avoid embarrassment, he often makes up things so
    others won't know he forgot. Maynard's disorder is probably: (p. 375)

    a. alcohol amnestic disorder.   c. alcohol withdrawal delirium.
    b. alcohol idiosyncratic intoxication. d. chronic alcoholic hallucinosis.

5. Goodwin and his colleagues concluded that which of the following situations put a son at
    greatest risk of becoming alcoholic?   (p. 376)

    a. being born to an alcoholic parent
    b. being born to nonalcoholic parents
    c. being raised by an alcoholic parent
    d. being raised by nonalcholic parents

6. The only personality characteristic that appears common to the backgrounds of most
    problem drinkers is: (p. 377)

    a. general depression.   c. inadequate sexual adjustment.
    b. emotional immaturity.   d. personal maladjustment.

7. A cultural attitude of approbation and permissiveness toward drinking, such as exists in France, generally: (p. 379)

    a. is correlated with a low rate of alcoholism and problem drinking.
    b. is a sign that alcoholism has been accepted as a normal behavior pattern.
    c. is associated with the common use of alcohol as a means of coping with stress.
    d. has no significant effect on either alcoholism or drinking behavior.

8. Extinction of drinking behavior by associating it with noxious mental images is a procedure called: (p. 382)

    a. Antabuse.
    b. systematic desensitization.
    c. covert sensitization.
    d. implosive therapy.

9. In their four year follow-up of a large group of treated alcoholics, Polich et al. (1981) found that _____ percent continued to show alcohol-related problems. (p. 383)

    a. 7
    b. 18
    c. 36
    d. 54

10. In an extensive comparative study of several different treatments for alcoholism, Brandsma found that the Alcoholics Anonymous treatment was: (p. 383)

    a. better than some treatments and worse than others.
    b. equally as effective as all others.
    c. less effective than all others.
    d. more effective than all others.

11. According to Marlatt's cognitive-behavioral view, alcoholic relapse is typically based upon: (p. 385)

    a. accidental "falling off the wagon."
    b. an overpowering psychological craving.
    c. small, apparently irrelevant decisions.
    d. sudden increases in stressor strength.

12. Cocaine is classified as a(an): (p. 385)

    a. hallucinogen.
    b. narcotic.
    c. sedative.
    d. stimulant.

13. The human body produces its own opiumlike substances called _____ in the brain and pituitary gland. (p. 390)

    a. antibodies
    b. dopamines
    c. endorphins
    d. phagocytes

14. Which of the following personality disorders has the <u>highest</u> incidence among heroin
    addicts?   (p. 390)

    a. antisocial   c. compulsive
    b. avoidant   d. dependent

15. Apparently, adipose cells (fat cells):   (p. 402)

    a. increase in number and size when an adult gains weight.
    b. have no relation to obesity.
    c. decrease in size, but not number, when an adult loses weight.
    d. change chemical structure in obese adults.

12

Sexual Disorders and Variants

OVERVIEW

Chapter 12 contains three separate sections that are related to sexual behavior: sexual dysfunctions, sexual variants and deviations, and homosexuality. These labels really don't describe anything about the personality characteristics of an individual. They describe one aspect of that individual's behavior. Many of the conditions may be seen in any kind of individual--normal or abnormal.

The first section concerns the sexual dysfunctions. These are problems that may interfere with an individual's full enjoyment of sexual relations. The sexual dysfunctions are not mental disorders but are simply behaviors that can be changed. The second section discusses behaviors that are considered "sex crimes." Most of these behaviors, such as pedophilia or voyeurism, are considered to be mental disorders as well.

The last section discusses homosexuality which is simply an alternative sexual preference and is not considered to be a mental disorder.

LEARNING OBJECTIVES

1. List and describe four sexual dysfunctions that affect men.

2. List and describe three sexual dysfunctions that affect women.

3. List and describe two sexual dysfunctions that may affect both men and women.

4. List and explain four factors that may cause sexual dysfunctions.

5. Describe the recent revolution in the treatment of sexual dysfunctions and explain why they are not normally disorders of individuals.

6. Differentiate between *victimless* and *nonconsent* types of sexual variations and list several examples of each.

7. Summarize the results of research concerning biological and psychosocial causes of gender identity disorders and evaluate sex reassignment surgery as a solution.

8. Define *paraphilias* and list nine examples recognized in DSM-III-R.

9. Define *fetishism*, give several examples, and summarize what is known about its causes.

10. Define *transvestic fetishism* and summarize what is known about its causes.

11. Define *voyeurism*, list two other terms that are synonyms, and summarize what is known about its causes.

12. Define *exhibitionism* and describe types of causes that may underlie the practice.

13. Define *sexual sadism* and describe three sets of causes for this disorder.

14. Define *sexual masochism* and summarize what is known about its causes.

15. Define *pedophilia* and describe four sets of causes for this disorder.

16. Define *incest*, describe five sets of causes for this disorder, and summarize what is known about the psychological effects on its victims.

17. Differentiate between *forcible* and *statutory rape* and describe three sets of motives which may influence the rapist.

18. Summarize what is known about the successful treatment of sexual variants and deviations.

19. Explain why homosexuality has been removed from the list of officially recognized mental disorders and explain your authors' dissatisfaction with this action.

20. Explain why it is impossible to classify everyone as either homosexual or heterosexual and evaluate the common practice of assuming that male and female homosexuals are similar.

21. Summarize what we know about five different sets of factors that may cause homosexuality.

22. Summarize the changes in society's attitudes toward homosexuality and evaluate the possible effects of AIDS on these trends.

23. Describe five problems associated with sexual disorders and variations that remain unresolved in our society.

TERMS YOU SHOULD KNOW

sexual dysfunction (p. 414)

sexual variants (p. 414)

erectile insufficiency, erectile disorder (formerly impotence) (p. 415)

primary insufficiency (p. 415)

secondary insufficiency (p. 415)

premature ejaculation (p. 415)

inhibited male orgasm (p. 415)

female sexual arousal disorder (formerly frigidity) (p. 416)

inhibited female orgasm (p. 416)

primary orgasmic dysfunction (p. 416)

functional vaginismus (p. 416)

dyspareunia (p. 416)

sexual desire disorders (p. 416)

spectator role (p. 417)

sexual moron (p. 418)

castrating females (p. 418)

variant sexual behavior (p. 420)

victimless sexual variants (p. 420)

gender identity disorder (pp. 420-421)

sex reassignment surgery (pp. 421-422)

paraphilia (p. 423)

fetishism (p. 424)

transvestic fetishism (pp. 424-425)

voyeurism (p. 426)

exhibitionism (pp. 426-427)

sadism (p. 428)

pathological sadists (p. 429)

masochism (p. 430)

pedophilia (p. 430)

incest (p. 432)

situational incest (p. 433)

rape (p. 434)

statutory rape (p. 434)

victim-precipitated rape (p. 435)

power-assertive type (of rapist) (p. 436)

power-reassurance type (of rapist) (p. 436)

anger-retaliation type (of rapist) (p. 436)

anger-excitation type (of rapist) (p. 436)

homosexuality (p. 438)

ego-dystonic homosexuality (p. 438)

continuum of sexual behavior (p. 439)

lesbianism (p. 440)

AIDS (p. 445)

(transsexualism) (p. 422)

(sexual efficiency) (p. 441)

(gay community) (p. 442)

(gay bar) (p. 442)

(Mattachine societies) (p. 442)

(Daughters of Bilitis) (p. 442)

CONCEPTS TO MASTER

1. Introduction
    a. The authors note several dimensions on which human sexual behavior has become more complicated than that of lower animals. The most important of these dimensions, they say, is the increasing _____
        as we move up the phylogenetic scale of development. Additional differences are the freedom of the human female from biologically based cycles of receptivity, and enormously increased adpatability in human sexual needs as a result of disengagement from their primary biological base.   (p. 414)

    b. These gains in flexibility have come at some cost--the gains in flexibility and adaptability of human sexual functioning have led to increased probability that sexuality will go awry. The two abnormalities of human sexuality dealt with in the chapter are the sexual _____ which involve inhibitions in sexual desire or functioning; and the sexual _____ which include those forms of sexual behavior that fall outside the range of generally accepted heterosexual activity.
                                                                                                                (p. 414)

2. Sexual Dysfunctions affecting the male
    The term *sexual dysfunction* refers to impairment either in the desire for sexual gratification or in the ability to achieve it. With some exceptions, these impairments are based on faulty psychosexual adjustment and learning.
    a. Explain the distinction between *primary* and *secondary* erectile insufficiency.
                                                                                                                (p. 415)

    b. Circle the correct term: Prolonged or permanent erective insugfficiency before the age of 60 is relatively: COMMON/RARE.   (p. 415)

    c.   Somewhere around _____percent of cases of erectile insufficiency are caused by
        organic or medical conditions including vascular disease, diabetes, etc.   (p. 415)

    d.   Can insufficiency due to organic causes be differentiated from psychogenic
        insufficiency by the presence of nocturnal erections?   YES OR NO   (p. 415)

    e.   LoPicolo's (1978) rule for determining when a male is a premature
        ejaculator is an inability to tolerate as much as _____minutes of stimulation
        without ejaculation. Younger men are notorious for their "quick trigger" and longer
        periods of abstinence unrelieved by masturbation increase the likelihood of premature
        ejaculation.   (p. 415)

    f.   It is thought that many more men experience retarded ejaculation than
        the number who seek the help of sex therapists. Why don't men seek help for this
        problem?   (p. 415)

3.   Dysfunctions affecting the female
    a.   What is the difference between a woman with "sexual arousal disorder" and one with
        "inhibited orgasm"?   (p. 416)

    b.   Vaginismus is an involuntary spasm of the muscles at the entrance to the vagina that
        prevents penetration and intercourse. In some cases women who suffer from
        vaginismus also have arousal insufficiency, possibly the result of conditioned fears
        associated with _____.   (p. 416)

4.   Dysfunctions affecting both sexes
    a.   The medical term for painful coitus (sexual intercourse) is _____.
        It can occur in the male but is far more common in the female.   (p. 416)

    b.   How is sexual desire disorder, which can affect either men or women, different from
        sexual arousal disorders?   (p. 416)

5.   Causal factors in sexual dysfunction
    The authors consider four causes of sexual dysfunction: (1) faulty learning,
    (2) feelings of fear and inadequacy, (3) interpersonal problems, and (4) social roles.
    Respond to the following questions regarding each causal factor:
    a.   Faulty learning
        1.   Kaplan (1974) has concluded that sexual education is too often left to chance.

Couples with sexual problems are typically practicing insensitive, incompetent, and ineffective _____.

(p. 417)

2. What two ideas may be part of a woman's early training about sex that subsequently exert a negative influence on her ability to fully enjoy sexual relations?   (pp. 416-417)

    a.

    b.

3. What may be the result of a young man having his first sexual experience under conditions where he is hurried and fears discovery?   (p. 417)

b. Feelings of fear

    1. Cooper (1969) reported that anxiety was a contributing factor in _____ percent of men with erectile difficulties.   (p. 417)

    2. Masters and Johnson (1975) have concluded that most sexual dysfunctions in males and females are due to fear and anxiety. This anxiety is based on mis-information in early sex training and later aversive experiences with actual sexual relations. An anxious person often adopts a _____ role during sex that leads him or her to become an observer of the sexual relations rather than a wholehearted participant. In this role the person often worries about the adequacy of his or her performance, and these anxieties serve as distractions and make the sexual performance even worse.   (p. 417)

c. Interpersonal problems
    Many investigators believe that an individual should be able to experience pleasure and orgasm with any "personally acceptable partner." However, some couples experience changes in their relationship that lead to a termination of their "acceptability" to each other. What are several situations that can lead to a lack of emotional closeness and a lack of "acceptability" as sexual partners?
    (p. 417)

    d. Social roles

How do the authors of the text believe that changes in the social roles of women have affected men's sexuality? How have these changes affected women's sexuality?   (p.418)

6. Treatment and outcomes

    a. Once the treatment of sexual dysfunctions was considered very difficult. However, a revolution in treating these difficulties has occurred and success rates approaching _____ percent are not unusual.   (pp. 418-419)

    b. Masters and Johnson's approach to treating sexual dysfunction, described in their book *Human Sexual Inadequacy,* combines elements of traditional and behavioral therapy and emphasizes direct intervention aimed at _____.

        (p. 419)

    c. After Masters and Johnson's pioneering book, many approaches to treating sexual dysfunction were developed. Most approaches are in general agreement about the major goals of treatment. Complete the following list of the goals of sex therapy:

        (p. 419)

      1. Removing crippling misconceptions, inhibitions, and fears

      2. Fostering attitudes and participation in sexual behavior as a

_____, _____, _____ human experience and not a test of personal adequacy or performance

    d. What do clinicians mean when they say that a particular sexual dysfunction (such as orgasmic dysfunction) is a "disorder of relationship"?   (p. 419)

    e. With competent treatment, success rates vary between approximately ___ percent and _____ percent, depending on the couple and the nature of the problem. What range of successful outcomes has been reported by sex therapists?

        (p. 419)

    f. Place the following sexual dysfunctions in the appropriate column to indicate how well they respond to treatment: erectile insufficiency, premature ejaculation, vaginismus, and orgasmic dysfunction.   (pp. 419-420)

High Success Rates   **Lower Success Rates**

7. Sexual variants and deviations
    Variant sexual behavior is behavior in which satisfaction involves a <u>nonmutual</u> sexual
    engagement with an adult, opposite sex partner.
    a. The authors distinguish between sexual variants which involve nonmutual sexual
        behavior and victimless sexual variants which do not infringe on the rights of others,
        are engaged in by mutual consent, and do not harm the partner. What variants do the
        authors place in the category of victimless sexual variants?   (p. 420)

    b. Treatment programs for sexual variants cannot focus solely on removing the deviant
        sexual behavior. According to writers such as Barlow (1974) and Adams and Sturgis
        (1977), in addition to techniques to stop the deviant sexuality, three other areas
        should receive attention in the treatment program. They are: (p. 420)

        1. The absence of a normal level of arousal to adults of the opposite sex

        2.

        3.

8. Gender identity: problems and disorder
    These disorders reflect confusion, uncertainty, or vagueness in a person's concepts of his or
    her identity as male or female.
    a. According to Money and colleagues (1980), how important is learning in determining
        whether a person adopts a male or female social role?   (p. 421)

    b. Complete this statement: While many poorly adapted people lack a strong
        identification with either male or female gender roles, the most functional men and
        women in our society demonstrate....   (p. 421)

    c. While psychosocial influences on gender identity and role are important, mounting
        evidence seggests that _____ factors are also important. These
        findings do much to explain why homesexuality, for example, has been maintained for
        centuries in human societies despite strong social disapproval.   (p. 421)

d. Gender identity disorder involves profound rejection of one's anatomical sex and is rare. The incidence in men is estimated to be less than _____ persons in 100,000. The incidence in women is even lower (<1/100,000). (p. 421)

e. Green (1974) studied transexual boys. She found that the boys shared parental indifference to or encouragement of feminine behavior, maternal overprotection, and dressing the child in female clothes. Later, Green (1985) recontacted these boys. Describe them in adulthood. (p. 421)

f. Has behavior therapy or psychotherapy been successful in altering gender identity? (p. 421)

g. Describe what procedures are involved in the following surgical changes of sex:
(pp. 421-422)

   1. male-to-female

   2. female-to-male

h. What do follow-up studies by Benjamin (1966) and Abramowitz (1986) reveal about the satisfaction of persons who have had sex-change surgery? (pp. 422-423)

i. Why is it recommended that a person seeking sex-change therapy spend a period of time cross-dressing and taking hormones? (p. 423)

9. The paraphilias
These are a group of persistent sexual arousal patterns in which unusual objects, rituals, or situations are required for sexual satisfaction to occur.

10. Fetishism
   a. In fetishism there is a centering of sexual interest on some body part or an inaminate object. Describe how fetishists get their desired objects and what they do with them once obtained. (pp. 423-424)

   b. What is most arousing to the fetishish, the fetish or the illegal act of obtaining the object? (p. 424)

   c. How can fetishes be developed through conditioning? (p. 424)

11. Transvestic fetishism
   a. Transvestic fetishism involves the obtaining sexual excitment by wearing the clothes of the opposite sex. Do transvestites see themselves as homosexuals? (p. 425)

   b. Bentler and colleagues (1969, 1970) administered a standardized psychological inventory to a large sample of transvestites and to a matched control group. Describe their findings. (p. 425)

   c. Gosslin and Eysenck (1980) asked male transvestites to take personality tests while wearing men's clothes and again when dressed as a woman. Describe their results. (p. 425)

12. Voyeurism
   a. Voyeurism, also known as scotophilia and inspectionalism, refers to obtaining sexual pleasure through looking at other people undressing or having sex. What age group commits the majority of voyeuristic acts? (p. 426)

   b. Many boys enjoy looking at attractive women. Under what conditions does this normal behavior become voyeurism ? (p. 426)

   c. If a voyeur is married, how well adjusted would he be expected to be in his sexual relationships with his wife? (p. 426)

d. Why doesn't pornography seem to satisfy most voyeurs?   (p. 426)

13. Exhibitionism
    a. Exhibitionsim involves obtaining sexual pleasure from exposing the genitals to others under inappropriate conditions such as in a public place. How common is exhibitionism in the following countries: (pp. 426-427)

        1.   United States

        2.   Europe

        3.   Japan

        4.   India

    b. The authors discuss three causes of exhibitionism: personal immaturity, interpersonal stress and psychopathology. Respond to the following questions about these causes:

        1.   Personal immaturity
             Witzig (1968) studied exhibitionists. He reported that approximately_____
             percent of them were immature. He also found that they possessed inadequate sexual information, were shy, had puritanical standards about masturbation, and felt inadequate to approach women.   (p. 427)

        2.   Interpersonal stress
             Exhibitionism may also be related to life stress. During periods of stress an individual may regress to adolescent _____
             _____.
                                                                            (p. 428)
        3.   Psychopathology
             Exhibitionism may occur in association with a variety of psychopathology including_____, senile brain deterioration, and psychopathic personality.   (p. 428)

14. Sadism
    a. Sadism refers to the achievement of sexual gratification through the infliction of physical pain, psychic pain, or humiliation on a sexual partner. Sometimes sadistic activities are associated with objects other than human beings such as
       _____.
                                                                            (pp. 428-429)

    b. What is a "pathological sadist"?   (p. 429)

c.   The authors mention three causal factors for sadism. Complete the following list:

(pp. 429-430)

1.   Negative attitudes toward sex: may help express contempt and punishment of the other person for engaging in sex

2.

3.   Association with other psychopathology including schizophrenia

15. Masochism
    a.   Masochism includes deriving pleasure from self-denial, physical suffering, and hardship in general. How do patterns of masochistic behavior usually develop?

(p. 430)

    b.   Explain how the clinical picture in maschoism is similar to that in sadistic practices.

(p. 430)

    c.   What does it mean to say that sadism and masochism require a "shared complementary interpersonal relationship"?   (p. 430)

16. Pedophilia
    a.   In pedophilia the sex object is a _____ and the intimacy usually involves _____.   (p. 430)

    b.   Most pedophiliacs are men. The average age of pedophiliacs is _____ years old. By a ratio of 2 to 1, _____ are most often victimized.   (p. 430)

    c.   Respond to the following questions: (p. 431)

        1.   Are most pedophiliacs known to their victims?   YES OR NO

        2.   Do most pedophiliacs use force?   YES OR NO

        3.   Is pedophilia usually a one-time event?   YES OR NO

        4.   Does the victim of a pedophiliac actively participate?   YES OR NO

d. Briefly describe each of the following types of offenders: (p. 431)

    1. The immature offender

    2. The regressed offender

    3. The conditioned offender

    4. The psychopathic offender

17. Other deviations: Incest and rape
    a. Incest
    Culturally prohibited sexual relations, up to sexual intercourse, between family members including brothers and sisters or parents and children. Describe the consequences of inbreeding among 12 brother-sister and 6 father-daughter matings as studied by Adams and Neel (1967).   (p.432)

    b. Incest is thought to be grossly underreported to authorities, but Meiselman (1978) estimates the incidence at 1-2 per _____ persons. In all studies, brother-sister incest is 5 times more common than father-daughter incest.   (p. 432)

    c. How common is mother-son incest compared to father-daughter?   (p. 432)

    d. The authors suggest five causal patterns for incest: situational incest, incest associated with psychopathology, incest associated with pedophilia, incest associated with a faulty paternal model, and incest associated with family pathology and disturbed marital relations. Respond to the following questions about the patterns.

        1. What is "situational incest"?   (p. 433)

        2. What forms of psychopathology may be related to incest?   (p. 433)

3. In pedophilic incest, a parent has an intense sexual craving for young children, including his or her own. Is this motivation a major factor in causing incest?

4. What impact does an incestuous relationship between father and daughter have on the sons of the family if they become aware of it?   (p. 433)

5. Is incest likely to occur in a home where the parents have a good marital relationship?   (p. 433)

e. Describe the fathers convicted of incestuous relations with their daughters who were studied by Cavillin (1966):   (pp. 433-434)

1. History of mental disorder

2. History of extramarital affairs

3. Average age of father

4. Average age of daughter

5. Father's feelings toward the mother

6. The feelings of the abused daughter

18. Rape
    a. What has happened to the incidence of rape over the last ten years?   (p. 434)

b.   The actual prevalence of rape is thought to be ten times higher than the number of incidents reported to the police. Why do rape victims fail to report their rape to the police?   (pp. 434-435)

c.   How old is the typical rapist?   (p. 435)

d.   Respond to the following questions by circling the appropriate answer: (p. 435)

1.   Rape is a young man's crime?   YES OR NO

2.   Rape is a repetitive activity?   YES OR NO

3.   Most rapes are planned?   YES OR NO

4.   A third of rapes involve more than one offender?   YES OR NO

5.   The closer the relationship between victim and offender, the
more brutally the victim may be beaten?   YES OR NO

e.   Far from being seductresses, the woman repeatedly victimized by rape was found by Calhoun et al. (1982) to be more likely a _____.
                                                                                                         (pp. 435)

f.   Although rape involves sexual relations, did Groth et al. (1977) discover a single case where sexual satisfaction was the rapist's primary motive?   (pp. 435-436)

g.   Briefly describe the following types of rapists: (p. 436)

1.   Power-assertive

2.   Power reassurance

3.   Anger-retaliation

4.   Anger-excitation

h. Label the following diagram to illustrate how frequently each of these types of rapist
    occur: (p. 436)

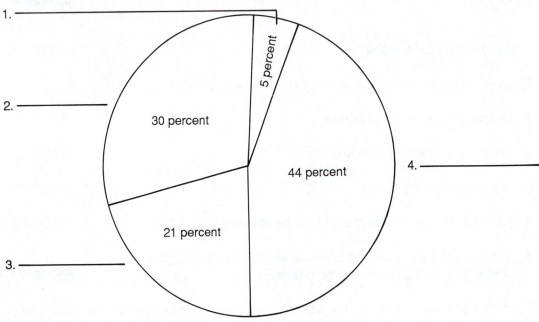

19. Treatment and outcomes
    a. Most sexually variant acts cannot be adequately conceptualized simply as aberrations of
        sexual arousal. In most instances we also need to look at: (pp. 436-437)

        1.

        2.

        3. Gender identity development

    b. How did Barlow and Abel (1976) (1) modify feminine gender role, (2) improve social
        skills, (3) increase arousal to heterosexual stimuli and (4) decrease arousal to
        homosexual stimuli in their treatment of a 17-year-old transsexual male?
                                                                             (p. 437)

20. Male and female homosexuality
    In 1973, the trustees of the American Psychiatric Association voted to remove homosexuality from the list of officially recognized mental disorders. However, the removal of stigma was incomplete. There are still circumstances under which homosexuality is considered to constitute a mental disorder according to the DSM-III. What are these circumstances? (p. 438)

21. Continuum of sexual behavior
    a. Kinsey (1948) surveyed the sexual behavior of white male subjects. How frequent were the following experiences? (pp. 439-440)

    _____ percent   1. Homosexual experience to the point of orgasm at least once during adolescence.

    _____ percent   2. As many homosexual encounters as heterosexual.

    _____ percent   3. Exclusively homosexual experience since adolescence.

    b. How do the homosexual experiences reported by women differ from those reported by men? (pp. 439-440)

    c. What have laboratory studies of arousal revealed about bisexuality? (p. 440)

    d. Taking all evidence into account, the authors of the text estimate that there are _____million people in the U.S. who consistently engage in homosexual acts although they are not exclusively homosexual. (p. 440)

22. The question of causal factors (of homosexuality)
    The authors consider five causal factors of homosexuality: genetic and hormonal factors, positive reinforcement of homosexual experiences, negative conditioning of heterosexual experiences, family patterns, and sociocultural factors. Respond to the following questions about each causal factor: (pp. 440-444)
    a. Genetic and hormonal factors
        Kallman reported a _____ percent concordance rate for homosexuality among identical twins. Pillard and Weinrich (1986) found that homosexuality was four time the expected rate among brothers of male homosexuals. Money and his associates have looked at male hormone levels during _____ to understand homosexuality. They believe that these hormonal influences may affect the formation of brain pathways, leading to propensities toward a relatively _____ or_____ behavioral orientation. (pp. 440-441)

b. Early homosexual experiences
    Early homosexual experiences are reported as pleasurableand many people engage voluntarily in them. Under what circumstances do they lead to adult homosexuality?   (p. 443)

c. Negative heterosexual experiences

    1. What circumstances could lead to the negative conditioning of heterosexual behavior?   (p. 443)

    2. How typical is it for a homosexual to have had heterosexual experience or even to have been married according to Bell & Weinberg, (1978)?   (p. 443)

d. Family patterns

    1. Describe the common family background Bieber et al. (1962) found among male homosexuals.   (pp. 443-444)

    2. Although these findings have been repeated a number of times, they have also been challenged. How do the authors conclude that family background is related to homosexuality?   (p. 444)

e. General sociocultural patterns

    1. Under what circumstances might the rate of homosexuality rise in a society?
                                                                (p. 444)

    2. Describe evidence provided by Stoller and Herdt (1985) from the Sambia people of New Guinea that challenges any simple social learning explanation of adult homosexuality.   (p. 444)

23. Homosexuality and society
    What does history teach us about the possibility of eradicating homosexuality from society?   (p. 445)

24. Unresolved issues on sexual disorders and variants
    The authors suggest that as a society we are failing to curb sexual exploitation, victimization, and assault. This failure results in serious short- and long-term consequences for victims. What do we need to know in order to do a better job of curbing such behavior?   (p. 446)

(25).   Sexual molestation of young children
    a.   Why don't professionals recognize even blatant cases of abuse?   (p. 434)

    b.   Who is most frequently the offender in child molestation cases?   (p. 434)

(26.)   Should homosexuality be treated?
    There are experts who argue that homosexuality should be treated and experts who argue that it should not be treated. Briefly present the views of both sides: (p. 439)

    a.   Psychologists should offer treatment to homosexuals because:

    b.   Psychologists should not offer treatment to homosexuals because:

(27.)   The Masters and Johnson (1979) perspective on homosexuality
    a.   Describe the sample studied by Masters and Johnson   (p. 441)

    b.   In what senses may this sample be unrepresentative of homosexuals in general?
                                                                               (p. 441)

    c.   How did Masters and Johnson find homosexuals and heterosexuals compared in the following areas?   (p. 441)
        1.   Sexual efficiency

    2.   Fantasies males have

    3.   Fantasies females have

    4.   Communication regarding sexual preferences and needs

    5.   Patterns of lovemaking

    d.   How successful were Masters and Johnson in achieving "reorientation" among the homosexuals who came to them for treatment?   (p. 441)

CHAPTER QUIZ

1. Impairment of either the desire for sexual gratification or of the ability to achievement is termed sexual: (p. 414)

    a. dysfunction.   c. perversion.
    b. incompetence.   d. variation.

2. According to the findings of Kinsey and his associates, about _____ of males become impotent by the age of 70.   (p. 415)

    a. one-fourth   c. two-thirds
    b. one-half   d. three-fourths

3. Most cases of sexual dysfunction seem traceable to _____ causes.   (p. 416)

    a. drug-related   c. psychological
    b. organic   d. sociocultural

4. According to Masters and Johnson, sexual dysfunctions are usually disorders of: (p. 419)

a. individuals as separate entities.
b. the psyche and its conflicts.
c. the relationships between individuals.
d. the society and its sexual rules.

5. An example of victimless sexual variants is: (p. 420)

a. voyeurism.   c. sadism.
b. exhibitionism.   d. transvestism.

6. An adult whose background was characterized by encouragement of feminine behavior, maternal overprotection, and lack of male friends would most likely receive which diagnosis? (pp. 420-421)

a. homosexuality   c. transvestism
b. gender identity disorder d. psychosexual dysfunction

7. Which of the following persons is most likely to engage in voyeurism? (p. 426)

a. a married woman who is unhappy with her sexual relations
b. a homosexual man who is "in between" lovers
c. an adolescent male who is shy and feels dominated by women
d. an elderly man who lives by himself

8. The most common sexual offense reported to the police is: (p. 427)

a. exhibitionism.   c. voyeurism.
b. obscene phone calls.   d. rape.

9. Most exhibitionists: (p. 427)

a. are adolescents who have never had sexual relations.
b. are immature married males.
c. are also aggressive and assaultive.
d. try to have sexual relations with their victims.

10. For the regressed pedophiliac, the most frequent event precipitating an offense is: (p. 431)

a. being humiliated by an adult sex partner.
b. having an erectile problem during intercourse.
c. seeing a child's underclothing.
d. the discovery that his wife or girlfriend is having an affair.

11. Which of the following types of pedophiliac offenders has had early sexual experiences with young boys often in reformatories?   (p. 431)

    a.   the conditioned offender
    b.   the personally immature offender
    c.   the psychopathic offender
    d.   the regressed offender

12. In Cavillin's study of incestuous fathers, all twelve reported that: (p. 433)

    a.   their daughters had seduced them.
    b.   they felt rejected and threatened by their wives.
    c.   they had always been sexually attracted to children.
    d.   they loved their daughters dearly.

13. Sgroi claims that even in the face of overwhelming evidence of sexual abuse, physicians are extremely reluctant to conclude that a child has been attacked apparently because:
                                                                           (p. 434)
    a.   it is considered "in bad taste."
    b.   it will just make more trouble for the child.
    c.   they are not legally bound to report sexual abuse.
    d.   they fear reprisal from the parents.

14. According to the authors, the fact that some homosexuals have high talent and multiple accomplishments shows that: (p. 439)

    a.   homosexuality causes superior functioning.
    b.   homosexuality is compatible with superior functioning.
    c.   homosexuals are normal rather than abnormal.
    d.   superior functioning is highly correlated with homosexuality.

15. Laboratory studies of arousal patterns of self-proclaimed bisexuals have shown that they respond: (p. 440)

    a.   differently in the laboratory than at home.
    b.   equally to homosexual and heterosexual stimuli.
    c.   more strongly to heterosexual than homosexual stimuli.
    d.   more strongly to homosexual than heterosexual stimuli.

13

Organic Mental Disorders
and Mental Retardation

OVERVIEW

Most mental disorders do not involve any known brain pathology. Those that do are discussed in this chapter. The chapter is divided into two major divisions: (1) organic mental disorders and (2) mental retardation.

The discussion of organic mental disorders begins with a description of the kinds of symptoms that may be seen as a result of brain pathology. Then, some of the specific causes of brain pathology, such as brain tumors, head injury, old age, etc., are described.

The section on mental retardation discusses the behavior that is characteristic of the different levels or degrees of mental retardation. The various causes of retardation are specified.

Both mental retardation and organic mental disorders are fairly common, so it is important to develop a familiarity with them.

LEARNING OBJECTIVES

1. Define *organic mental disorders*, describe three major conditions that underlie them, and give general principles of acute and chronic brain disorders.

2. Define *syndromes* and describe four types that are typical of persons with organic brain pathology.

3. Explain the organic cause of general paresis, list its symptoms, and summarize what we know about its treatment.

4. Define *tumor*, describe the symptoms of tumors in various areas of the brain and indicate the nature of treatment.

5. Indicate the incidence of brain damage resulting from head injuries, describe some symptoms that result from damage of various areas of the brain and summarize what is known about its treatment.

6. Differentiate between *senile* and *presenile dementias* and describe the organic pathology that underlies Alzheimer's disease and multi-infarct dementia.

7. Compare the symptoms of Alzheimer's disease and multi-infarct dementia, giving four clinically distinguishing features of the two disorders.

8. Describe some biological, psychosocial and sociocultural factors that influence the development of the dementias of old age.

9. Summarize what is known about the treatment and outcomes of the old-age dementias.

10. Define *mental retardation* and describe its classification by DSM-III-R.

11. List and describe the behavior of four levels of mental retardation and explain their distribution in the United States.

12. List five biological conditions that may lead to mental retardation and describe four clinical types that have been identified.

13. Distinguish between two subtypes of mental retardation that are caused by sociocultural deprivation, summarize what is known about the cultural-familial type, and explain why mental retardation is so difficult to assess.

14. Summarize what is known about educational and therapeutic methods that have been successful in helping mentally retarded individuals.

15. Describe two new frontiers in the prevention of mental retardation and explain the three-pronged "broad spectrum" approach to providing a more supportive sociocultural setting for children.

16. Describe some unresolved issues involving the old-age dementias and cultural-familial mental retardation.

TERMS YOU SHOULD KNOW

mental retardation (pp. 449 and 472-473)

organic mental disorders (pp. 449-450)

acute (p. 452)

chronic (p. 452)

acute brain disorder (p. 452)

chronic brain disorder (pp. 452-453)

syndromes (p. 453)

delirium (p. 453)

dementia (pp. 453-454)

amnestic syndrome (p. 454)

confabulation (p. 454)

hallucinosis (p. 454)

organic delusional syndrome (p. 455)

organic mood syndrome (p. 455)

organic anxiety syndrome (p. 455)

organic personality syndrome (pp. 455-456)

general paresis (p. 456)

chancre (p. 456)

great pox (p. 456)

cluster testing (p. 459)

tumor (p. 459)

malignant (p. 459)

benign (p. 459)

metastasis (p. 459)

chocked disc (p. 459)

"lilliputian hallucinations" (p. 460)

retrograde amnesia (p. 462)

intracerebral hemorrhage (p. 463)

petechial hemorrhages (p. 463)

encephalopathy (p. 463)

punch drunk (p. 463)

senile dementia (p. 464)

presentile dementia (p. 464)

Alzheimer's disease (p. 464)

plaques (p. 464)

neurofibrillary tangles (p. 464)

"hardening" of the arteries (p. 467)

cerebrovascular insufficiency (p. 467)

intracerebral hemorrhage (p. 467)

small stroke (p. 467)

multi-infarct dementia (pp. 467-468)

role obsolescence (p. 471)

expectancies of mutual gratification (p. 472)

mild mental regardation (educable) (p. 475)

moderate mental retardation (trainable) (p. 475)

severe mental retardation (dependent retarded) (p. 475)

profound mental retardation (life support retarded) (p. 475)

hypoxia (p. 476)

Down's syndrome (p. 477)

trisomy (p. 479)

amniocentesis (p. 479)

phenylketonuria (PKU) (p. 479)

cretinism (p. 480)

myxedema (p. 480)

macrocephaly (p. 481)

microcephaly (p. 481)

hydrocephalus (p. 481)

cultural-familial retardation (pp. 482-483)

mainstreaming (p. 486)

(Luria-Nebraska neurophychological battery) (p. 452)

(sensorimotor area) (p. 452)

(receptive) (p. 452)

(expressive) (p. 452)

(tactile) (p. 452)

(Pick's disease) (p. 455)

(Huntginton's chorea) (p. 465)

(Tay-Sach's disease) (p. 478)

(Turner's syndrome) (p. 478)

(Klinefelter's syndrome) (p. 478)

(Niemann-Pick's disease) (p. 478)

(Bilirubin encephalopathy) (p. 478)

(rubella, congenital) (p. 478)

(wild boy) (p. 485)

CONCEPTS TO MASTER

1. Introduction
   a. When gross structural defects in the brain occur before birth or at a very early age, the typical result is _____, the severity of which depends on the severity of the defect. Such individuals fail to develop an optimal level of various skills that underlie the ability to independently cope with environmental demands. Virtually all severely retarded individuals have demonstrable brain defects but many more mildly retarded persons do not have gross brain damage. (p. 449)

   b. Does it matter whether the brain damage occurs in early life before life skills have been developed or in adulthood after life skills have been mastered? (p. 449)

2. Organic mental disorders
   a. Organic mental disorders that have resulted in interference with brain functioning may cause limited to gross psychopathology depending on three variables. Complete the following list of them: (p. 450)

   1.

   2.

   3. The individual's life situation

   b. There are three clues for the clinician that organic patholgoy may underlie a person's psychological symptoms. Complete the following list of them: (p. 450)

1. The psychopathology is especially severe and includes prolonged catatonia or other movement disorder, anorexia, or is the first psychotic episode for a person 50 years or older.

2.

3.

c. Respond true or false to the following statements:

1. Most neurologically impaired individuals develop psychiatric symptoms?
   TRUE OR FALSE   (p. 450)

2. A person can have physical changes without psychological and social disturbance.
   TRUE OR FALSE   (p. 450)

3. Cell bodies and neural pathways in the brain have the power of regeneration but it is slow.   TRUE OR FALSE   (p. 450)

4. The central nervous system abounds with back-up aparatus.
   TRUE OR FALSE   (p. 450)

5. The location of damage is or great significance in predicting the impact of an injury because the parts of the human brain are specialized in their function.
   TRUE OR FALSE   (pp. 450-451)

d. It is possible to make certain generalizations about the likely effects of damage to particular parts of the brain. Complete the following chart that summarizer these relationships.   (p. 451)

Area of the Brain Damaged	Probable Clinical Picture
frontal areas	either passivity and apathy or impulsiveness and distractibility
right parietal area	
left parietal area	

temporal area

occipital area

e. Place the words *acute* and *chronic* where they belong in the blanks in the chart below.
                                                                    (p. 452)

Type of Organic Disorder	Characteristics
_____ organic mental disorders	1. Are caused by diffuse impairment of the brain. 2. Causes include high fevers and drug intoxication. 3. Delirium, hallucinations, and stupor predominate clinical picture. 4. Prognosis for recovery is good.
_____ organic mental disorders	1. Are caused by permanent destruction of some brain tissue. 2. Impairment of orientation, memory, learning, emotion, ethical controls, and personal hygiene are predominant symptoms.

f. What three words are used to indicate the severity of a particular case of organic
    mental disorder?   (p. 453)

    1.

    2.

    3.

g. Psychiatric and personality disorders are classified on axes I and II of DSM-III-R.
    Where are the organic mental disorders are classified?   (p. 453)

3. Organic symptom syndromes
    The clusters of symptoms based on brain damage listed in the DSM-III-R are grouped
    by the authors into four clusters: (1) delirium and dementia; (2) amnestic syndrome
    and hallucinosis; (3) organic delusional, mood, and anxiety syndromes; and (4) organic
    personality symdrome.   Respond to each of the following questions about these symptom
    clusters:
    a. What processes are most seriously disturbed in dementia?   (p. 453)

    b. Match the following: (p. 453)

        1. delirium   a. Caused by repeated strokes, infections, tumors,
                                        and injuries.
        2. dementia
                                    b. Caused by head injury, abuse of alcohol or other
                                        drugs, and lack of oxygen to the brain.

    c. Which of the following would a person with amnestic syndrome have the most problem
        remembering?   (p. 453)

        1. The name of the doctor who just introduced herself one second before.
        2. What he or she had for breakfast.
        3. Details of his or her childhood from 50 years ago.

    d. Is overall cognitive functioning impaired in the amnestic syndrome as it is in dementia?
                                                                                   (p. 453)

    e. Is the most common form of amnestic syndrome, those due to alcohol or barbiturate
        addiction, considered reversible?   (p. 454)

    f. Fill in the following chart which summarizes the most common causes of the following
        organic syndromes: (pp. 453-454)

                Organic Syndrome   Common Etiological Factors

                delirium   head injury, toxic or metabolic disturbances,
                                                        oxygen deprivation, insufficient blood to
                                                        brain, or alcohol and drugs in an addicted
                                                        person

                dementia

amnestic syndrome

hallucinosis

organic mood syndrome

organic personality syndrome

4. General paresis
    a. The following are the stages in the development of general paresis. Answer the following
        questions regarding them.   (p. 456-457)

        Stage 1 - A chancre appears at the point of contact with the infected person.
        Stage 2 - A generalized skin rash appears.
        Stage 3 - Spirochetes multiply and are carried in the bloodstream to various parts
                  of the body, but no outward symptoms are observed.
        Stage 4 - A wide range of disabilities begin to appear gradually, including mental
                  problems related to brain damage.

        1. How many people who contract syphilis (Stage 1) eventually get general paresis
            (Stage 4)?

        2. How long does it usually take to progress from Stage 1 to Stage 4?

        3. What are the various physical problems that may be seen at Stage 4?

4. General paresis is associated with a wide range of behavioral and psychological symptoms. In the early phase the individual typically is careless and inattentive. Accompanying these symptoms is a blunting of affect so that individuals seem unable to realize the seriousness of their behavior. Paralleling these physical symptoms is a progressive personality deterioration. What three types of emotional reactions are observed ?
   a.

   b.

   c.

5. Who is more likely to progress from Stage 1 to general paresis?   (p. 458)
   a.   Males or females?

   b.   Blacks or whites?

b. Desribe procedures used to try to prevent cases of general paresis.   (p. 458)

5. Disorder involving brain tumors
   a. The clinical picture seen among individuals with brain tumors is quite variable. What two factors determine the degree of impairment any given tumor will produce?
                                                                                 (p. 459)
      1.

      2.

   b. The most frequent early symptoms among people who were later found to have brain tumors include persistent headache, vomiting, memory impariment, listlessness, depression and _____, which is a retinal anomaly. Underline the most frequent symptom in brain tumor cases accouding to Levin (1949).
                                                                                 (p. 459)

   c. Describe the symptoms that may be seen as the tumor progresses.   (p. 459)

d. Describe the usual results of a tumor in the following areas of the brain:

(p. 460)

1. Frontal lobe

2. Special sensory areas

3. Temporal lobe

4. Olfactory pathways

e. About how many brain tumors are curable according to German (1959)?

(p. 461)

6. Disorders involving head injury
    a. Why do people with emotional problems often remember a time when they received a blow to the head?   (p. 461)

    b. What causes people to experience retrograde amnesia after accidents?   (p. 462)

    c. Why is boxing potentially dangerous?   (p. 463)

    d. Common aftereffects of moderate brain injury are chronic headaches, anxiety, irritability, dizziness, easy fatigability, and impaired memory. How common is epilepsy after a head injury?   (p. 463)

    e. List seven factors in the following short example suggesting that the patient has an unfavorable prognosis?   (pp. 463-464)

"An 18-year-old male who had several run-ins with the law during high school received a serious head injury in a motorcycle accident. He was in a coma for almost a month. The patient is currently suffering some paralysis and is very angry and depressed. He refuses to cooperate with his physical therapist. His parents, who live in a remote rural area where no rehabilitation facilities are available, will take him back home but are rather unenthusiastic about the prospect."

1.

2.

3.

4.

5.

6.

7.

7. Dementias usually associated with aging
   Two causes of dementia are discussed: Alzheimer's Disease, and multi-infarcts.
   a. What are the major differences between *senile* and *presenile dementia?*
   (p. 464)

   b. The neurological degeneration that occurs in Alzheimer's disease includes degenerative changes in neurons (senile plaques and meurofibrillary tangles) and a gradual loss of neurons in the basal forebrain--the area responsible for the production of acetycholine. Current theory emphasies _____ as the most likely cause of the disease? (p. 464)

   c. How common is Alzheimer's disease: (p. 464)

      1. Among persons over 65 years old?

      2. Among nursing home residents?

d. Describe the onset of Alzheimer's disease.   (p. 464)

e. Approximately _____ of Alzheimer's disease patients show a course of
    simple deterioration, that is, they gradually lose mental capacities. Symptoms of
    psychopathology are brief and unsystematized.   It is less frequent but not uncommon for
    Alzheimer's disease patients to develop a decidedly paranoid orientation becoming
    markedly suspicious and developing jealousy delusions.   (p. 465)

8. Clinical picture in multi-infarct dementia
    a. Subsequent to the deposit of large patches of fatty and calcified material inside the blood
        vessels, circulation becomes sluggish or may even be blocked altogether. This blocking
        may result in cerebrovascular insufficiency or intracerebral hemorrhage. Answer the
        following questions about this clinical picture: (pp. 467-468)

        1. Impairment of circulation in the brain leads to areas of _____ which are seen
            in some 90% of patients suffering from arteriosclerotic brain disease.

        2. A sudden blocking or rupture in a small vessel is referered to as a
            _____.

        3. When a series of small strokes occur, the condition is known as
            _____ dementia, the underlying cause of 10% of all
            dementia.

        4. In about half of the cases of multi-infarct dementia, symptoms appear suddenly.
            Characteristic symptoms include:

        5. When the onset of symptoms is gradual, early sumptoms include depression,
            dizziness, fatigue, memory defect, a slowing up of activity and a loss of
            _____ in living.

    b. By the time hospitalization occurs, the clinical picture in Alzheimer's disease is almost
        indistinguishable from the clinical picture in multi-infarct dementia. In fact, the two
        conditions often are mixed in the same individual. However, some features may guide
        physicians in distinguishing the two in some cases. These features include the
        observation that Alzheimer's disease is more likely to involve (1) gradual but
        progressive deterioration, and (2) more pronounced intellectual impariment and

paranoid concerns. Alzheimer's disease is <u>less likely</u> to involve (1) headaches, dizziness, depression and seizures; and pronounced _____ in symptoms. (p. 468)

9. Causal factors in the dementias of old age
The authors discuss three causal factors: biological, psychosocial, and sociocultural.
a. Biological factors

1. Is it realistic to consider genetic factors as primary causes of Alzheimer's and arteriosclerotic brain disease? YES OR NO (p. 469)

2. Are there reports of Alzheimer's disease showing a familial transmission pattern? YES OR NO (p. 469)

3. An excess accumulation of the protein _____has been found in the brains of Alzheimers's patients. (p. 469)

4. An unusual protein, called A68, has been found in the _____ of Alzheimer's patients. (p. 469)

5. Gal (1959) did a study in which postmortem examinations were performed on the brains of 104 people who had died naturally of old age. Some of these people had shown signs of extensive brain damage . How was the extent of brain damage correlated to the behavioral symptoms the person had exhibited when alive? (p. 469)

b. Psychosocial factors
The authors of the text discuss two psychosocial factors that play a causal role in seniliform psychoses: prepsychotic personality and presence of stressors characteristic of old age. Respond to the following questions about these factors.

1. Describe the types of personality characteristics that may predispose a person to psychoses and other mental disorders in old age. (p. 469)

2. It is suggested in the text that negative environmental changes are more harmful to older persons than organic changes. Complete the following list of three environmental factors that occur in aging that may prove stressful for older persons. (p. 470)

      a.   Retirement and reduced income

      b.

      c.

c.   General sociocultural conditions
      The sociocultural context provides the climate in which aging takes place.
      Describe the climate for aging in an urban industrial society.   (p. 471)

10. Treatment and outcomes for the old-age dementias
    a.   Why is hospitalization of the older person showing confusion, depression, etc.
       considered a last resort?   (p. 471)

    b.   Medical treatment includes diagnostic procedures, dietary changes to improve overall
       health, and antipsychotic and antianxiety drugs to control psychotic symptoms and
       alleviate anxiety. There are also favorable reports on the use of psychotherapy.
       Refer to the interesting study by Volpe and Kastenbaum (1967) with a group of older
       men who were so physically and psychologically incapacitated that they required
       around-the-clock nursing care.   (pp. 471-472)

      1.   Describe what happened on a ward of older men with seniliform psychoses when
         the were dressed in more formal clothes and given beer everyday.

      2.   How did the researchers explain these changes?

    c.   The greatest number of deaths and the greatest number of improvements among
       hospitalized elderly psychotic patients occurs during the first _____ after
       admission. For patients who require continued care in the hospital, about _____
       percent die within the first 5 years.   (p. 472)

    d.   List four favorable indications in the following short description that suggest a positive
       treatment outcome is likely.   (p. 472)

"After his wife's death, a 74-year-old former college professor became increasingly confused and depressed. His children finally had him hospitalized. At the hospital, doctors found minor cerebral arteriosclerosis and no other serious health problems, such as obesity, alcoholism, or hypertension. After his hospitalization, the professor's children planned to send him to an excellent retirement center only blocks from his former university."

1.

2.

3.

4.

11. Mental retardation
    a.   The AAMD (American Association on Mental Deficiency) has defined mental retardation as "significantly subaverage general intellectual functioning existing concurrently with deficits in adaptive behavior, and manifested during the developmental period. The IQ cutoff for mental retardation recommended by the AAMD is below _____, which represents about 6.8 million persons in the U.S.   (p. 473)

    b.   Explain why the incidences of mental retardation increase markedly between ages five to six, peak at 15, and drop off sharply after that.   (p. 473)

12. Levels of mental retardation
    a.   An IQ of 70 represents a score 2 standard deviations below the population mean. It represents a point below which _____ percent of the population scores.
         (pp. 473-474)

    b.   Generally, IQ tests measure an individual's likely level of success in dealing with
_____.   (p. 474)

    c.   Although an IQ test score lower than 70 tends to be the predominant consideration in the diagnosis of mental retardation, additional evidence is required. What additional evidence is required to make a diagnosis of mental retardation?   (p. 475)

    d.   Fill in the missing information in the following chart that summarizes the educational

potential, level of care required, and the degree of physical deformities characteristic
of each level of retardation: (pp. 475-476)

Level of Retardation	Description
Mild (IQ 52-68)	Person in this group are considered "educatable." They can master simple academic and occupational skills and become self-supporting. Physically, these individuals are normal.
Moderate (IQ 36-51)	Persons in this group are considered _____. They can gain partial independence in self-care, learn acceptable behavior, and work within the family or sheltered workshop. These indivudals appear physically ungainly.
Severe (IQ 20-35)	Persons in this group are called "dependent retarded." They can _____ _____. Physical handicaps are common.
Profound (IQ below 20)	Persons in this group are considered _____. They are capable of only the simplest tasks, and speech does not develop. They must remain in custodial care their whole lives. Serious physical deformities are common.

e. Which levels of retardation can be diagnosed readily in infancy?   (p. 475)

f. The distribution of intelligence should look like a perfect normal curve as shown by
    Graph A below, but it actually looks like Graph B. Why does this bulge at the lower
    end of the intelligence distribution, which indicates that there are more mentally
    retarded people than extremely intelligent people, occur?   (p. 476)

A. **Theoretical Distribution of Intelligence**

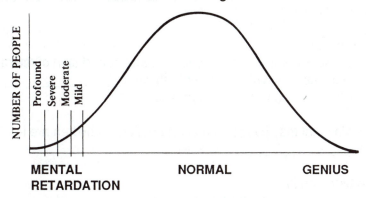

B. **Actual Distribution of Intelligence**

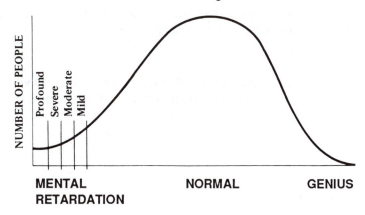

13. Mental retardation and organic brain dysfunction
   a. Mental retardation is associated with known organic pathology in _____ percent of the cases. In cases with organic pathology, retardation is virtually always moderate and is often severe. Profound retardation is fare and never occurs in the absence of obvious organic damage. (p. 476)

   b. The authors of the text list five biological conditions that may lead to mental retardation. They are presented below. Complete the requested information. (pp. 476-477)

      1. Genetic-chromosomal factors
         Mental retardation tends to run in families but _____ and _____ do, also. Exposure to social disadvantage may lead to retardation even in children who have inherited average intellectual potential.

In some rare types of mental retardation such as _____,
genetic factors play a clear role.

2. Infections and toxic agents
    Illnesses of the pregnant woman that can cause mental retardation of the offspring
    include German measles and syphillis. After birth, viral _____
    in the newborn child may lead to mental retardation.

    Environmental toxins that may cause mental retardation in children are lead and
    excess maternal _____ intake.

3. Prematurity and birth trauma
    Brain damage leading to mental retardation occurs in 1 birth out of _____.

4. Ionizing radiation
    The list of sources of harmful radiation includes diagnostic x-rays, leakages at
    nuclear power plants, and nuclear weapons testing.

5. Malnutrition
    _____ deficiencies in the mother's diet during pregnancy as well
    as in the baby's diet after birth have been pinpointed as particularly potent
    causes of lowered intelligence.

c. Down's Syndrome
    Down's Syndrome is the most common condition that leads to moderate and severe mental
    retardation. It occurs in 1 in every 600 babies born in the U.S.

    1. Describe some of the physical characteristics of children born with Down's
        syndrome.   (p. 477)

    2. Provide the following information about the clinical picture of Down's syndrome:
                                                                   (pp. 477-479)
        a. How common are cataracts in Down's syndrome children?

        b. How long do these children live?

        c. What level of mental retardation is usually present in children with Down's
            syndrome?

    d.   Is the intellectual defect consistent across abilities?

    e.   Are these children atypically placid and affectionate?

3.   Down's syndrome is caused by an extra chromosome, number 21. (Normal children have 23 pairs of chromosomes--46 total. Down's syndrome children have 23 pairs also, but "pair" 21 has three chromosomes instead of the normal two--47 total.) Where does the extra chromosome come from?   (p. 479)

4.   The risk of having a child with Down's syndrome is high if the mother is age _____ or older or the father is age _____ or older.   (p. 479)

d.   Phenylketonuria
PKU is a rare metabolic disorder occuring in about 1 in 20,000 births; about 1 in 100 retarded individuals in institutions suffer from PKU. Respond to the following questions about PKU.

    1.   A child with phenylketonuria (PKU) appears normal until six to twelve months of age. Explain the reason for this finding.   (pp. 479-480)

    2.   What level of retardation is likely if PKU goes untreated?   (p. 480)

    3.   PKU can be identified by a simple test of the infant. Once found, how is PKU treated?

                     (p. 480)

e.   Cretinism
Cretinism is a form of mental retardation that usually results from malnutrition.

    1.   What was missing in the diets of cretins?   (p. 480)

    2.   How can this form of malnutrition be avoided?   (p.480)

3. Treatment of iodine babies with severe thyroid deficiency with thyroid gland extract must begin in the first year of life. It it doesn't, what happens?

(p. 480)

f. Cranial anomalies
Mental retardation is associated with a number of gross alterations in head size and shape such as microcephaly (small-head) and hydrocephalus (enlarged head).

1. How severely retarded are microcephalic children?   (p. 481)

2. What are the causes of microcephaly?   (p. 481)

3. What is the outcome for hydrocephalic children today?   (p. 481)

14. Mental retardation and sociocultural deprivation
Mental retardation was formerly believed to always be the result of faulty genes or other physical pathology. Recently, it has become apparent that adverse environments, particularly those involving deprivation, play a primary role in the cause of mental retardation. In fact, the *majority* of all cases of mental retardation are cultural-familial and are *not* due to chromosomal abnormalities, diseases, radiation, etc.

a. Culturally-familially mentally retarded persons usually fall into the _____ level of retardation.   (p. 483)

b. When is cultural-familial mental retardation usually diagnosed?   (p. 483)

c. What proportion of mentally retarded children come from socially, economically, and culturally deprived homes?   (p. 483)

d. Complete the following list of the three factors that usually account for errors in measuring an individual's IQ:

(p. 483)

1. Errors were made in administering the test

2.

3. Limitations within the tests themselves to evaluate an individual compared to others in his/her social class and ethnic group; and to take social competence into account.

15. Treatment, outcomes, and prevention
   a. Few retarded children are institutionalized today. Those likely to be institutionalized include two types. What are they?   (p. 484)

      1.

      2.

   b. Are services for the mentally retarded adequate, and are all affected individuals being reached by specialized services?   (p. 484)

   c. Describe some of the forms of care for the mentally retarded that are alternatives to institutionalization according to Tylor & Bell (1984).   (p. 485)

   d. Today, educational training procedures are often based on a behavioral approach. First, an assessment is carried out to determine which areas a person needs to improve. These areas are referred to as target areas. Typical target areas include personal grooming, social behavior, basic academic skills, and
      _____ for retarded adults.   (p. 486)
      Within each area, the skills the individual needs to learn are broken down to their simplest components, and each component is taught separately.

   e. The "mainstreaming" approach to the education of retarded children has pros and cons. Among the disadvantages are the fact that the programs are hard to launch and administer, and any educational gains obtained may come at the expense of self-esteem. What is a reasonable conclusion about mainstreaming at this point?
                                                                       (p. 486)

   f. List the three areas of emphasis President Kennedy's Committee on Mental Retardation suggested to alleviate sociocultural conditions that deprive children of the stimulation, motivation, and opportunity for normal learning. (p. 487)

1.

2. Community services including efforts to reach high-risk children early with intensive cognitive stimulation including Head Start and TV programs like *Sesame Street.*

3.

g. What group of youngsters seem to benefit most from programs like *Sesame Street* and *The Electric Company* ? (p. 487)

16. Unresolved issues
As long as conventional academic success is the ticket of admission to economic wellbeing, what are the chances of Blacks and other minority group members of receiving equal opportunity? (pp. 487-488)

(17.) Dementia in 417 patients fully evaluated for dementia
In what proportion of cases of dementia is Alzheimer's disease the cause?
(p. 455)

(18.) Presenile dementias
What are two presenile dementias other than Alzheimer's disease? (p. 455)
a.

b.

(19.) Incidence of mental retardation
Which of the following degrees of retardation is by far the most common?
a. Profound (p. 473)
b. Moderate
c. Severe
d. Mild

(20.) Difficulties of mentally retarded people in learning basic academic skills
Describe the three major difficulties faced by mentally retarded children in learning
basic academic skills.   (p. 474)
a.

b.

c.

(21.) The wild boy of Aveyron
What was the outcome Pinel achieved after devoting 5 1/2 years to teaching the wild
boy?   (p. 485)

(22.) Two innovative deinstitutionalization approaches
Describe how each of the following programs operate: (p.486)
a. MORC "Community training homes"

b. ENCOR houses and apartments

CHAPTER QUIZ

1. When gross structural defects in the brain occur before birth or at a very early age, the
typical result is: (p. 449)

    a. mental retardation.   c. dementia.
    b. delirium.   d. amnesia.

2. Approximately how many acutely disturbed hospitalized psychiatric patients show the
presence of contributory organic disease?   (p. 450)

a.   75 percent   c.   25 percent
b.   50 percent   d.   15 percent

3.   In DSM-III-R, physical disorders are coded on Axis: (p. 453)

a.   I   c.   III
b.   II   d.   IV

4.   A noteworthy deterioration in intellectual functioning occurring after the completion of
     brain maturation is called: (p. 453)

a.   amnestic syndrome.   c.   delirium.
b.   confabulation.   d.   dementia.

5.   A benign brain tumor causes abnormal behavior because it: (p. 459)

a.   attracts and destroys spinal fluid.
b.   changes the electrical nature of the brain's pathways.
c.   destroys the brain tissue in which it arises.
d.   exerts pressure on the brain.

6.   If a head injury is sufficiently severe to result in unconsciousness, the person may
     experience retrograde amnesia or inability to recall: (p. 462)

a.   events immediately following the injury.
b.   events immediately preceding and following the injury.
c.   events immediately preceding the injury.
d.   names or faces of friends.

7.   Alzheimer's disease accounts for _____ percent of all cases of dementia.
                                                                                  (p. 464)
a.   10   c.   50
b.   30   d.   70

8.   Which of the following is the most common behavioral manifestation of Alzheimer's disease?
                                                                                  (p. 465)
a.   jealousy delusions   c.   psychopathological symptoms
b.   paranoid delusions   d.   simple deterioration

9.   Multi-infarct dementia involves a(an):   (pp. 467-468)

a.   appearance of senile plaques.
b.   continuing recurrence of small strokes.

c. increase in neurofibrillary tangles.
d. loss of neurons in the basal forebrain.

10. All of the following are stressors characteristic of old age <u>except</u>:   (p. 470)

a. fear of invalidism and death.
b. isolation and loneliness.
c. retirement and reduced income.
d. the empty nest syndrome.

11. Although the outcome of the old-age dementias has been considered unfavorable because of the irreversibility of the brain damage, evidence indicates that behavioral recovery or improvement is possible in about _____ of the cases.   (p. 472)

a. one-fourth   c. one-half
b. one-third   d. two-thirds

12. By far the <u>greatest</u> number of mentally retarded individuals have IQs between:

(p. 473)

a. 0 and 19.   c. 50 and 70.
b. 20 and 49.   d. 70 and 90.

13. Most states have laws providing that individuals with IQs below _____ who behave in a socially incompetent or disapproved way can be classified as mentally retarded and committed to an institution.   (p. 473)

a. 30   c. 70
b. 50   d. 90

14. The term "idiot savant" refers to a retarded individual who: (p. 475)

a. acts more like a savage than a civilized person.
b. enjoys waiting on other people.
c. has a high level of skill in some specific behavior.
d. is musically inclined.

15. About _____ percent of the cases of mental retardation occur with known brain pathology.   (p. 476)

a. 5   c. 25
b. 15   d. 35

14

Behavior Disorders of
Childhood and Adolescence

OVERVIEW

Many of the mental disorders described in previous chapters do not develop until early or middle adulthood. In dealing with children, the mental health worker is faced with some problems that are unique to childhood, such as hyperactivity, and with others, such as withdrawal, that may be forerunners of serious adult problems with depression or schizoid behavior. The types of problems seen in children are described in this chapter as well as the treatments typically used for each one. In each instance, there is an attempt to indicate what the long-range outcome for the problem usually is. It's important to place emphasis on the treatment of children and adolescents, because successful treatment at these stages prevents the occurrence of more serious pathology and spares years of suffering.

LEARNING OBJECTIVES

1. List several ways in which childhood disorders are different from those of other ages.

2. List and explain several special vulnerabilities of childhood.

3. Explain three reasons why early childhood diagnostic systems were inadequate and describe two kinds of systems that have been used.

4. List three goals which guided the revision of DSM-III-R for childhood disorders and explain the changes that were made to reach these objectives.

5. List and describe four clusters which Quay believes will account for most problem behavior of children, and explain the structure of the Child Behavior Checklist (CBCL) developed by Achenbach and his colleagues.

6. Explain three ways in which categorical and dimensional approaches to diagnosing childhood disorders differ.

7. Define *hyperactivity* and describe its clinical picture.

8. List several of the multiple causes of hyperactivity and summarize what is known about its treatment.

9. Define *conduct disorders* and describe their clinical picture including the three subtypes noted by DSM-III-R.

10. Describe the family patterns that contribute to childhood conduct disorders and summarize what is known about their treatment.

11. Define *delinquency,* describe some of the forms it takes, and explain several key variables which may be involved in the development of delinquent behavior.

12. Describe and evaluate several systems that have been used to deal with delinquency.

13. List several general characteristics of anxiety disorders in childhood and adolescence, and describe two subclassifications noted by DSM-III-R.

14. Explain four causal factors that have been emphasized in explanations of childhood anxiety disorders, and summarize what is known about their treatment.

15. Summarize what is known about *functional eneuresis, functional encopresis, sleepwalking,* and *tics* as they occur in children and adolescents.

16. Explain why autistic disorder is classified as a *pervasive developmental disorder* and describe its clinical picture.

17. Summarize what is known about the causes and treatments of autistic disorders, giving special attention to behavioral and structural therapy.

18. List and explain six special factors which must be considered in relation to treatment for children.

19. Define *advocacy* and evaluate the success of several governmental agencies and private groups that have tried to provide this function for children.

20. Describe the current controversy over whether childhood depression should be considered a separate clinical syndrome.

TERMS YOU SHOULD KNOW

categorical strategy (of classification) (p. 493)

dimensional strategy (of classification) (p. 493)

presenting symptoms (p. 493)

conduct disorder (p. 494)

anxiety-withdrawal (p. 494)

immaturity (p. 494)

socialized aggressive disorder (p. 494)

Child Behavior Checklist (CBCL) (pp. 494-495)

internalizing (p. 495)

externalizing (p. 495)

attention deficit-hyperactivity disorder (or hyperactivity) (p. 496)

conduct disorders (p. 500)

juvenile delinquency (p. 500)

social rejects (p. 507)

recidivism rate (p. 509)

juvenile status offenders (p. 509)

separation anxiety disorder (p. 510)

overanxious disorder (p. 510)

functional eneuresis (p. 513)

functional encopresis (p. 513)

sonambulism (sleepwalking) (p. 514)

tics (p. 514)

Tourette's syndrome (pp. 514-515)

coprolalia (pp. 514-515)

pervasive developmental disorder (p. 515)

autistic disorder (p. 516)

echolalic repetition (p. 516)

self-stimulation (p. 516)

maintenance of sameness (p. 517)

emotional refrigerators (pp. 517-518)

structural therapy (p. 518)

treatment contracts (p. 519)

change agents (p. 519)

mature minors (p. 519)

emancipated minors (p. 519)

double deprivation (p. 522)

advocacy (p. 525)

Children's Defense Fund (p. 526)

individual case advocacy (p. 526)

class advocacy (p. 526)

anaclitic depression (p. 526)

(minimal brain dysfunction--MBD) (p. 498)

(token reinforcement program) (p. 500)

(fading) (p. 500)

(fire-setting) (p. 502)

(run from's) (p. 504)

(run to's) (p. 504)

CONCEPTS TO MASTER

1. Introduction

Wunsch-Hitzig, Gould, and Dohrenwend (1980) compared the incidence of childhood maladjustment in the United States and Great Britain. The rates in both countries were quite similar; in the U.S. it was 11.8%. In both countries, maladjustment among boys was _____ than the rate of maladjustment among girls; and higher for adolescents than children.   (p. 491)

2. Maladaptive behavior in different life periods

Childhood disorders differ from adult disorders on the following two dimensions. Briefly answer the following questions pertaining to these differences.   (p. 492)

Differences between Childhood and Adult Disorders

differences in clinical picture

In general, how does the clinical picture in childhood disorders differ from adults?
a. Some disorders, such as autism, are only seen in childhood.
 b. Problems tend to reflect the developmental level of the person experiencing them.
In fact, emotional disturbances of children tend to be short-lived, undifferentiated, and _____ compared to those of later life periods.

special vulnerability
of children

Children do not have a clear-cut view of themselves and their _____.
As a result they have more difficulty coping with stress. They have a limited perspective and explain events with child-like concepts. On the

other hand, children tend to recover
_____ from their hurts.

3. Classification of childhood and adolescent disorders
    a. Kraepelin's (1883) classic text on classification did not include childhood disorders. In
        1952, a classification system for childhood was made available but it was inadequate.
        The authors list several reasons for the inadequacy of early childhood diagnostic
        systems; complete the following list of these reasons: (p. 493)

        1. In the past, the same categories used to classify adults were used for children.

        2. Children's symptoms are highly influenced by the family's acceptance or rejection
            of the behavior.

        3. Normal developmental changes...

    b. The DSM-III-R is a <u>categorical</u> classification system. Two axes are used to classify
        children's disorders.   (p. 494)

        1.   Axis I of the DSM-III-R covers symptomatic disorders including
             disruptive behavior disorders, anxiety disorders , eating disorders, gender identity
             disorders, tic disorders, elimination disorders, and speech disorders.

        2. Axis II of the DSM-III-R includes a broad range of disorders to account for
            disturbances in the _____ of cognitive, language, motor,
            or social skills. Examples of these disorders include pervasive developmental
            disorders, mental retardation, and specific developmental disorders. This axis is
            controversial since many of these disorders, such as " developmental reading
            disorder," are normally treated in educational settings, not in mental health
            facilities.

    c. An alternative to the categorical classification system is a dimensional system. Quay
        (1979) reviewed all of the dimensional classification studies and concluded that four
        dimensions are generally typical. Complete the following list of the four dimensions of
        child behavior disorders: (p. 494)

Dimension	Behavior Which is Included
1. conduct disorder	1. includes aggressive behavior and resistive behavior
2.	2.
3. immaturity	3. includes behaviors that reflect a general lack of adaptive skills
4. socialized-aggressive disorder	4.

4. A comparison of categorical and dimensional approaches

    a.   The general goals and methods employed by categorical and dimensional approaches are different and it is unlikely that they will ever totally agree in their classification of children althought there will be overlap. Place a C next to the choices on the following chart that characterize the categorical approach to classification of childhood disorders. Place a D next to the choices that characterize the dimensional approach to the classification of childhood disorders. (p. 495)

Strategy	Characteristics
categorical strategy such as DSM-III-R	1. Follows the disease model of psychopathology clinical study
	2. Based on the idea that behaviors are continuous and are found even among mornals
dimensional strategy such as Quay (1979)	3. Uses arbitrary classes or types as the basis for classification
	4. Strives for broad coverage and includes ever very rare conditions
	5. Emphasizes depth rather than depth
	6. Developed through cluster analysis of symptom checklists

b. Match the following investigators with the diagnostic symptom clusters they created using dimensional strategies: (p. 494)

Investigator		Clusters Identified
1. Petersen (1961)	a.	Unsocialized aggressive, socialized aggressive, overinhibited
2. Hewitt and Jenkins (1946)	b.	Conduct disorder, anxiety-withdrawal, immaturity, socialized aggressive disorder
3. Quay (1979)	c.	Conduct problems, personality problems

5. Hyperactivity
   a. Attention deficit-hyperactivity disorder, more commonly known as hyperactivity is characterized by maladaptive behavior that interferes with effective task-oriented behavior in children. Hyperactivity is the most frequent reason children are referred to mental health facilities. It is estimated that between _____ and _____ percent of elementary school aged children manifest the symptoms of hyperactivity. The disorder occurs with greatest frequency before age _____, although some residual effects may persist until adolescence.   It is 6 to 9 times more common in boys than girls. (p. 496)

   b. Describe the clinical picture in hyperactivity in the following areas: (p. 496)

      1. Muscular activity

      2. Attention

      3. Impulsive control

      4. Responsibility

5. Intelligence

6. Parental relationships

c. Why has Quay (1979) argued that the diagnostic category of hyperactivity has
    little meaning?   (p. 496)

d. Complete the following summary of current thinking regarding the possible causes of
    hyperactivity: (p. 497)

    1. Biological basis--There is no compelling evidence for a biological basis.

    2. Diet

    3. Parental personality problems--There are no clearly established psychological
        causes but some evidence points to parental personality problems, particularly
        diagnoses of personality disorder or hysteria.

e. The authors conclude that the hyperactive syndrome has multiple causes and multiple
    symptoms. Thus, the diagnosis of hyperactivity doesn't really indicate much about a
    child. And, the label of hyperactivity may have harmful effects. What are they?
                                                                         (p. 497)

f. Amphetamines, such as Ritalin, have been used to treat hyperactivity. Are they
    effective?   (p.497)

g. What possible harmful side effects do they have according to a longitudinal study of
    hyperactivie children performed by Safer and Allen (1973)?   (p. 497)

h.   Another effective approach to treating hyperactive children involves behavior therapy techniques . What techniques does a behavioral therapy involve?   (p. 498)

i.   Why are cognitive-behavioral techniques used with hyperactive children? What do these techniques accomplish?   (p. 498)

j.   What treatment approach was identified as most effective by Pelham et al. (1980)?   (p. 499)

k.   What did Weiss et al. (1979) report regarding the adult adjustment of formerly hyperactive children?   (p. 499)

l.   A recent follow-up of previously hyperactive boys was conducted by Gittleman, Mannuzza, Shenker, And Banagura (1985). These authors concluded that the "most striking finding is the degree to which the syndrome consisting of _____, _____, and _____ persisted."   (p. 500)

6. Conduct disorders
   a.   The authors conclude that the terms *conduct disorder*, a *predelinquent pattern*, and *early stages of* _____ are difficult, if not impossible to distinguish.   (p. 500)

   b.   The essential symptomatic behavior in conduct disorders involves: _____and _____. Approximately 9 percent of boys and _____ percent of girls have conduct disorder problems.   (p. 501)

   c.   In DSM-III-R, conduct disorders are contain three subtypes. Complete the following chart that summarizes these three types: (p. 501)

Subtype of conduct disorder   **Characteristic behavior**

   group type   conduct problems occur in group activity

_____   conduct problems are individual acts and are
                            directed against both adults and children

undifferentiated type   features of both the two types above are mixed

d. Describe what is known regarding the following causal factors of conduct disorder:
                                                                (pp. 501-502)

   1. Family setting

   2. Institutionalization

e. Therapy for conduct disorders is ineffective unless _____.
    Fareta (1981) reported that many conduct disordered children grew up to be adults
    who _____. Robins (1970)
    found that antisocial aggressive behavior in childhood is highly predictive of
    sociopathic behavior in later adolescence and adulthood.   (p. 502)

f. How is behavior therapy used to assist the parents of conduct disordered children?
                                                                (pp. 502-503)

g. However, parents often have difficulty carrying out the program. How did Shoemaker
    and Paulson (1976) try to overcome these difficulties among mothers of aggressive
    children?   (p. 503)

7. Delinquent behavior
    a. Delinquency is a legal term that refers to acts committed by individuals under the age of
        16-18 that call for some punishment or corrective action. Between 1972 and 1981,
        the frequency of serious juvenile crimes rose _____ percent. In 1981, juveniles
        accounted for 1 out of every _____ arrests for robbery and crimes against
        property, and 1 out of every 6 rapes.   (p. 503)

    b. The form of juvenile delinquency differs between male and female adolescents.

1. For what crimes are girls commonly arrested? (p. 503)

2. For what crimes are boys most often arrested? (p. 503)

c. According to Dintz and Conrad (1980), are juvenile criminals dangerous and violent?
(p. 503)

8. Causal Factors in delinquency
The authors highlight four causal factors in deliquency: personal pathology, pathogenic
family patterns, undesirable peer relationships, and general sociocultural factors. Fill
in the missing information on the following chart that summarizes the research on
the causal factors of juvenile delinquency. (pp. 504-508)

Causal Factors in Juvenile Delinquency

Personal Pathology

genetic determinants	Schulsinger (1980) found adopted psychopathic criminals more often had psychopathic fathers than non-psychopathic criminals.
brain damage and mental retardation	Less than _____ percent of delinquents have been found to have brain damage that could lead to lowered inhibitory controls and violent behavior.
	Moffitt et al. (1980) found that some delinquents mentally retarded and are unable to foresee the consequences of their actions or understand the significance of what they are doing.
neurotic and psychotic disorders	In a small portion of cases, delinquent acts are performed by a neurotic individual. The neurotic acts often represent deviant _____ gratification.

psychopathic traits

A sizable number of habitual delinquents appear to share traits typical of psychopathic persons, such as _____ .

_____ .

Pathogenic Family Patterns

broken homes

Delinquency seems to be more common in homes broken by _____ or _____ than in homes broken by death of a parent.

parental rejection
and faulty discipline

When the father rejects a boy, the following may occur: _____ .
Bandura and Wlaters (1963) studied boys whose fathers rejected them, used inconsistent discipline, and were physically punitive. Describe the end result of such a pattern.

_____

_____ .

psychopathic parental models

Psychopathic behaviors found in the fathers of delinquents included: _____

_____ .
Psychopathic fathers and mothers may contribute to the delinquency of girls by:

_____

_____ .

limited parental relationships
outside the family

Children's oppositional behavior (negativism) is greater when parents have few friendly contacts outside the home.

Undesirable Peer Relationships

About _____ percent of delinquent acts involved one or two other persons, and most of the remainder involved three or four other persons.

General Sociocultural Factors

alienation and rebellion   Alienation from family and from the borader
                                  society allows teenagers to become captives of
                                  their _____.

social rejects   Social rejects have discovered that they are not
                                  _____ by our society.

gang cultures   What type of feelings does belonging to a gang
                                  give a delinquent? _____
                                  _____.

9. Dealing with delinquency
    a. Refer to the California Youth Authority five-year experiment
        called "The Community Treatment Project."   (pp. 508-509)

        1. The rebahilitation success rate at the 15-month follow-up was
            _____ percent.

        2. In the nontreated control group that was released on probation, the rehabilitation
            success rate was only _____ percent. How did these results compare to data
            from the control group?

    b. The overall recidivism rate for juvenile offenders, as estimated by *Time*
        magazine, is as high as _____ percent.   (p. 509)

    c. Institutionalization of a juvenile is particularly questionable in the case of
        _____ offenders.   (p. 509)

    d. Clarke (1985) published a provocative review of the limitations and inadequacies of
        programs aimed at reducing juvenile crime by psychological therapies, which he
        maintains have fallen far short of success. Consequently, juvenile crime in Britain is
        viewed as a rational act that should be dealt with through environmental means rather
        than through psychological treatment. Give some examples of environmental or
        "situational" means to reduce crime among juveniles.   (p. 509)

10. Anxiety disorders of childhood and adolescence
    In the DSM-III-R, anxiety disorders include two subtypes: separation anxiety disorder and
    overanxious disorder.

a. Separation anxiety disorder
    Separation anxiety is characterized by unrealistic fears and worry especially in
    new _____.   (p. 510)

b. Overanxious disorder
    The overanxious disorder is characterized by excessive worry and persistent fear;
    however the fears are usually not specific and are not due to a

    _____.   (p. 510)

c. Causal factors in anxiety disorders
    The authors list four general causal factors of anxiety disorders: (pp. 510-511)

    1. Unusual sensitivity, easy conditionability, and a build-up of
        _____.

    2. Undermining of self-adequacy and security by early
        _____, _____, or _____.

    3. Modeling by an overanxious parent who sensitizes the child to
        _____ in the outside world.

    4. Detached or indifferent parents who fail to provide adequate
        _____.

d. Treatment and outcomes

    1. The anxiety disorders of childhood may continue into adolescence and adulthood but
        this is not usually the case. Peers and school teachers are likely to provide
        corrective experiences such as making _____ and succeeding at tasks.
                                                                    (p. 511)

    2. Behavior therapy procedures employed in structured group experiences at school
        can often speed up favorable outcomes. Included here are
        _____ training and desensitization. Desensitization using
        imagination is limited in application to children, however, because
        _____.
        However, _____ methods using graded real life situations can be
        effective with young children.   (pp. 511-512)

11. Other symptom disorders
    a. Functional eneuresis
        The term eneuresis refers to the habitual involuntary discharge of urine after the age of
        expected continence (toilet training), which is age 5.

1. Estimates of the prevalence of enuresis reported in DSM-III-R are _____
    percent for boys and _____ percent for girls at age 5. In a study conducted in
    Holland, Verhulst et al. (1985) determined that between the ages of 5 and 8, the
    rates of enuresis among boys are _____ times higher than the rates among
    girls.   (p. 513)

2. Although enuresis may result from a variety of organic conditions, the authors
    emphasize three psychosocial factors. Complete the requested information in the
    following list of causes of eneuresis: (p. 513)

    Causal Factor   **Description**

    a. faulty learning   results in a failure to acquire the inhibition reflex of
                                         bladder emptying.

    b.   associated with or stems from emotional problems

    c. disturbed family   particularly situations that lead to sustained anxiety
        reactions   or hostility. Also, regression when a new
                                         _____ arrives.

3. Conditioning procedures have proven successful in the treatment of eneuresis.
    Describe how this treatment is conducted.   (p. 513)

4. What happens to the incidence of eneuresis as the child gets older if it is
    untreated?   (p. 513)

b. Functional encopresis
    Encopresis refers to the absence of appropriate toleting habits for bowel movements
    after age 4. Respond TRUE or FALSE to the following statements about encopresis:
                                                                        (pp. 513-514)

    1. Regular soiling after age 3 is encopresis.   TRUE OR FALSE

    2. One third of encopretic children are eneuretic.   TRUE OR FALSE

    3. Six times more boys than girls are encopretic.   TRUE OR FALSE

    4.   A common time for encopresis is after school.   TRUE OR FALSE

    5.   Most children know they need to have a bowel movement.   TRUE OR FALSE

    6.   Many encopretic children suffer from constipation.   TRUE OR FALSE

  c. Sleepwalking (somnambulism)
Sleepwalking involves repeated episodes in which a person leaves his or her bed and walks around without being conscious of the experience or remembering it later.

    1.   The onset of a sleeping disorder is usually between _____ years of age. It is estimated that _____ percent of children experience regular or periodic sleepwalking episodes.   (p. 514)

    2.   During sleepwalking, the eyes are partially or fully open and obstacles are avoided. Episodes usually last from _____ minutes to half an hour.   (p. 514)

    3.   How have researchers determined that sleepwalking is related to an anxiety-arousing situation that has just occurred or is expected to occur?   (p. 514)

    4.   Does a fully described and evaluated treatment program exist for sleepwalking?   (p. 514)

  d. Tics
A tic is a persistent muscle twitch usually limited to a localized muscle group.

    1.   Tics occur most frequently between the ages of _____.   (p. 514)

    2.   An extreme tic disorder involving multiple motor and vocal patterns is called _____ syndrome. About one-third of individuals with this syndrome manifest _____ which is a complex vocal tic that involves the uttering of obscenities. Most cases of this symdrome onset before age _____, which suggests an organic basis for it.   (p. 514)

12. Developmental disorders
The term pervasive developmental disorder, including autistic disorder, are contained on Axis II of DSM-III. Their inclusion along with mental retardation recognizes the significant impairment in the development of social, cognitive, and communication skills that impact on the evaluation and treatment of individuals with pervasive developmental disorders.

a. Autism afflicts some 80,000 American children and is 4-5 times more frequent among boys than girls.   Autism may be diagnosed in a child as young as a few _____ old but is almost always diagnosed before _____ months of age.   (p. 516)

b. The clinical picture in autistic disorders: complete the following chart by writing a brief description of austic children's behavior in each area: (pp. 516-517)

Area of Behavior	Characteristics of Autistic Children
interactions with parents	Mothers remember them as never being cuddly. They do not evidence any need for affection or contact.
use of speech	Speech is absent or severly restricted. Ecolalic repetition of a few words may be observed. There are suggestions that autistic children do comprehend language, but they do not use it to express themselves.
self-stimulation	
interactions with objects	
cognitive or intellectual tasks	Compared to other children, impariment is seen. While some investigators have viewed autistic children as retarded, others such as Koegel and Mentis (1985) have raised the possibility that the deficits result from motivational differences; autistic children can perform tasks at higher levels if motivation for a task is found.

c. Circle YES, NO, or MAYBE as appropriate to indicate whether each of the following factors is currently thought to be an important cause of autism: (pp. 517-518)

1. Brain pathology   YES   NO   MAYBE

2. Genetic basis   YES   NO   MAYBE

3. Chromosome abnormalities   YES   NO   MAYBE

4. Defect in perceptual/cognitive functions   YES   NO   MAYBE

5. Personality characteristics of parents   YES   NO   MAYBE

d. Tinbergen (1974) has viewed autism as an approach-avoidance conflict in which the child's natural tendency to _____ has been overbalanced by aversive experiences and fear.   (p. 518)

e. Bettleheim (1974) has used warm, loving, acceptance and reinforcement procedures to treat autism. Ward (1978) used structural therapy.   Describe structural therapy.
                                                                    (p. 518)

f. Bartak et al. (1973), at the Maudsley Hospital, compared three different approaches to treating autism: an approach emphasizing formal schooling, a structured form of play therapy, and free play therapy. Which approach was found to be most successful?
                                                       (pp. 518-519)

g. Rutter (1985) has used parents as therapists to treat their own autistic children.
                                  YES OR NO   (p. 519)

h What is the prognosis for autism in children who show symptoms before age 2?
                                                      (p. 519)

i. How many children who receive treatment attain even a marginal adjustment in adulthood?   (p. 519)

13. Special factors associated with treatment for children
    a. In what ways do children have difficulty seeking assistance for emotional problems?
                                                        (p. 519)

b. What does it mean to say a child from a pathogenic home is "double deprived"?
(p. 522)

c. What is meant by the expression, "using parents as 'change agents'"? (p. 523)

d. Give some reasons that placement of a child in a foster home often works out less than ideally for the child. (pp. 523-524)

14. Child-advocacy programs
   a. In 1970 the National Institute of Mental Health estimated that fewer than _____ percent of disturbed children in the United States were receiving any kind of help, and only half of those receiving help were receiving adequate treatment. (p. 525)

   b. One approach to meeting children's mental health needs is advocacy. Twice in recent years the federal government has established a National Center for Child Advocacy. What happened both times? (p. 525)

   c. Currently the physical welfare of children is the responsibility of the _____, the mental health needs of children are the responsibility of the _____, and juvenile delinquency is handled by the Justice Department. This fragmentation means that there is no government agency which considers the whole child and plans comprehensively for children who need help. (p. 525)

   d. Define the following two forms of advocacy: (p. 526)

      1. Individual case advocacy

      2. Class advocacy

15. Unresolved issues on childhood depression
   There are arguments for and against the proposition that childhood depression is separate and different from adult depression. What decision did the DSM-III-R make on childhood depression? (p. 526)

(16.)   Drug therapy with children
   a.   What criticism has been made about the way children are selected to receive drugs?
                                                                    (p. 498)

   b.   What criticism has been made about the purposes for which drugs are used in children?   (p. 498)

   c.   What do we know about the long-range side effects of drug therapy on children?
                                                                    (p. 498)

(17.)   Token reinforcement programs in the classroom
   a.   How do these programs work?   (p. 500)

   b.   How is "fading" accomplished?   (p. 500)

   c.   What behavioral problems are positively affected by token reinforcement?
                                                                    (p. 500)

(18.)   Fire-setting: An extreme conduct disorder?
   a.   Estimates of the prevalence of fire-setting by children are as high as _____ percent of all recorded fires. Fire-setting is more common among boys by about _____ to one.   (p. 502)

   b.   Children who set fires tend to have the following personality characteristics:_____
        _____.
        However not all children with these personality characteristics set fires. Why some do is not known.   (p. 502)

(19.)   Problems that lead children to run away
   a.   What is the average age of a runaway child?   (p. 504)

b. Of runaways reported to the police, _____ percent are eventually located.

(p. 504)

c. Is it common for parents of a runaway child to fail to call the police?   (p. 504)

(20.) Television and violence
    a. Describe the findings of Lefkowitz et al. (1977).   (p. 507)

b. Does this study prove a direct, causal link between violence and TV?   (p. 507)

c. How can TV be viewed as a "precipitating cause of aggressive behavior"?

(p. 507)

(21.) Do children develop psychologically based somatic disorders?
    Refer to a recent investigation by Routh and Ernst (1984) that establishes
    the likelihood of the occurence of somatization disorder in children and evaluated the
    possibility of parental influence on the development of these disorders.

(p. 511)

a. What methods did the investigators use?

b. What did they find?

c. What possibilities are raised by this study?

(22.) The problem of child abuse in contemporary society
    a. How often does child abuse result in serious injury?   (p. 522)

b. The most frequent cases of child abuse involve children under _____ years of
    age.   (p. 522)

c. What proportion of children have suffered serious abuse according to Gelles (1978)?

(p. 522)

d. What differences emerge when abused children are compared to nonabused children?

(p. 522)

e.   What common factors have been found among families with abusing parents?

(p. 522)

f.   Describe the study of high risk families for child abuse. What has been learned so far?

(p. 522)

g.   Describe the various approaches to prevention of child abuse that are available:

(p. 522)

1.

2.

3.

4.

5.

(23.)   Freeing children for permanent placement
   a.   Describe the project undertaken in Oregon at the Regional Research Unit.

(p. 524)

   b.   What changes in usual procedure were made for purpose of the study?   (p. 524)

CHAPTER QUIZ

1. In a study by Wunsch-Hitzig and others in 1980, the incidence of childhood maladjustment in the United States was found to be _____ percent. (p. 491)

   a. 1.8
   b. 11.8
   c. 21.8
   d. 31.8

2. Compared to a categorical system for classifying childhood and adolescent disorders, a dimensional strategy: (p. 493)

   a. assesses fewer behaviors for each category.
   b. has more diagnostic categories.
   c. ignores presenting symptoms in favor of case studies.
   d. requires more symptoms to make a diagnosis.

3. The inclusion of developmental problems on Axis II of DSM-III-R is controversial since several of these conditions are: (p. 494)

   a. extremely rare among children and adolescents.
   b. largely medical in nature.
   c. normally dealt with in educational settings.
   d. the same for adults as for children.

4. Under which of Quay's four problem clusters does childhood depression belong?
   (p. 494)

   a. anxiety-withdrawal
   b. conduct disorder
   c. immaturity
   d. socialized-aggressive disorder

5. According to Swanson, hyperactivity is difficult to differentiate from: (p. 496)

   a. anxiety disorders of childhood.
   b. autistic disorders.
   c. conduct disorders.
   d. functional encopresis.

6. One focus of cognitive-behavior treatment is to help hyperactive children learn to:
   (p. 498)

   a. behavior more reflectively.
   b. imitate children who are not hyperactive.
   c. shift attention more frequently.
   d. think more positively of themselves.

7. Gittelman and associates found that in comparison to a control sample of nonhyperactive boys, hyperactive boys: (p. 500)

   a. showed diminished symptom patterns in later adolescence.
   b. were less likely to develop conduct disorders.
   c. were less likely to develop later psychiatric disorders.
   d. were more likely to marry before age 21.

8. In 1981, about one teenager out of every _____ in the nation was arrested. (p. 503)

   a. 5   c. 25
   b. 15   d. 35

9. A sizable number of habitual delinquents share the traits typical of the _____ personality. (p. 505)

   a. antisocial   c. narcissistic
   b. obsessive-compulsive   d. passive-aggressive

10. Haney and Gold found that most delinquent acts were committed: (p. 506)

    a. alone, without any help.
    b. in association with one or two other persons.
    c. with three or four other persons.
    d. with five or six other persons.

11. Alienation from family and the broader society causes juveniles to become more vulnerable to: (p. 507)

    a. incest and related sexual crimes.
    b. negative influences of TV and other media.
    c. peer pressures to engage in delinquent acts.
    d. solitary acts of violence.

12. Children diagnosed as suffering from anxiety disorders usually attempt to cope with their fears by: (p. 509)

    a. becoming overly dependent on others.
    b. denying the existence of fearful things.
    c. developing compulsive behaviors.
    d. indulging in "guardian angel" fantasies.

13. Typically, children with anxiety disorders: (p. 511)

   a. become adolescents with maladaptive avoidance behavior.
   b. become adults with idiosyncratic thinking and behavior.
   c. become suicidal when they reach 30.
   d. have experiences that reduce their fears and help them feel more adequate.

14. Systematic desensitization is difficult to use in reducing anxieties of young children
   because they: (pp. 511-512)

   a. are afraid of strange therapists.
   b. are unable to relax while imagining an emotionally charged stimulus.
   c. do not understand the word *relax.*
   d. have no imagination.

15. All of the following are true of infantile autism except: (p. 516)

   a. it afflicts about 1 child in 2,500.
   b. it is usually identified before the child is 30 months old.
   c. it occurs much more frequently in boys than in girls.
   d. most cases are found in the upper classes.

15

Clinical Assessment

OVERVIEW

The clinical assessment process is described in this chapter. Clinical assessment includes the use of psychological tests but also depends on data from other sources, such as observation and interview. Psychological tests have a mystique in our society and have recently come under serious public scrutiny. Questions regarding the validity of tests as predictors of academic performance have been raised. Also, concerns have been voiced publicly that tests may invade privacy and reveal things about an individual that he or she did not realize were being revealed. Chapter 15 describes what the different types of tests are, how they are constructed, and what types of information can be obtained from them. The chapter concludes with a discussion of how assessment information is put together with data obtained by other members of the clinical team.

LEARNING OBJECTIVES

1. Explain the difference between diagnosis and clinical assessment and list several components that must be integrated into the dynamic formulation.

2. Describe several medical and neuropsychological procedures that can be used for the physical evaluation of clients and explain why each type of data is gathered.

3. Describe the characteristics of a good assessment interview and list some advantages and disadvantages of the interview method.

4. Describe several techniques and instruments that are used to make clinical observations of client behavior.

5. Explain the kind of data gathered by psychological tests and list two types that are commonly used.

6. List and describe several intelligence tests used by clinicians and explain how this information can be used in assessment.

7. Explain the assumptions behind the use of projective tests and describe the use of the Rorschach Test and the Thematic Apperception Test (TAT) in clinical assessment.

8. Define *objective tests* and describe the Minnesota Multiphasic Personality Inventory (MMPI) and its uses in clinical assessment.

9. Explain what is meant by the actuarial approach used to interpret the MMPI and describe three methods of obtaining computer-based interpretation.

10. Cite some general objectives of personnel screening and describe the use of some psychological tests to accomplish these goals.

11. List and explain three questions which must be addressed before implementing a psychological assessment program for preemployment screening.

12. Summarize the psychological case study of Esteban, noting the various types of clinical assessment that were used to build the dynamic formulation.

13. Explain the functions of a staff conference in integrating the assessment data and making decisions about the client.

14. Describe the controversy over computerized psychological assessment including the debate over Matarazzo's criticisms.

15. Describe three possible reasons for the underutilization of computer-based assessment procedures.

TERMS YOU SHOULD KNOW

clinical assessment (p. 531)

dynamic formulation (p. 532)

electroencephalogram (EEG) (p. 534)

dysrhythmias (p. 534)

computerized axial tomography (CAT scan) (p. 534)

positron emission tomography (PET scan) (p. 534)

neurophychological test battery (p. 534)

Halsted-Reitan battery (p. 534)

Luria-Nebraska battery (pp. 534-535)

structured interview (p. 536)

self-report (p. 537)

self-report schedule or problem checklist (p. 537)

direct observation (p. 537)

Brief Psychiatric Rating Scale (BPRS) (p. 537)

role playing (p. 538)

self-monitoring (p. 538)

psychological tests (p. 539)

Wechsles Intelligence Scale for Children-Revised (WISC-R) (p. 539)

Stanford-Binet Intelligence Scale (p. 539)

Wechsler Adult Intelligence Scale -Revised (WAIS-R) (p. 539)

general information (p. 539)

picture completion (p. 539)

personality tests (p. 539)

projective tests (pp. 539-540)

Rorschach Test (p. 540)

Thematic Apperception Test (TAT) (p. 540)

sentence completion tests (p. 541)

objective tests (p. 542)

Minnesota Multiphasic Personality Inventory (MMPI) (p. 542)

"Minnesota normals" (p. 542)

MMPI profile (p. 542)

validity scales (p. 542)

diagnostic standard (p. 542)

descriptive diagnosis (p. 542)

content interpretation (p. 542)

clinical scales (p. 544)

factor analysis (pp. 544-545)

Sixteen Personality Factor Questionnaire (16PF) (p. 545)

actuarial procedures (p. 546)

Computer based MMPI interpretation (p. 546)

mail-in service (p. 546)

teleprocessing (p. 546)

on-site microprocessing (p. 546)

personnel selection (p. 547)

personnel screening (p. 547)

(Halstead Category Test) (p. 535)

(Tactual Performance Test) (p. 535)

(Rhythm Test) (p. 535)

(Speech Sounds Perception Test) (p. 535)

(Finger Oscillation Task) (p. 535)

(MMPI clinical scales including: Hypochondriasis, Depression, Hysteria, Psychopathic Deviate, Masculinity-feminity, Paranoia, Psychasthenia, Schizophrenia, Hypomania, Social Introversion) (p. 543)

(MMPI special scales including: Anxiety, Repression, Ego-strength, MacAndrew addiction scale) (p. 543)

(faking good) (p. 544)

(cultural bias) (p. 555)

CONCEPTS TO MASTER

1. Introduction
   a. The goal of clinical assessment is to identify and understand an individual's
      _____ within the context of his or her overall level of
      _____ and _____.   (p. 531)

   b. Data from clinical assessment is used for two purposes. First, it serves as a basis for
      treatment decisions. Later, it can serve as a _____
      against which to evelute progress made during and following treatment.   (p. 531)

2. The information sought in assessment
   a. Although there has been a trend against overdependence on labeling because of their
      potential to create self-fulfilling prophecies, accurate classification is needed for three
      reasons: (1) for insurance reimbursement, (2) for treatment decisions, and
      (3)_____.   (p. 532)

   b. For clinical purposes, however, knowledge about an individual's _____,
      _____, personality characteristics, and environmental pressures
      and resources (including   excesses and deficits in behavior as well as its
      appropriateness) is more important than a formal diagnosis.   (p. 532)

   c. The material gained through assessment is integrated into a consistent and meaningful
      picture, often called the dynamic formulation, that should lead to an explanation of why
      the person is engaging in maladaptive behavior; it should lead to hypotheses about the
      person's _____ behavior as well.   (pp. 532-533)

3. Interdisciplinary sources of assessment data
   What assessment techniques would be favored by a: (p. 533)
   a. Biologically oriented clinician

   b. Psychoanalytically oriented clinician

   c. Behaviorally oriented clinician

   d. Humanistically oriented clinician

4. Physical evaluation
    a. Medical examinations are necessary in some situations to rule out physical abnormalities or to determine the extent to which physical problems are involved. The two types of medical examinations that may be performed include the general _____ examination and the _____ examination. (p. 534)

    b. List several diagnostic procedures that might be obtained as part of a specialized neurological exam. (p. 534)

    c. Sometimes psychological tests will be used to detect the presence of organic damage or disease. These tests are referred to as a _____ test battery. (p. 534)

    d. The Halstead-Reitan is a highly regarded neurophychological test. However, if time is at a premium, the _____ could be used. (pp. 534-535)

5. Psychosocial Assessment
    Psychosocial assessment attempts to provide a realistic picture of the individual in interaction with the _____. (p. 535)

6. Assessment interviews
    a. In order to minimize sources of error, an assessment interview is often carefully structured in terms of goals, content to be explored, and the type of _____ the interviewer attempts to establish with the subject. (p. 536)

    b. Nevertheless, the clinical interview been criticized as an unreliable source of information on which to base clinical decisions. What type of evidence is used to demonstrate that interviews are unreliable? (p. 536)

    c. To improve reliability, structured interviews were developed. How do judgments based on the use of structured interviews and rating scales compare to the accuracy of judgments based on clinical interviews? (p. 536)

    d. Give an example of a structured interview for children that has been developed for computer administration. (p. 536)

    e. A type of assessment that is related to interview is _____. One of the

most efficient instruments for obtaining specific information about an individual's
problem area is the problem checklist. (p. 537)

7. Clinical observation of behavior
   a. The main purpose of direct observation is to find out more about the person's
      psychological makeup and level of functioning through observations, ideally, in the
      individual's natural environment. A commonly used method to allow the observer to
      indicate not only the presence or absence of a trait or behavior but also its prominence
      is _____. (p. 537)

   b. What is the most widely used rating scale for recording observations in clinical practice
      and psychiatric research? (p. 537)

   c. How did Paul and his colleagues (1977, 1978, 1979, 1982) use observational rating
      scales? (pp. 537-538)

   d. Jones, Reid, and Patterson (1975) have developed a method of coding and quantifying
      observations of _____ at _____ and
      at _____. This method provides the clinician with
      information about the stimuli that are controlling the child's interactions. (p. 538)

   e. Describe how the following techniques are used to obtain observational data:
      (p. 538)

      1. Role playing

      2. Self-monitoring

8. Psychological tests
   a. Psychological tests are standardized sets of procedures to obtain samples of a subject's
      behavior that can be compared to the behavior of other individuals usually through the
      use of test _____. (pp. 538-539)

   b. Among the characteristics about which the clinician can draw inferences from
      psychological tests are intellectual capacity, motive patterns, personality
      characteristics, role behaviors, values, level of depression or anxiety, and
      _____. (p. 539)

   c. Match the following psychological tests with the appropriate description of each test's
      purpose: (pp. 539-542)

Psychological Test	**Purpose**
1. Rorschach Test	a. Rating scale based on standardized interview
2. Thematic Apperception Test	b. Intelligence scale for children
3. Minnesota Multiphasic Personality Inventory (MMPI)	c. Intelligence scale for adults
4. WAIS-R	d. Projective test using inkblots
5. WISC-R	e. Projective test using pictures
6. Brief Psychiatric Rating Scale (BPRS)	f. Structured personality test
7. 16PF	g. Personality test for normal subjects
8. Sentence Completion Test	h. Test that pinpoints topics that should be explored

d. Individual intelligence tests
   Individual intelligence tests such as the WISC-R or the WAIS-R require two to three hours to administer, score, and interpret; in many clinical situations, there is not sufficient time or funcing to use these tests in every assessment situation. (p. 539)

   1. In what type of cases would an individual intelligence test be indicated?

   2. In which cases would an individual intelligence test be unnecessary?

e. Personality Tests
   There are basically two kinds of personality test: objective and projective.

   Projective tests are unstructured in that they rely on various ambiguous stimuli, such as inkblots, rather than questions and answers. It is assumed that in trying to make sense out of the stimuli, the respondents "project" their own problems, motives, and wishes into the situations.

1. The Rorschach Test
   Which of the following are among the reasons that the use of the Rorschach Test has declined over the last 20 years? Circle the correct response.   (p. 540)

   a. The Rorschach takes too long to administer.   YES OR NO

   b. The Rorschach is often of low or negligible validity
       except in the hands of a skilled interpreter.   YES OR NO

   c. The results of the Rorschach are unreliable.   YES OR NO

   d. The Rorschach results in behavioral
       descriptions rather than in a formulation
       of personality dynamics.   YES OR NO

2. The Thematic Apperception Test
   The TAT has been criticized for its dated pictures, lengthy administration, and the fact that interpretation is often _____.
                                                                            (p. 541)

Objective tests are structured, that is, they typically use questionnaires, self-report inventories, or rating scales in which questions are carefully phrased and possible responses are specified.

1. The Minnestoa Multiphasic Personality Inventory
   a. Place a 1, 2, or 3 in front of the following steps to indicate the sequence in which the step appeared during the construction of the MMPI.   (p. 542)

      _____ Scales are constructed.

      _____ Items analyses are performed.

      _____ Items are administered to large groups of normal subjects and
                psychiatric patients.

   b. What is a validity scale for?   (p. 542)

   c. How is the MMPI used as a diagnostic standard?   (p. 542)

   d. What criticisms have been made of the MMPI?   (pp. 542-543)

2. The Sixteen Personality Factor Questionnaire
   The 16PF was constructed by factor analysis. What does this mean?
   (pp. 544-545)

f. Complete the chart below that compares the overall strengths and weaknesses of projective and objective tests. (pp.545-546)

Test	Strengths	Weaknesses
projective		interpretations are subjective, unreliable, and difficult to validate, require trained staff to administer and score
objective	cost effective, reliable, objective, administered and scored by computer	

g. Computer interpretation of objective personality tests is possible and a number of highly sophisticated MMPI interpretation systems have been developed. Computer-based MMPI interpretation systems typically employ an _____ procedure. Describe how this procedure works. (p. 546)

h. There are three ways to obtain computer-basd MMPI interpretation: mail-in service, teleprocessing, and _____. (p. 546)

9. Use of psychological tests in personnel screening
   a. The potential for job failure or for becoming psychologically maladjusted under stress is so great for individuals in some occupations that measures need to be taken in the preemployment hiring process to evaluate potential candidates for emotional _____ and to determine their capability of performing the job. (p. 547)

   b. The use of personality tests in personnel screening has a long tradition. The first formal use of a standardized personality scale took place in _____ to screen draftees who were psychologically unfit for military service. (p. 547)

c. Place the following words in the correct blanks: Personnel selection, personnel
    screening.   (p. 547)

    1. Screening out is called _____.   This type of
        selection is done to alert employers to possible maladjustment that would impact
        adversely upon the way in which the individual would function in a critical job.

    2. Screening in is called _____. This type of
        selection is done when the employer believes that certain personality
        characteristics are desirable for a particular job.

d. Before personality tests are used in personnel screening, the psychologist needs to
    consider three issues: (1) how much weight should the test be given, (2) determine if
    the job is critical enough to justify the invasion of privacy involved in the use of
    psychological testing, and (3)_____.
                                                                                  (p. 547)

10. Integration of assessment data
    In a clinic or hospital setting, assessment data is usually evaluated in a
    _____ attended by members of the
    interdisciplinary team who are concerned with the decision to be made
    regarding treatment.   (p. 554)

11. Unresolved issues
    a. Concerns have been raised by Matarazzo (1986) that the widespread use of
        computer-based assessment procedures is not sufficiently supported by the research
        and that there is substantial overselling of unvalidated measures. Butcher and Fowler
        (1986) replied that there are already controls in place, specifically the APA guidelines
        for _____.   (p. 555)

    b. Is is appropriate for practitioners to employ computer-based interpretations as their
        final report on a client according to APA guidelines?   (p. 556)

    c. The authors suggest that computer-based assessment procedures are actually
        underutilized. Complete the following list of reasons why this may be so:
                                                                                  (p. 556)

        1. Practitioners trained prior to the microcomputer age may not have the time to
            become familiar with these machines and may be uncomfortable with them.

        2.

        3.

(12.) Neuropsychological examination: determining brain-behavior relationships
Match the following subtests of the Halstead-Reitan neuropsychology battery with the
correct description of its purpose: (p. 535)

Subtest

Purpose

1. Halstead category test

a. Determines if an individual can identify spoken words.

2. tactual performance test

b. Measures a patient's ability to learn and remember.

3. rhythm test

c. Gives clues to the extent and location of brain damage.

4. speech sounds perception test

d. Measures attention and sustained concentration.

5. finger oscillation test

e. Measures motor speed, response to the unfamiliar, and the learning of tactile and kinesthetic cues.

(13.) Limitations of psychological assessment
Describe *how* each of the following factors *may* limit the accuracy of psychosocial
assessment: (p. 555)
a. Cultural bias

b. Overemphasis on internal traits

c. Theoretical orientation of the clinician

CHAPTER QUIZ

1. In assessing a client's social context, all of the following are pertinent except:
(p. 532)
a. environmental demands.
b. interpersonal skills.
c. sources of emotional support.
d. special stressors.

2. Therapists with which of the following orientations will <u>typically</u> use interview techniques to discover areas of blocked or distorted personal growth? (p. 533)

   a. behavioral
   b. humanistic

   c. interpersonal
   d. psychoanalytic

3. A neurological diagnostic aid that reveals how an organ is functioning by measuring metabolic processes is the: (p. 534)

   a. PET scan.
   b. CAT scan.

   c. EEG.
   d. angiogram.

4. Which of the following is the <u>most highly regarded</u> six-hour neurolotical test? (p. 534)

   a. Halstead-Reitan
   b. Luria-Nebraska

   c. Stanford Binet
   d. Wechsler Adult Intelligence Scale

5. If a clinical researcher wanted to group patients into treatment groups on the basis of similarity of clinical symptoms, he or she could easily use the: (p. 537)

   a. Thematic Apperception Test (TAT).
   b. Brief Psychiatric Rating Scale (BPRS).
   c. Record of Clinical Behavior (RCB).
   d. Rorschach test.

6. Two general categories of psychological tests used in clinical practice are: (p. 539)

   a. intelligence and personality.
   b. philosophy and religion.
   c. speech perception and reaction time.
   d. tactual performance and auditory perception.

7. An instrument used to measure the present level of intellectual functioning in adults is the: (p. 539)

   a. WICS-R.
   b. WAIS-R.

   c. TAT.
   d. MMPI.

8. Personality tests are often grouped into two categories: (p. 539)

   a. projective and structured.
   b. behavioral and psychodynamic.
   c. conscious and unconscious.
   d. verbal and performance.

9. The aim of a projective test is to: (pp. 539-540)

   a. predict a patient's future behavior.
   b. compare a patient's responses to those of persons who are known to have mental disorders.
   c. assess the role of organic factors in a patient's thinking.
   d. assess the way a patient perceives ambiguous stimuli.

10. All of the following are structured personality tests except the: (p. 540)

    a. MMPI.   c. Sixteen Personality Factor Questionnaire.
    b. Q Sort.   d. TAT.

11. A clinical researcher devises a new psychological test that assesses neuroticism. She is concerned with the possibility that some individuals might not answer the questions in a straightforward, accurate way. To determine whether an individual is honest, she should: (p. 542)

    a. factor analyze the responses.
    b. make use of actuarial interpretation.
    c. construct a validity scale.
    d. test the instrument on a group of college students.

12. Behaviorists have criticized the MMPI for being too: (p. 543)

    a. action-oriented.   c. objective.
    b. "mentalistic."   d. superficial.

13. Advantages of the MMPI and other self-report inventories include all of the following except: (p. 545)

    a. they are cost effective.
    b. they are highly reliable and objective.
    c. in the hands of a skilled interpreter they can be quite useful in uncovering psychodynamic problems.
    d. they can be administered, scored, and interpreted by computers.

14. Which of the following personality tests would most likely be used for personnel screening for a dangerous job? (p. 547)

    a. California Psychological Inventory
    b. MMPI
    c. 16 PF
    d. Strong Vocational Inventory

15. The APA guidelines on computer-based assessment assume that computerized test results will be used as: (p. 556)

    a.   a last resort only.
    b.   final recommendations.
    c.   the sole basis for diagnosis.
    d.   working hyptheses.

16

Biologically Based Therapies

OVERVIEW

Many states have passed laws during the past few years allowing or requiring pharmacies to post prices for the most frequently used prescription drugs in order to help consumers comparison shop. When such signs were posted, it surprised quite a few people to learn that several of the most frequently used drugs are chemicals that alter the emotional state and not drugs for "physical disease." Because of this widespread use of psychoactive drugs, an informed person should have some understanding of what such drugs can really accomplish and the trade-offs involved in using them.

Chapter 16 presents details about the major types of drugs used for mental disorders: antianxiety, antipsychotic, antidepressant, and antimania, discussing their major effects, side effects, modes of action, and effectiveness. Other biological treatments, such as electric shock and psychosurgery, are also described briefly.

LEARNING OBJECTIVES

1. Briefly summarize the early history of attempts at biological intervention and explain why medical treatment for physical diseases is far more advanced than medical treatment for behavior disorders.

2. Describe the use of insulin coma therapy and explain why it has largely disappeared.

3. Describe the discovery and use of electroconvulsive therapy (ECT) and its positive and negative effects on the patient.

4. Explain the controversy about using ECT and the reasons for its continued use.

5. Describe prefrontal lobotomy and its effects on the patient.

6. Compare the psychosurgery of today with its earlier forerunners and describe the current debate over "brain-disabling" therapies.

7. Define *psychopharmacology* and list four types of chemical agents now commonly used in therapy for mental disorders.

8. List several antipsychotic compounds and describe their effects and side effects in the treatment of behavior disorders.

9. List several antidepressant compounds and describe their effects and side effects in the treatment of mental disorders.

10. List several antianxiety compounds and describe their effects and side effects in the treatment of maladaptive behavior.

11. Describe the use of lithium in the treatment of bipolar mood disorders and list its effects and side effects.

12. List some of the drugs that have been used in treating maladaptive behavior in children, and explain a danger of using drug therapy for hyperactive youngsters.

13. List some of the overall advantages and disadvantages of using pharmacological therapy for treating behavior disorders.

14. Describe megavitamin therapy and summarize the conclusions of the American Psychiatric Association Task Force which was formed to evaluate it.

15. Describe hemodialysis therapy and evaluate its results in treating schizophrenic patients.

TERMS YOU SHOULD KNOW

insulin coma therapy (p. 561)

electroconvulsive therapy (ECT) (p. 561)

tonic (extensor) seizures (p. 561)

clonic (contractile) seizures (p. 561)

unilateral ECT (p. 563)

prefrontal lobotomy (p. 563)

cingulotomy (p. 564)

informed consent (p. 565)

pharmacology (p. 565)

psychotropic drugs (p. 565)

antipsychotic compounds (major tranquilizers) (p. 565)

reserpine (p. 566)

chlorpromazine (Thorazine) (p. 566)

tardive dyskinesia (p. 566)

target dosing (p. 567)

antidepressant compounds (p. 569)

monoamine oxidase inhibitors (MAO) (p. 569)

tricyclics (p. 569)

antianxiety compounds (minor tranquilizers) (p. 569)

benzodiazepines (p. 570)

lithium (p. 570)

megavitamin therapy (p. 574)

hemodialysis (p. 574)

(reuptake mechanism) (p. 567)

CONCEPTS TO MASTER

1. Early attempts at biological intervention
    List several treatments in medicine that involve substantial disruption of biological
    processes (and suffering to the patient).   (p. 559)

2. Coma and convulsive therapies

   a. Insulin coma therapy is no longer practiced. Why was it abandoned? (p. 561)

   b. Electroconvulsive therapy (ECT) is much more widely used than insulin therapy, mostly because of its effectiveness in alleviating depressive episodes. Describe what happens during ECT. (p. 561)

   c. After awakening several minutes after ECT, the patient has amnesia for the period immediately preceeding the therapy. With repeated treatments, usually administered 2-3 times weekly, the patient gradually becomes generally disoriented. It is possible that each single electroconvulsive treatment administered to the person destroys a varying number of central nervous system _____. (p. 561)

   d. Why did the citizens of Berkeley, California try to ban ECT although their efforts were overturned in court? (p. 562)

   e. In 1985, the National Institute of Mental Health sponsored a Consensus Development Conference on electroconvulsive therapy.

      1. The panel recognized a number of potential risks associated with the use of ECT. What were the risks? (p. 562)

      2. With present techniques, the death rate from ECT is _____ per 10,000 patients. (p. 562)

      3. Complete the following information about the kinds of cases where the panel concluded that ECT might be beneficial. (p. 562)

       a. Depression, particularly _____ and _____.

       b. Some types of manic disorders, particularly _____.

    4. The panel concluded that relapse rates following ECT were high unless the treatment was followed up by _____.   (p. 562)

    5. The mechanism by which ECT accomplishes therapeutic effects is still unknown.
                                         TRUE OR FALSE   (p. 562)

  f. Provide the following information about unilateral ECT: (p. 563)

    1. What is unilateral ECT?

    2. Is it widely employed?

3. Psychosurgery
  a. After initial enthusiasm, doctors began to recognize that the results of psychosurgery could be very undesirable. What are some of the undesirable results that were found?
                                         (pp. 563-564)

  b. The discovery of _____ caused an almost immediate halt to psychosurgical procedures.   (p. 564)

  c. In the mid 1970s the United States Congress conducted a special investigation into the effects of psychosurgery. They concluded that some psychosurgery resulted in surprisingly beneficial effects but also warned that such benefits were often achieved at the expense of the loss of _____.
                                         (p. 564)

4. Emergence of pharmacological methods
    Pharmacology is the science of _____.   (p. 565)

5. Types of drugs used in therapy
  a. Fill in the missing information in the following chart that summarizes the four types of drugs commonly used for mental disorders: (pp. 565-571)

Class of Drugs	Biological Effect	Behavioral Effect	Example
antipsychotics		reduce the intensity of schizophrenic symptoms (including delusions and hallucinations) and have a calming effect	Thorazine
antidepressant-tricyclics	increase concentration of biogenic amines at synapses		
antianxiety-benzodiazepines	selectively diminish generalized fear		
lithium		resolve 70 percent of manic episodes and may also be useful in depression of bipolar type	

b. Antipsychotic compounds

    1. The following is a schematic diagram of the antipsychotic class of drugs that illustrates the two general types of antipsychotics, official clinical names for these drugs, and the trade names under which they are sold in the drugstore (by prescription only). Fill in the missing trade names.

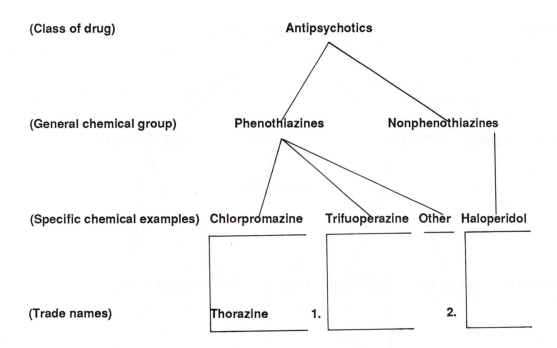

(Class of drug)   **Antipsychotics**

(General chemical group)   **Phenothiazines**   **Nonphenothiazines**

(Specific chemical examples) **Chlorpromazine   Trifuoperazine   Other   Haloperidol**

(Trade names)   **Thorazine   1.   2.**

2. Compared to anything we have known before, the effects of the antipsychotic
    compounds in the treatment of schizophrenia are remarkable. At the same time we
    must acknowledge that the behavioral residual is still less than impressive. In what
    ways are the behavioral results of treatment with antipsychotic drugs "less
    than impressive"?   (p. 567)

c. Antidepressant compounds
    1. The following is a schematic diagram of the antidepressant class of drugs that
        illustrates the three general types of antidepressants, the official chemical names
        for these drugs, and the trade names under which they are sold in the drugstore (by
        prescription only). Fill in the missing trade names. Regardless of the chemical
        makeup, it is believed that all antidepressants accomplish a similar biochemical
        result--increasing the concentrations of the neurotransmitters serotonin and
        norepinephrine at pertinent synaptic sites in the brain.   (p. 569)

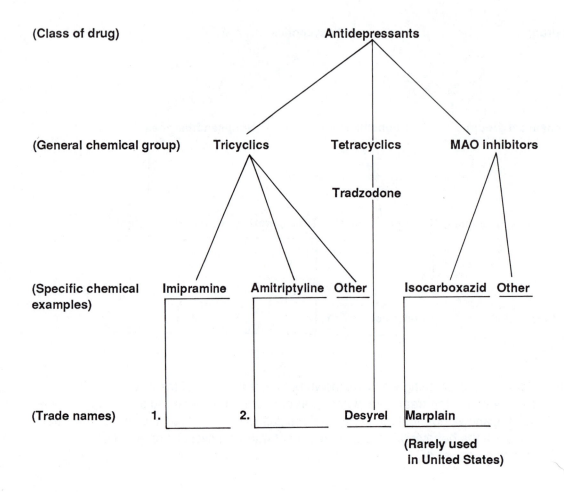

(Class of drug) — Antidepressants

(General chemical group) — Tricyclics, Tetracyclics, MAO inhibitors

Tradzodone

(Specific chemical examples) — Imipramine, Amitriptyline, Other, Isocarboxazid, Other

(Trade names) — 1. , 2. , Desyrel, Marplain

(Rarely used in United States)

2.   To date, little progress has been made in identifying _____ or other _____ that relate to treatment success by a given drug or treatment method.   (p. 569)

   d.   Antianxiety compounds

      1.   A schematic diagram follows of the antianxiety class of drugs that illustrates the three general types of antianxiety drugs, the official chemical names for the drugs, and the trade names under which they are sold in the drugstore (by prescription only). Fill in the missing information next to numbers 1, 2, 3, and 4:
                                                                                     (p. 570)

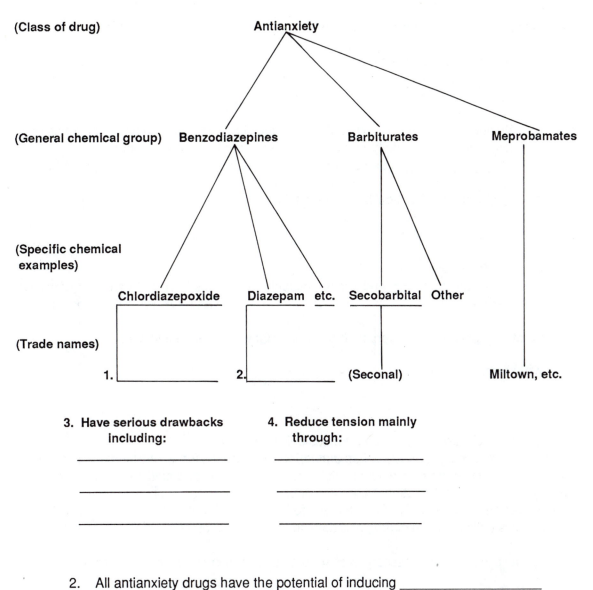

(Class of drug) — Antianxiety

(General chemical group) — Benzodiazepines — Barbiturates — Meprobamates

(Specific chemical examples) — Chlordiazepoxide — Diazepam — etc. — Secobarbital — Other

(Trade names)

1. _____ 2. _____ (Seconal) Miltown, etc.

3. Have serious drawbacks
including:

_____

_____

_____

4. Reduce tension mainly
through:

_____

_____

_____

2. All antianxiety drugs have the potential of inducing _____
when used unwisely or in excess.   (p. 570)

3. The range of application of antianxiety compounds is quite broad. List some of the
conditions in which tension and anxiety may be significant components.
                                                         (p. 570)

    e.   Lithium for the bipolar mood disorders

        1.   Why is lithium difficult to use?   (p. 570)

        2.   Although lithium was slow to catch on in the U.S., there can be no doubt at this point concerning its remarkable effectiveness in promptly resolving about _____ percent of all manic states.   (p. 571)

        3.   What is the biochemical basis of the therapeutic effect of lithium?   (p. 572)

6.   Drug therapy for children
    a.   Antianxiety, antipsychotic, and antidepressant medications have all been used effectively with children.   TRUE OR FALSE   (p. 572)

    b.   What is a "paradoxical reversal effect," and what would cause it to occur?
                                                                  (p. 572)
    c.   What is Ritalin?   (p. 572)

7.   A biopsychosocial perspective on pharmacological therapy
All in all, pharmacological therapy has outmoded more drastic forms of treatment and has led to a much more favorable hospital climate for patients and staff alike. However, there are a number of limitations in the use of psychotropic drugs even in addition to their undesirable side effects. Complete the following list of limitations: (p. 573)
    a.   It is difficult to match drug and dosage to the needs of the patient.

    b.   It is sometimes necessary to change medications in the middle of treatment.

    c.   The use of medications in isolation from other treatment methods for psychological disorders is usually inappropriate and ineffective, since drugs themselves do not _____ disorders.

8.   Unresolved issues
    a.   What conclusion did the American Psychiatric Association reach regarding the effectiveness of megavitamin therapy for schizophrenia?   (p. 574)

b.   What is the latest information available on the effectiveness of hemodialysis as a
      treatment for schizophrenia according to a study by Schultz et al. (1981)?

                                                                            (p. 575)

(9.)   Chemically induced sleep: is it worth the risks?
      a.   How did the Institute of Medicine evaluate the safety of the benzodiazepines (e.g.
            Valium, Librium, Dalmane) as sleeping medication?   (p. 571)

      b.   Should older people who complain of insomnia be given sleeping pills?   (p. 571)

CHAPTER QUIZ

1.   Electroconvulsive therapy (ECT) was developed as a result of speculation by Von Meduna,
     a Hungarian physician, that: (p. 561)
     a.   electricians who were severely shocked often became epileptic.
     b.   epileptics rarely developed schizophrenia.
     c.   schizophrenics often had seizures.
     d.   survivors of lightening strikes seldome became schizophrenic.

2.   Criticisms of the use of ECT for depression include all of the following except:

                                                                            (pp. 561-562)

     a.   it is ineffective.
     b.   benefits may be short-lived.
     c.   it causes demonstrable brain damage.
     d.   it is undertaken too routinely.

3.   The 1985 NIMH Consensus Panel concluded that relapse rates following electroconvulsive
     therapy (ECT) were high unless the treatments were followed by: (p. 562)

     a.   changes in the patient's psychosocial environment.
     b.   maintenance doses of antidepressant medication.
     c.   regular psychodynamic therapy sessions.
     d.   sedative and muscle relaxant medication.

4.   The great majority of psychiatrists employ an unnecessarily damaging, inefficient form of
     ECT. Which of the following treatments is still effective, but without as many distressing
     side effects as the damaging, outdated method?   (p. 563)

    a.   ECT accompanied by muscle stimulants
    b.   bilateral ECT
    c.   unilateral ECT
    d.   cerebellar ECT

5.   Which of the following caused an <u>almost</u> immediate halt in the widespread use of psycho-
    surgical procedures in this country?   (p. 564)

    a.   a 1951 law banning all such operations
    b.   the advent of electroconvulsive therapy (ECT)
    c.   the advent of the major antipsychotic drugs
    d.   the unusually high mortality rate

6.   Contemporary uses of psychosurgery include: (p. 564)

    a.   treatment of "psychic pain."
    b.   reduction of depression
    c.   modification of schizophrenia.
    d.   treatment of some forms of retardation.

7.   A modern psychosurgical technique known as "cingulotomy" is used to remove the
    subjective experience of: (p. 564)

    a.   depression.   c.   mania.
    b.   guilt.   d.   pain.

8.   Antipsychotic, antidepressant, antianxiety, and lithium compounds are all referred to
    as _____ drugs.   (p. 565)

    a.   hallucinogenic   c.   narcotic
    b.   mind-expanding   d.   psychotropic

9.   Which of the following is a trade name for a major antipsychotic drug?   (p. 565)

    a.   Haldol   c.   Dyserl
    b.   Valium   d.   Synaquon

10. The <u>unique</u> quality of antipsychotic drugs is their ability to: (p. 565)

    a.   calm patients down.
    b.   put patients to sleep.
    c.   reduce patients' anxiety.
    d.   reduce the intensity of delusions and hallucinations.

11. Virtually all of the antipsychotic drugs accomplish the same biochemical effect, which is:

(p. 566)

    a.   blocking dopamine receptors.
    b.   blocking the production of noradrenalin.
    c.   stimulating the production of endorphins.
    d.   stimulating the production of glutamic acid.

12. Pharmacological treatment of depression with tricyclics is believed to: (p. 567)

    a.   reduce central nervous system arousal.
    b.   reduce intracranial pressure by absorbing cerebral spinal fluid.
    c.   increase the availability of lithium in the central nervous system for absorption.
    d.   increase the concentration of seritonin and norephinephrine at synaptic sites.

13. One of the most commonly used tricyclic drugs in the treatment of depression is:

(p. 569)

    a.   methylpenidate (Ritalin).
    b.   imipramine (Tofranil).
    c.   chlordiazepoxide (Librium).
    d.   haloperidol (Haldol).

14. Lithium compounds are used in the treatment of: (p. 570)

    a.   anxiety.
    b.   hyperactivity and specific learning disabilities.
    c.   bipolar affective psychosis.
    d.   hallucinations and delusions.

15. The reported success of megavitamin therapy and the orthomolecular approach is probably because of `the: (p. 573)

    a.   relief of synaptic pathway blockages.
    b.   blockage of norepinephrine at neural transmitter sites.
    c.   increase of seritonin level in the bloodstream.
    d.   placebo effect.

17

Psychologically Based Therapies

OVERVIEW

This chapter describes in some detail what mental health professionals do about all the types of problems discussed in the earlier chapters. There are a wide variety of techniques available, and often completely different approaches have been developed for the same problem behavior. These various approaches to treatment are all outgrowths of the different models of psychopathology described earlier. This material is confusing at first because of the natural tendency to feel that one approach might be right and the others wrong. In reality, no general approach to psychotherapy has proved capable of handling the wide range of problems seen clinically. Consequently, the inclination to identify strongly with one approach or another is decreasing. Today, many therapists are familiar with a variety of techniques chosen from several therapeutic approaches and use them depending on the type of problems the client is having. Some therapists, however, prefer to use only one type of treatment. In this case, they try to develop a professional reputation as a specialized therapist so that only clients appropriate to their chosen orientation are referred to them.

LEARNING OBJECTIVES

1. List and explain several reasons why people enter psychotherapy and describe three types of mental health professionals who are trained in the identification and treatment of mental disorders.

2. Describe four general types of therapy and explain the "continuous loop" perspective.

3. List and describe the four basic techniques of psychoanalysis, summarize the changes that have taken place since Freud, and evaluate the effectiveness of the psychodynamic approach to the treatment of maladaptive behavior.

4. Explain the principle of extinction and describe several therapeutic techniques which make use of this phenomenon.

5. Explain the learning principles underlying systematic desensitization and list three steps in its application to maladaptive behavior.

6. Define *aversion therapy* and give several examples of its use to treat behavioral disorders.

7. Define *modeling* and explain how it can be used in the treatment of mental disorders.

8. Explain what is meant by systematic use of positive reinforcement and describe three general techniques based on this plan.

9. Describe *assertiveness therapy* and explain the learning principles that are involved in its use.

10. List three steps in the biofeedback approach to therapy and describe several of its applications to maladaptive behaviors.

11. List and explain three advantages that behavior therapy has over other psychotherapies and indicate why it cannot be a cure-all.

12. Define *cognitive-behavior therapy* and describe several techniques used by rational-emotive therapists to treat mental disorders.

13. Describe Beck's cognitive-behavior therapy for depression and explain the theory on which it is based.

14. Describe the three stages of stress-inoculation therapy and give some examples of the use of this strategy.

15. Compare the outcomes of cognitive-behavior therapy with other psychotherapies and describe some trends in its use.

16. Describe Carl Rogers' client-centered therapy and indicate some differences in the way it is practiced today.

17. List several important concepts that underlie existential psychotherapy and describe its application to maladaptive beavhior.

18. Explain the main goals of Gestalt therapy and describe several techniques used by Perls and others to treat mental disorders.

19. List some criticisms of the humanistic-experiential therapies and point out some of their positive contributions to the field.

20. Describe several foci of couple counseling, and indicate some of its difficulties and outcomes.

21. Describe two types of family therapy and give some examples of their use to treat maladaptive beavhior.

22. List and explain the three "ego states" that are the basis for transactional analysis and indicate the significance of the games people play.

23. List Kendall's four reasons for the current interest in integrating behavior therapy with other methods and explain three problems that he sees in achieving this goal.

24. List five sources of information necessary to evaluate the effectiveness of treatment and describe some of the limitations they impose on the process.

25. Describe the controversy centering around possible conflicts between the role of the therapist and the values of society.

26. Describe three unresolved issues in psychotherapy that are discussed by the authors.

TERMS YOU SHOULD KNOW

psychotherapy (p. 579)

"YAVIS" phenomenon (p. 581)

physician (p. 581)

clergy (p. 581)

clinical psychologist (p. 581)

psychiatrist (p. 581)

psychiatric social worker (p. 581)

therapeutic relationship (p. 583)

expectation (of receiving help) (p. 583)

class I therapies (p. 583)

class II therapies (p. 583)

class III therapies (p. 583)

class IV therapies (p. 583)

causal primacy (p. 584)

psychodynamic therapy, psychoanalytically-oriented therapy (or psychoanalysis) (p. 585)

psychoanalyst or analyst (p. 585)

free association (p. 586)

analysis of dreams (p. 587)

manifest content (p. 587)

latent content (p. 587)

resistance (p. 587)

analysis of resistance (p. 587)

transference (p. 587)

analysis of transference (p. 587)

transference neurosis (p. 587)

countertransference (p. 587)

time limited dynamic psychotherapy (p. 589)

behavior therapy (p. 589)

behavior therapists (p. 589)

extinction (p. 590)

flooding, or in vivo procedures (p. 590)

implosive therapy (p. 590)

systematic desensitization (p. 591)

training in relaxation (p. 591)

construction of hierarchies (pp. 591-592)

aversion therapy (p. 592)

differential reinforcement of other responses (DOR) (p. 593)

modeling (p. 593)

response shaping (p. 593)

token economics (p. 594)

behavioral contracting (pp. 594-595)

assertiveness therapy (p. 595)

biofeedback (p. 596)

thermistors (p. 596)

coverants (p. 597)

cognitive-behavioral therapy (p. 597)

rational-emotive therapy (RET) (p. 597)

cognitive behavioral therapy for depression (p. 598)

selectively perceive (pp. 598-599)

overgeneralize (p. 598)

magnify (p. 598)

stress-inoculation therapy (p. 600)

cognitive preparation (p. 600)

skill acquisition and rehearsal (p. 600)

humanistic-experiential therapies (p. 602)

(alcohol or drug-abuse counselor) (p. 582)

(team approach) (p. 582)

(individual/group) (p. 586)

(cognitive change/behavior change) (p. 586)

(directive/nondirective) (p. 586)

(inner control of behavior/outer control of behavior) (p. 586)

(brief/long term) (p. 586)

(historical focus/here-and-now emphasis) (p. 586)

(hypnosis) (p. 588)

(induction) (p. 588)

(age regression) (p. 588)

(dream induction) (p. 588)

(post-hypnotic suggestion) (p. 588)

(psychodrama) (p. 603)

(contingencies) (p. 608)

(conflict resolution) (p. 608)

(utility matrices) (p. 608)

(contingency contracting) (p. 608)

CONCEPTS TO MASTER

1. Introduction
   a. Psychotherapy is based on the assumption that even in cases where physical pathology is present, changes in _____, _____, _____, and coping strategies will have to occur if

recovery is to take place. The belief that individuals can _____ is the underlying assumption of all psychotherapy approaches.   (p. 579)

b. There are six general goals of psychotherapy. Following are four of the goals; fill in the missing two: (p. 579)

    1. Changing maladaptive behavior

    2. Changing environmental conditions that may be causing or maintaining the maladaptive behavior

    3. Improving interpersonal skills

    4. Resolving inner conflict

    5.

    6.

c. It has been estimated that there are several _____ "therapeutic" approaches in existence, ranging from psychoanalysis to Zen meditation.(p. 580)

2. An overview of psychological treatment
All psychotherapies share an orientation that is directed toward change. Affecting the nature and direction of the change are the individuals involved, specifically the therapist and the _____. Some theorists have even argued that the therapist's _____ is as important to patient improvement as the therapist's training and background.   (p. 580)

3. Who receives psychotherapy
    a. Describe the obvious clients for psychotherapy.   (p. 581)

    b. What types of individuals are likely to be reluctant or resistant clients?

        (p. 581)

    c. Clients who do the best in psychotherapy are often "YAVIS" types. Explain this statement.   (p. 581)

4. Who provides psychotherapuetic services
    Fill in the blank spaces in the following chart that summarizes the training and
    special duties of the professionals on the mental health team: (p. 581)

Professional	Training	Special Duties
psychiatrist	MD degree plus three-year residency of hospital	
clinical psychologist		
psychiatric social worker	BA and MA in social sciences	family evaluation

5. The therapeutic relationship
    a. Describe the patient's major contribution to the therapeutic relationship.
    (p. 583)

    b. The patient's "expectation of receiving help" is also important to the outcome of
        therapy and may operate to some degree as a placebo does in medicine. Explain this
        statement.   (p. 583)

    c. Are a therapist's personality characteristics directly related to the outcome of
        therapy?   YES OR NO   (p. 583)

6. A perspective on therapeutic pluralism
    The authors discuss a continuous loop of relationships among (1) the client conceived as
    a system of integrated cognitions and affects; (2) his/her abnormal behavior which is
    assumed to be the product of (3) the client interacting with the environment. Respond
    to the following two questions about this continuous loop: (p. 584)
    a. What is causal primacy?

    b. In order to effect positive overall therapeutic outcome, where in the loop should the
        therapist intervene?

7. Psychodynamic therapy
    a. Psychodynamic therapy is a treatment approach that focuses on individual personality dynamics from a _____. As developed by Freud, psychoanalytic therapy is an intensive, long-term procedure for uncovering repressed memories, thoughts, fears, and conflicts--presumably stemming from problems in early _____ --and helping the individual come to terms with them in light of adult reality.   (p. 585)

    b. There are four basic techniques of psychoanalysis: free association, dream interpretation, analysis of resistance, and analysis of transference. Briefly explain how the analyst uses each technique: (pp. 586-587)

Technique	How it is Used
free association	
dream interpretation	
analysis of resistance	
analysis of transference	

    c. How do most modern analysts like Mann and Strupp differ in emphasis from strict Freudian psychoanalysis?   (p. 589)

8. Evaluation of psychodynamic therapy
    a. Indicate whether each of the following statements represents a valid criticism of psychodynamic therapy. Circle the correct response: (p. 589)

        1. It's time consuming and expensive.   TRUE OR FALSE

        2. It's based on a questionable theory of human nature.   TRUE OR FALSE

        3. It neglects the patient's current problems.   TRUE OR FALSE

4. There is inadequate proof of its effectiveness. TRUE OR FALSE

b. For whom is psychodynamic therapy the treatment to choose? (p. 589)

9. Behavior therapy
The behavioristic perspective views the maladjusted person as one who has:
(1) failed to acquire competencies, or (2)learned faulty coping. Instead of exploring past
traumatic events or inner conflicts, behavior therapists manipulate environmental
contingencies to alter maladaptive behavior.
    Fill in the requested information in the following chart that summarizes several of
the commonly used behavioral therapy techniques:

Behavioral Therapy Technique	**Description**
1. simple extinction (p. 590)	a. This technique is based on the observation that learned behavior patterns weaken over time if not _____. b. It works best on behavior that is being _____ _____ reinforced.
2. implosive therapy and flooding (p. 590)	a. These techniques rely on the principle of _____. b. With implosion, the problematic behavior is removed by the therapist deliberately trying to _____ anxiety rather than to minimize it. c. What techniques can be used with patients who are not able to realistically imagine scenes? d. Which technique is more effective: implosion, in vivo or flooding in imagination? e. What unfavorable results have been reported from implosion therapy?
3. systematic desensitization (p. 591)	a. The technique is designed to eliminate behaviors that are being _____ reinforced but can be used for other types of problems. b. The procedure consists of three steps. What are they?

1.

2.

3.

c.   The procedure doesn't work well with the following types of clients:

4. aversion therapy   a. This approach involves modification of behavior by
    (p. 592)   _____ which can be of two types.
                                  These two types are:

                              1.

                              2.

                          b. The use of electric shock as an aversive stimulus has
                              decreased recently because of what two reasons?

                              1.

                              2.

                              What method is often used instead of electric shock by
                              clinicians such as Lovaas?

5. modeling   a. Modeling involves learning skills through _____.
    (p. 593)
                            b. Modeling may be used in clinical situations such as
                                _____.

6. systematic uses of   a. Briefly describe each of the following techniques:

positive reinforce-
ment (pp. 593-594)

      1. Response shaping

      2. Token economy

b. What are the goals of a token economy program?

7. behavioral
     contracting
     (pp. 594-595)

a. A behavioral contract often specifies _____
as well as the responsibilities of the other person to provide
tangible rewards in return.

b. Briefly list some of the ways a behavioral contract can
facilitate therapy.

8. assertiveness therapy
     (p. 595)

a. Assertiveness is used both as a method of _____
and as a means of teaching more effective coping techniques.

b. Assertiveness training works because each act of intentional
assertion inhibits the _____ associated
with the situation.

9. biofeedback treatment
     (pp. 595-596)

a. Biofeedback consists of three steps. What are they?

     1.

     2.

     3.

b. Biofeedback is commonly used on the following types of
problems:

c. Is there unequivocal data supporting the effectiveness of
biofeedback with conditions such as migraine headaches?

      d. How does the effectiveness of biofeedback (which requires expensive machinery) compare to the effectiveness of relaxation training (which requires next to no special equipment)?

10. Evaluation of behavior therapy
    a. Respond true or false to the following statements about behavior therapy (p. 596)

       1. The treatment is precise.   TRUE OR FALSE

       2. Behavior therapy is successful in the treatment of childhood autism, schizophrenia, and severe depression.   TRUE OR FALSE

       3. Behavior therapy techniques are important in the treatment of sexual dysfunction.   TRUE OR FALSE

    b. Behavior therapy techniques are differentially effective. Fill in the technique that seems most useful to treat the following problems: (p. 596)

Technique	**Behavior Problem**
_____	conditioned avoidance responses
_____	establishing impulse control
_____	acquisition of complex responses

11. Cognitive-behavioral therapy
    a. How have behavioral therapists recently changed their thinking so that many are now labeled "cognitive-behavioral therapists"?   (p. 597)

    b. At present, there are several alternative approaches to cognitive-behavioral therapy, but two main themes seem to characterize them all. Complete the following list of these two themes.   (p. 597)

       1. The conviction that cognitive processes influence both motivation and behavior

     2.

c. The chart below summarizes three different cognitive-behavioral therapies. Fill in the requested information:

Therapeutic Approach   **Description**

1. rational-emotive   a. This approach was developed by _____.
    therapy (RET)   Today, it is one of the most widely used therapeutic
    (pp. 597-598)   approaches.
                              b. Why does Ellis believe that many of us behave irrationally
                                  and feel unnecessarily that we are failures?

                                  How have Arnhoff and Glass (1982) criticized this
                                  viewpoint?

                              c. To change this situation, the RET therapist disputes these
                                  false beliefs through _____ and
                                  brings about changed thoughts and behaviors through the
                                  use of _____ techniques.

2. cognitive-behavioral   a. This therapy was developed by _____
    therapy for   for the treatment of _____.
    depression   b. A basic assumption of this approach is that problems like
    (pp. 598-600)   depression result from a person's negative views about
                                  himself or herself, the world, and the future. Such behavior
                                  typically includes features such as the following. Briefly
                                  describe each one:

                                  1. Selective perception

                                  2. Overgeneralization

                                  3. Magnification

                                  4. Absolutistic thinking

     c. Describe how Beck's approach to changing irrational thinking differs from Ellis' RET.

     d. Cognitive restructuring may involve other techniques as well. Briefly describe each one:

        1. Schedule of daily activities

        2. Discovery of automatic thoughts

3. stress-inoculation therapy (pp. 600-601)

     a. This approach was developed by _____.

     b. Stress-inoculation training usually involves three stages. Briefly describe what happens at each of the stages:

        1. Cognitive preparation

        2. Skill acquisition and rehersal

        3. Application and practice

     c. This approach has been successfully employed in the following cases:

        It is particularly suited to increasing the adaptive capacities of individuals who have shown a vulnerability to:

12. Evaluation of cognitive-behavioral therapy
     Indicate whether each of the following statements is true or false by circling the appropriate response: (p. 602)
     a. Data on RET and cognitive therapy for depression indicate they are more successful than drug treatment in promoting change.   TRUE OR FALSE

b.   There are questions whether cognitive-behavioral therapy is
     really "behavioral."   TRUE OR FALSE

13. Humanistic-experiential therapies
    a.   These approaches have developed in reaction to behavioral and psychodynamic therapies
         which are believed to fail to accurately account for either the
         _____ or _____.
                                                                        (p. 602)

    b.   Humanistic-experiential therapies are based on a major assumption. What is it?
                                                                        (p. 602)

    c.   How do behavioral therapists differ from humanistic therapists on this assumption?

    d.   The chart below summarizes the major approaches to psychotherapy that are
         humanistic-experientially oriented. Fill in the requested information: (pp. 602-606)

Therapeutic Approach   **Description**

1.   client-centered   a.   This therapy was originated by _____
     (nondirective)   in the 1940s as an alternative to psychoanalysis. In this
     (pp. 602-604)   therapy, the psychoanalytic view of humans as irrational
                                       and the idea that the proper role of the therapist is to be the
                                       director of therapy are rejected.
                                  b.   The primary role of client-centered therapy is to remove
                                       "incongruence." What is incongruence and how does it come
                                       about?

                                       How does the client-centered therapist remove
                                       incongruence?

                                  c.   "Pure" client-centered therapy is rarely used today, but it
                                       has been influential. How are the experiential therapies of
                                       today similar to client-centered therapy, and how are they
                                       different?

2. existential therapy
    (pp. 604-605)

    a. Existential therapists do not follow any rigidly prescribed procedures, but they all emphasize the _____ of each individual.

    b. In contrast to the behavioral therapist, the existential therapist _____ his or her feelings and values with the client.

    c. For what types of clients is this therapy indicated?

3. Gestalt therapy
    (pp. 605-606)

    a. This therapy was originated by _____ as a means of teaching clients to recognize _____ and emotional modalities that they had been _____.

    b. The main goal of Gestalt therapy is to increase _____.

    c. Gestalt therapy sessions focus on the more obvious elements of a person's behavior; thus the sessions are often called _____ training.

    d. What is "taking care of unfinished business"?

    e. Gestalt therapy is said to have become widely used because it blends many of the strong points of psychoanalysis, behavioral therapy, and humanistic-existential therapy. Indicate what Gestalt therapy shares with each of these therapies.

14. Evaluation of the humanistic-experiential therapies
    Complete the following list of the three major criticisms that have been made of humanistic-experiential therapies. (Ironically, that points of criticims are seen by proponents of humanistic-experiential therapies as the strengths of their approach.)
    (p. 606)

    a. Lack of a highly systematized model of human behavior

    b.

    c.

15. Therapy for interpersonal relationships
    These therapeutic techniques focus on relationships rather than individuals and emphasize the role of faulty communication in causing maladaptive behavior. The following chart summarizes the major forms of interpersonal therapy. Fill in the missing information: (pp. 607-611)

Therapeutic Approach

Description

1. couple counseling
    (marital therapy)
    (pp. 607-609)

    a. Can improvements in marital relationships usually be accomplished by undertaking therapy with one member but not the other?

    b. How do happily married couples differ from unhappily married couples?

    c. How are videotapes useful in couple counseling?

    d. How effective are marital therapies at resolving crises according to Cookery (1980)?

2. family therapy
    (pp. 609-610)

    a. How did family therapy originate?

    b. Who does the family therapist view as the "patient" in family therapy?

    c. The most widely used approach to family therapy is _____ developed by Satir (1967). This therapy emphasizes improving family communication and interactions.

    d. Another approach is called "structured family therapy" and was developed by _____. This therapy assumes that if the family context changes, then the individual members will change. Thus, an important goal is to change the family organization so that family members will behave:

Structured therapy has been used successfully with:

e. Which approach to family therapy has been found to be most effective by Gurman, Kniskern, & Pinsof (1986)?

f. How does the success of family therapy compare to individual therapy?

3. transactional analysis (pp. 610-611)

a. What happens if one party stops playing a game?

b. Describe each of the following games people may play:

1. "Why don't you--yes but"

2. "Wooden leg"

3. "Now I've got you, you son of a bitch"

c. What is the purpose of analyzing the "games" people play?

16. Integration of therapy approaches
a. What have psychodynamic therapists had to acknowledge about behavioral techniques?
(p. 612)

b. What have behavioral therapists had to acknowledge about relationship factors?
(p. 612)

c. Kendall (1982) has summarized the reasons there is interest in integrating the approaches to psychotherapy, but he has also noted the obstacles to integration. Summarize these arguments in the following chart: (p. 612)

Reason for Integration of Therapeutic Approaches	**Obstacles to Integration of Therapeutic Approaches**
1.	1.
2.	2.
3.	3.
4. Integration would require members of schools to reevaluate their assumptions and could promote a broad reappraisal of therapy from different perspectives.	4.

17. Evaluation of success in psychotherapy
    a. The chart below lists some of the sources of information that can be used to gauge the outcome of psychotherapy and also note the bias inherent in each source. Fill in the missing information: (p. 613)

Source	**Bias**
therapist	wants to see him/herself as competent and successful
patient	
	may tend to see what they want to see but are often more realistic than therapist or client

    b. Changes in _____ appear to be the safest measures of outcome, but even this criterion is subject to limitations because changes in therapy may not generalize to other situations. In addition, the changes selected often reflect the goals of the therapist. (p. 613)

c. Some abnormal behavior patterns such as _____ and _____ appear to run a predictable course that is not influenced one way or another by psychotherapy. (p. 613)

d. The rate of improvement in most studies of therapy outcome regardless of approach is _____ percent compared to untreated controls. (p. 613)

e. Underline the correct phrase: The largest proportion of the gain in treatment occurs (in the beginning, in the middle, close to the end) of psychotherapy according to Howard et al. (1986). (p. 613)

f. How can psychotherapy be viewed as "the guardian of the status quo"? (p. 614)

18. Unresolved issues

a. In _____ percent of client therapist relationships, the client ends up worse off than before treatment. (p. 615)

b. List some of the types of patients who are notoriously hard to treat. (p. 615)

c. What therapist styles can be dangerous to client functioning, particularly when it is unmodulated by warmth and empathy. (p. 615)

d. Even with a treatable problem and a skilled therapist, negative events such as _____ , can impact negatively on the course of therapy. (p. 615)

e. Discuss the following points in reference to sexual relationships between therapist and clients: (p. 615)

1. Are such relationships ethical for the therapist to participate in under certain circumstances?

2. Are sexual relationships a serious cause of malpractice claims? (p 615)

f.   The authors suggest a "trial" interview. What is this?   (p. 615)

g.   Why don't all therapists practice a multifaceted, multitargeted approach to every case?
                                                                                (p. 616)

(19.)   Descriptive comparison of various approaches to psychotherapy
        Using the letters provided below, place each therapeutic approach along each of the
        following continua :   (p. 586)

        P   psychodynamic
        B   behavioral
        CB   cognitive-behavioral
        HE   humanistic-existential
        I   interactional

Individual   **Group**
_____

Cognitive   **Behavior**
change   **change**
_____

Directive   **Nondirective**
_____

Inner control   **Outer control**
of behavior   **of behavior**
_____

Historical   **Here and now**
focus   **focus**
_____

Brief   **Long term**
_____

(20.)   The use of hypnosis in therapy
    a.   Describe how a hypnotic trance is induced.   (p. 588)

    b.   Hypnosis may be used to accomplish the following outcomes. Briefly describe what
         each one is: (p. 588)

         1.   Recall of buried memories

         2.   Age regression

         3.   Dream induction

         4.   Post-hypnotic suggestion

    c.   Is there any evidence that hypnosis really works for anything?   (p. 588)

    d.   How might drugs sometimes be used in the hypnotic procedure?   (p. 588)

(21.)   Group therapy
         What school of psychotherapy does group therapy follow?   (p. 603)

(22.)   Structured behavioral therapy for couples
         Weiss (1975) has developed a brief, highly structured form of couple therapy. Briefly
         describe the major things he tries to teach couples.   (p. 608)

CHAPTER QUIZ

1. Individuals who seek therapy because they feel overwhelmed by sudden highly stressful situations typically respond best to: (p. 580)

    a. existential approaches that reduce alienation.
    b. long-term psychodynamic analysis.
    c. short-term, directive, crisis-oriented treatment.
    d. therapies that employ confrontational methods.

2. Clients who are reluctant to see a therapist in spite of their obvious need: (pp. 580-581)

    a. have no real reason for undergoing therapy.
    b. may not be amenable to therapy at that time.
    c. usually have an excellent prognosis.
    d. will probably never enter therapy voluntarily.

3. The member of the mental health team who has specialization in personality theory, psychological assessment, and psychotherapy is a: (p. 581)

    a. psychiatrist.   c. psychiatric social worker.
    b. clinical psychologist.   d. pastoral counselor.

4. The patient's major contribution to the therapeutic relationship is his/her: (p. 583)

    a. motivation.   c. expectation of receiving help.
    b. financial incentives for therapist.   d. suggestibility.

5. All of the following are key dimensions that can be used to describe various approaches to psychotherapy except: (p. 586)

    a. cognitive change/behavioral change.
    b. directive/nondirective.
    c. individual/group.
    d. successful/unsuccessful.

6. A son of a critical father comes to therapy one day and with no provocation is extremely hostile in his remarks to the therapist. The therapist might consider that _____ is occurring. (p. 587)

    a. free association   c. transference
    b. countertransference   d. positive transference

7. Contemporary psychodynamic treatment differs from Freudian psychoanalysis by placing more emphasis on: (p. 589)

   a. early repressed sexuality.
   b. current ego functioning.
   c. long-term treatment.
   d. childhood events.

8. Both implosive therapy and flooding focus on: (p. 590)

   a. bombarding maladaptive behavior with aversive stimuli.
   b. exploding inner conflicts.
   c. extinguishing the conditioned avoidance of anxiety-arousing stimuli.
   d. inundating a person with positive reinforcement.

9. All of the following are steps in Wolpe's approach to systematic desensitization except: (p. 591)

   a. asking the client to imagine anxiety-producing situations while relaxing.
   b. constructing a hierarchy of anxiety-producing situations.
   c. placing the client in anxiety-producing life situations.
   d. training the client to relax.

10. Aversion therapy reduces maladaptive behavior by following it with: (p. 592)

   a. a request for the client to avert his or her eyes from the stimulus.
   b. negative reinforcement.
   c. punishment.
   d. stimuli which divert the client's attention.

11. Which of the following statements regarding biofeedback is true? (p. 596)

   a. Biofeedback is a more elaborate means of teaching relaxation.
   b. Biofeedback is more effective than relaxation training.
   c. The effects of biofeedback are often generalized outside the laboratory.
   d. Recent well-controlled studies of biofeedback have shown a treatment effect for migraine patients.

12. According to Aaron Beck (1979), individuals maintain false beliefs even in the face of contradictory evidence because: (pp. 598-599)

   a. they are reinforced for doing so.
   b. of biologically-based drives to do so.
   c. of a strong regressive pull to be a "child" or a "parent" rather than an "adult."
   d. they engage in selective perception and overgeneralization.

13. Not only was Carl Rogers rated as one of the most influential psychotherapists of his time, but he was also a pioneer in: (p. 604)

   a. advocating health insurance for mental illness.
   b. carrying out empirical research on psychotherapy.
   c. initiating broad spectrum mental health program.
   d. reorganizing mental hospital procedures.

14. The rate of improvement given in most studies of therapy outcome, regardless of approach, is usually about _____ percent. (p. 613)

   a. 20   c. 60
   b. 40   d. 80

15. According to one report, _____ percent of claim funds paid by a national mental health malpractice insurer from 1976 to 1986 involved complaints of therapist sexual misconduct. (p. 615)

   a. 11.8   c. 44.8
   b. 22.8   d. 66.8

18

Contemporary Issues
in Abnormal Psychology

OVERVIEW

Previous chapters have catalogued the many forms of mental disorders and have briefly described various treatment programs, most of which focus either directly on the patient or involve only immediate family members.   Chapter 18 is different. Here "primary prevention" is emphasized which includes programs and research at the level of the broader society in order to prevent maladaptive behavior in the first place. The chapter discusses how the U.S. government is involved both nationally and internationally in improving mental health. The chapter also addresses controversial legal issues. Many people were shocked when John Hinkley was found not guilty of shooting President Ronald Reagan, especially since we all saw him do the shooting right on television. The chapter attempts to describe the maze of laws pertaining to the insanity defense and other pertinent legal issues.

LEARNING OBJECTIVES

1. Define *primary prevention* and list several biological, psychosocial, and sociocultural measures that need to be taken.

2. Define *secondary prevention* and list three interventions that can be used.

3. Define *crisis intervention* and describe two types that are in use.

4. Explain how mental health professionals are able to reach a larger group through the process of consultation and the education of intermediaries.

5. List and explain three general therapeutic principles that guide the milieu approach to treatment and compare the relative effectiveness of three treatment approaches.

6. Define *tertiary prevention* and describe several aftercare programs that perform this function.

7. List four conditions that must be met before involuntary commitment to a mental institution can occur and describe the legal process that follows.

8. Describe the incidence of assaultive patients and explain three dilemmas involved in trying to identify or predict dangerousness in psychiatric patients.

9. Describe some methods for assessing a patient's potential for dangerousness and explain the implications of the Tarasoff decision on a therapist's duty to warn persons that a patient is planning to harm.

10. Expalin what is meant by the insanity defense in criminal cases and describe four established precedents defining this plea.

11. Define *deinstitutionalization,* briefly describe its history, and list eight principles upon which successful programs have been based.

12. List and describe four major functions of the National Institute of Mental Health (NIMH).

13. List several professional organizations in the mental health field and explain three key functions that they perform.

14. Describe some of the major functions of the National Association for Mental Health (NAMH).

15. Explain why private industry is interested in mental health, and describe Control Data Corporation's Employee Advisory Resource (EAR).

16. Describe the functions of WHO, UNESCO, and the World Federation for Mental Health.

17. Explain the need for social planning in the mental health field and describe some of the factors that inhibit the process.

18. List eight value assumptions with which we must come to grips as we make decisions about the future of mental health.

19. Describe several opportunities that individuals have to contribute to the advancement of mental health and list five facts that should help them to succeed in those endeavors.

20. Summarize Okin's criticisms of state mental hospitals and explain why these shortcomings will be difficult to remedy.

TERMS YOU SHOULD KNOW

restorative (p. 619)

primary prevention (p. 620)

secondary prevention (p. 620)

tertiary prevention (p. 620)

epidemiological studies (p. 621)

crisis intervention (pp. 621-622)

short-term crisis therapy (p. 623)

hot line (p. 623)

consultation and education (of intermediaries) (pp. 623-624)

therapeutic community (p. 624)

milieu (p. 624)

social learning program (p. 625)

aftercare programs (p. 627)

day hospital (p. 627)

halfway house (p. 627)

forensic psychology (p. 628)

civil commitment procedures (p. 628)

voluntary hospitalization (p. 628)

involuntary commitment (p. 628)

hold order (p. 629)

dangerousness (p. 629)

"overcontrolled" person (p. 631)

duty-to-warn doctrine (p. 631)

insanity defense (p. 632)

M'Naughton rule (p. 632)

irresistible impulse (p. 633)

Durham rule (p. 633)

diminished capacity (p. 633)

deinstitutionalization (p. 633)

National Institute of Mental Health (NIMH) (p. 637)

National Institute on Alcohol Abuse and Alcoholism (NIAAA)(p. 637)

National Institute on Drug Abuse (NIDA) (p. 637)

National Association for Mental Health (NAMH) (p. 639)

National Association for Retarded Children (NARC) (p. 640)

employee assistance programs (p. 640)

World Health Organization (WHO) (p. 641)

United Nations Educational, Scientific, and Cultural Organization (UNESCO)
 (p. 641)

(bibliotherapy) (p. 625)

(occupational therapy) (p. 625)

(music therapy) (p. 625)

(art therapy) (p. 625)

(hospitalization syndrome, or social breakdown syndrome) (p. 626)

(the sick role) (p. 626)

(right to treatment) (p. 629)

(freedom from custodial confinement) (p. 629)

(right to compensation) (p. 629)

(right to legal counsel) (p. 629)

(right to live in the community) (p. 629)

(right to refuse treatment) (p. 629)

(right to less restrictive treatment) (p. 629)

CONCEPTS TO MASTER

1. Introduction
   Why are funds targeted for prevention programs likely to be cut during periods of
   economic conservatism and restraint?   (p. 619)

2. Primary prevention
   Primary prevention involves research into the conditions that foster mental disorders.
   Primary prevention also involves the eradication of negative conditions and institution
   of circumstances that foster mental health. Fill in the missing information on the
   following chart that illustrates various primary prevention measures:

Form of Primary Prevention	Example
biological (p. 620)	Examples of biological prevention include:
psychosocial (pp. 620-621)	Examples of psychosocial prevention include preparation for:

sociocultural (p. 621)

Sociocultural prevention is focused on making the _____ as "nourishing" as possible. Examples of sociocultural prevention include:

3. Secondary prevention
    a. Epidemiological studies
        Secondary prevention emphasizes early identification and treatment of maladaptive behavior before it can become seriously disabling. How do epidemiological studies assist in secondary prevention?   (p. 621)

    b. Crisis intervention

        1. Crisis intervention is an attempt at secondary prevention that aims at delivering prompt treatment. Complete the list of ways by which prompt services are given.
                                                                              (pp. 621-622)
            a.

            b. Telephone hot line

        2. The sole concern of short-term crisis therapy is the current problem with which the individual or family is having difficulty. How long does such therapy last?   (p. 623)

        3. The Telephone hot line is another form of crisis intervention service delivery. The range of problems for which people call is astounding. Both face to face and telephone hot line crisis intervention are discouraging for the therapist. Explain.
                                                                              (p. 623)

    c. Consultation and education
        What does "consultation and education of intermediaries" mean?   (pp. 623-624)

d. Therapeutic community

    1. Describe the following aspects of a therapeutic community: (p. 624)
       a. Staff expectations

       b. Do-it-yourself attitude

       c. Group cohesivensss

    2. A persistent danger with hospitalization is that the hospital will become a permanent refuge. To keep the focus on returning the patient to the community and on preventing the disorder from becoming chronic, hospital staffs try to establish _____ and to maintain a _____ attitude. Between _____ and _____ percent of patients treated this way can be discharged within a few weeks or at most a few months.   (p. 625)

e. Pauland Lentz (1977) performed an evaluation of the relative effectiveness of three treatment approaches for chronic hospitalized patients: milieu therapy, social-learning treatment program, and traditional mental hospital treatment. Respond to the following questions about this study: (pp. 625-626)

    1. Briefly describe each of the three treatments that were compared:
       a. Milieu therapy

       b. Social-learning treatment

       c. Traditional mental hospital treatment

    2. Describe how the study was carried out.

    3. Who were the subjects?

4. The results of this study were quite impressive. Both milieu therapy and social learning therapy produced significant improvement in overall functioning and resulted in more successful hospital releases than the traditional hospital care. However, _____ was clearly superior to the more diffuse program of _____ . The relative improvement rates for the different treatments were _____ percent of the social-learning program, _____ percent of the milieu therapy group, and _____ percent of the traditional treatment group remained continuously in the community.

4. Tertiary prevention
   a. Many studies have found that as many as _____ percent of schizophrenic patients have been rehospitalized within one year of their discharge. Aftercare programs reduce the rehospitalization. Describe the following aftercare programs: (p. 627)

      1. Halfway house

      2. Day hospitals

   b. Does adequate aftercare reduce the chances of rehospitalization, according to Glasscote (1978)?   (p. 627)

   c. Penk, Charles, & Van Hoose (1978) showed that _____ in a day treatment center resulted in as much improvement as full inpatient psychiatric treatment at a lower cost.   (p. 627)

   d. One of the chief problems of halfway houses is that of gaining the _____ and _____ of community residents.   (p. 627)

5. The commitment process
   a. In most cases people are sent to state mental hospitals voluntarily. However, there are four conditions on which a person can be formally committed. Complete the following list of them: (p. 628)

      1. Dangerous to him or herself

      2.

3. Unable to make responsible decisions about hospitalization

4.

b. Commitment is a civil court proceeding that varies slightly from state to state.
    In a typical procedure, a court order must be obtained for commitment. If there is
    imminent danger, howerer, the law allows emergency hospitalization without a formal
    commitment hearing. In such cases a physician must sign a statement. The person can
    then be picked up--usually by the police--and detained under a _____
    for 72 hours.   (p. 629)

6. Assessment of "dangerousness"
    a. How many individuals did Tardiff and colleagues (1984, 1985) state are confined
        because they are dangerous?   (p. 629)

        1. In private psychiatric hospitals: _____percent

        2. In state hospitals: _____percent

        3. In outpatient clinics:_____percent

    b. McNeil and Bindfer (1986) reviewed the rates of violence preceding hospitalization for
        a ten-year period. They found that while there was not a significant increase in the rate
        of violence among patients, there was a significant increase in the use of
        _____ as a grounds for civil commitment.   (p. 630)

    c. Violent acts are particularly difficult to predict. Complete the following list of critical
        dilemmas involved in prediction of dangerousness among psychiatric patients:
                                                                              (p. 630)
        1. Some people are definitely capable of uncontrolled violence

        2. Mental health professionals must have some faith in the people they rehabilitate

        3.

    d. Violent acts are difficult to predict because they are determined as much by
        _____ circumstances as they are by the personality traits
        of the individual. Mental health professionals typically err on the conservative side
        when assessing violence proneness.   (p. 631)

    e. The two major sources of personality information for the prediction of dangerousness
        are _____ and _____ _____.   (p. 631)

7. Duty-to-warn: implications of the Tarasoff decision
    a.   When does a clinician have a "duty-to-warn"?   (p. 632)

    b.   Does the doctrine extend to suicidal cases?   (p. 632)

8. The insanity defense
    a.   How frequently is the insanity plea used?   (p. 632)

    b.   How does the time served by the criminal sent to a psychiatric hospital compare to time served by criminals sent to prison?   (p. 632)

    c.   The established precedents that define the insanity defense are listed below. Briefly describe each one.   (p. 633)

        1.   The M'Naghten Rule

        2.   The irrestible impulse

        3.   The Durham Rule

        4.   Diminished capacity

9. Deinstitutionalization
    a.   Since 1955 what has happened to the number of persons hospitalized in state mental hospitals? What accounts for the changes?   (p. 634)

    b.   List five unforeseen problems have arisen in the effort to deinstitutionalize the mentally ill?   (p. 634)

        1.   Many residents of mental institutions had no families or homes to go to.

        2.

3.

4.　Many patients had not been carefully selected for discharge and were ill-prepared for community living.

5.　Many of those who were discharged were not followed-up sufficiently to ensure successful adaptation.

c.　The NIMH epidemiological survey was administered to transient and homeless people. It was found that _____ percent of homeless people had been hospitalized for psychiatric problems compared to only 5 percent of the control sample.

(p. 635)

d.　One of the most significnt problems in the maintenance of discharged patients outside the hospital involves preventing the individual from developing what has been referred to as the "chronic social breakdown syndrome." Describe the chronic social breakdown syndrome.　　　　　　　　　　　　　　　　　　　　　　(p. 636)

e.　Bachrach (1980) has developed a program to reintegrate chronic mental patients into the community. Of what elements does it consist? Describe the following elements of the program:　　　　　　　　　　　　　　　　　　　(p. 636)

1.　Targeting chronic patients

2.　Linkage with other services

3.　Cultural and ethnic-group relevance

4.　Hospital liason

f.　In order to improve the readjustment of the former mental patient to society, a new case-management approach has been initiated over the past few years. The effectiveness of the case-management approach was recently studied by Franklin et al. (1987). How did the case-management approach compare to the no-management condition at the 12 month follow-up?　　　　　　　　　　　　　　　　　　　(p. 636)

10. Organized efforts for mental health
a.　The extent of mental disorders was brought to public attention during World War II.
How?　　　　　　　　　　　　　　　　　　　　　　　　　(p. 637)

b. Following is a diagram of the government's mental health departments. Fill in the missing information: (p. 637)

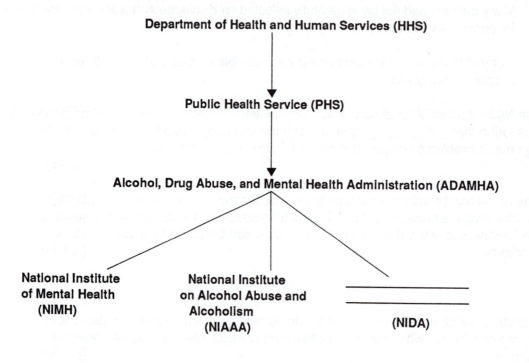

Department of Health and Human Services (HHS)

Public Health Service (PHS)

Alcohol, Drug Abuse, and Mental Health Administration (ADAMHA)

**National Institute
of Mental Health
(NIMH)**

**National Institute
on Alcohol Abuse and
Alcoholism
(NIAAA)**

_____
_____
(NIDA)

c. What type of activities does the NIMH do?   (p. 637)

d. Does the federal government directly supervise: (p. 637)

1. Local community services?

2. State hospitals?

3. What has happened to these programs in recent years compared to the 1960s and 1970s?

e. What is the role of voluntary groups in regard to mental health needs?   (pp. 639-640)

f.   Private industries also have a role in mental health services. Describe how the
      Control Data Corporation meets employees' mental health needs.   (p. 640)

11. International efforts for mental health
    a.   It has been estimated that over _____ million people worldwide are affected by
          alcoholism, drug abuse, mental retardation, organic brain disorders, and mental
          disorders. (The population of the United States is only around 220 million.)
                                                                                    (p. 640)

    b.   Briefly describe the efforts of the folowing international organizations to improve
          mental health: (p. 641)

          1.   World Health Organization (WHO)

          2.   United Nations Educational, Scientific, and Cultural Organization (UNESCO)

12. Challenges for the future
          To some people in our society, social planning seems contrary to the American way of
          life and the ideal of individual freedom. How does NIMH respond to this view?
                                                                                    (p. 642)
          "Social planning does not imply authoritarian control; ..."

13. The individual's contribution
    a.   List some constructive courses of action open to each citizen to work for improved
          health in society.   (p. 644)

    b.   Indicate whether each of the following is true or false by circling the appropriate
          response: (p. 644)

          1.   From time to time, *everyone* has serious difficulty coping with
                problems.   TRUE OR FALSE

2. During such a crisis, professional assistance may be needed.   TRUE OR FALSE

3. Such difficulties can happen to *anyone* if the stress is severe.   TRUE OR FALSE

4. Early detection and treatment is important to prevent chronic
conditions.   TRUE OR FALSE

14. Unresolved issues
   a. Okin (1983) has written a provocative critique of state mental hospitals. He considers hospitals to be _____ institutions that encourage
   _____ rather than restoration of
   functioning.   (pp. 644-645)

   b. Okin (1983) concluded that statemental hospital care is deficient not because of inferior quality but because hospital care is the wrong kind of
   _____.   (p. 645)

(15.)   Primary prevention following a crisis
In 1977, 154 people were held hostage at three locations in Washington. Describe the program of care offered by the Health Maintenance Organization to the hostages after release.   (p. 622)

(16.)   The hospitalization syndrome
   a. Describe the elements of the social breakdown syndrome: (p. 626)

      1. Deficiency in self-concept

      2. Social labeling

      3. The sick role

      4. Atrophy of work and social skills

      5. Development of chronic sick roles

   b. Are characteristics of the patient thought to interact with the hospital milieu in formation of the social breakdown syndrome?   (p. 626)

CHAPTER QUIZ

1. Over the years most efforts toward mental health have been largely geared toward helping people only after they have already developed serious problems. The authors' term for this is: (p. 619)

   a. crisis intervention.
   b. in vivo treatment.
   c. restorative.
   d. retrospective.

2. According to Kessler and Albee, everyting aimed at improving the human condition, at making life more fulfilling and meaningful may be considered part of _____ prevention of mental or emotional disturbance. (p. 620)

   a. primary
   b. secondary
   c. tertiary
   d. fourth level

3. Biological measures for primary prevnetion of mental disorders includes all of the following except: (p. 620)

   a. drug treatment of hyperactive children.
   b. family planning.
   c. genetic counseling.
   d. in utero treatment of genetic defects.

4. All of the following are sociocultural efforts toward primary prevention of mental disorders except: (p. 621)

   a. economic planning.
   b. penal systems.
   c. public education.
   d. social security.

5. All of the following groups are at high risk for mental disorders except: (p. 621)

   a. elderly people living alone.
   b. married people between 25 and 35.
   c. recently divorced people.
   d. the physically disabled.

6. Allen Jones is a middle-aged factory worker, husband, and father of five children. He has never previously been involved in psychotherapy until his home is destroyed in a tornado. While he attempts to find housing for his family, he discovers that his wife wants a divorce. He immediately becomes quite depressed and is unable to follow through on his house-seeking. Allen Jones is a prime candidate for: (pp. 621-622)

   a. day hospitalization.
   c. psychoanalysis.

b.   crisis intervention.   d.   milieu therapy.

7.   The purpose of consultation work by community mental health professionals is:

(p. 623)

a.   crisis intervention.
b.   to reach individuals in need of help who would otherwise never be identified by
     any community agency.
c.   tertiary prevention.
d.   to reach a larger group of persons in need by working with intermediary agents.

8.   Milieu therapy is: (pp. 625-626)

a.   the temporary substitution of one treatment mode by another until adequate
     resources can be acquired to provide the treatment of choice.
b.   a general term for any form of preventive treatment.
c.   the establishment of a hospital environment itself as a therapeutic community.
d.   the integration of any two distinct forms of treatment.

9.   All of the following are steps in the development of the social breakdown syndrome
     except: (p. 626)

a.   atrophy of work and social skills.
b.   deficiency in self-concept.
c.   fear of hospital staff.
d.   social labeling.

10. Typically, the first step in committing an individual to a mental hospital involuntarily is:

(p. 628)

a.   appointing a physician and a psychologist to examine the client.
b.   filing a petition for a commitment hearing.
c.   holding a commitment hearing.
d.   notifying the police.

11. Research shows that mental health professionals typically: (p. 631)

a.   are correct in their judgments of "dangerousness" about 50 percent of the time.
b.   are incorrect in their judgments of "dangerousness" about 75 percent of the time.
c.   judge patients as less dangerous than they really are.
d.   judge patients as more dangerous than they really area.

12. A clear implication of the Tarasoff decision is that a therapist must: (p. 632)

a.   inform the police when a client has made global threats.
b.   warn a person whom his or her client has specifically threatened to harm.

c. warn anyone whom he or she believes might be in danger from a client.
d. warn the authorities when a client threatens suicide.

13. Studies have confirmed that individuals acquitted of crimes by reason of insanity typically spend _____ time in psychiatric hospitals as(than) individuals convicted of crimes spend in prison. (p. 632)

a. less
b. more

c. the same amount of

14. Under which of the following precedents holds that individuals might not be responsible for their acts, even though they knew what they were doing was wrong, if they had lost the power to choose between right and wrong? (p. 633)

a. Diminished Capacity (1978)
b. The Durham Rule (1954)
c. The irresistible impulse (1887)
d. The M'Naghten Rule (1843)

15. In the 1960s and 1970s, state governments favored deinstitutionalization because it could: (p. 634)

a. better meet the needs of mental patients.
b. lower hospital population to manageable numbers.
c. reduce state funding.
d. rid society of an unwelcome evil.

ANSWER KEY

Chapter 1 **Abnormal Behavior in Our Times**

1. c
2. a
3. c
4. c
5. b

6. b
7. c
8. d
9. a
10. b

11. b
12. c
13. a
14. d
15. c

Chapter 2 **Historical Views of Abnormal Behavior**

1. b
2. d
3. b
4. a
5. b

6. d
7. b
8. a
9. b
10. b

11. a
12. d
13. c
14. d
15. c

Chapter 3 **Biological, Psychosocial, and Sociocultural Viewpoints**

1. d
2. b
3. c
4. a
5. b

6. b
7. d
8. b
9. d
10. d

11. c
12. c
13. a
14. b
15. c

Chapter 4 **Causal Factors in Abnormal Behavior**

1. c
2. b
3. b
4. d
5. d

6. c
7. a
8. b
9. c
10. d

11. d
12. d
13. a
14. d
15. b

Chapter 5 **Stress and Adjustment Disorders**

1. d
2. b
3. b
4. c
5. c

6. b
7. b
8. c
9. a
10. a

11. a
12. d
13. b
14. a
15. a

Chapter 6 Anxiety-Based Disorders (Neuroses)

1.	b	6.	b	11.	a
2.	b	7.	c	12.	c
3.	a	8.	b	13.	b
4.	b	9.	c	14.	c
5.	b	10.	a	15.	c

Chapter 7 Personality Disorders

1.	d	6.	b	11.	a
2.	a	7.	a	12.	c
3.	b	8.	d	13.	b
4.	b	9.	a	14.	b
5.	a	10.	c	15.	d

Chapter 8 Psychological Factors and Physical Illness

1.	d	6.	a	11.	a
2.	d	7.	b	12.	b
3.	b	8.	d	13.	d
4.	b	9.	a	14.	c
5.	c	10.	a	15.	c

Chapter 9 Mood Disorders and Suicide

1.	a	6.	a	11.	b
2.	c	7.	d	12.	d
3.	a	8.	b	13.	d
4.	a	9.	d	14.	b
5.	c	10.	a	15.	d

Chapter 10 Schizophrenias and Delusional (Paranoid) Disorders

1.	a	6.	d	11.	a
2.	b	7.	b	12.	b
3.	c	8.	c	13.	c
4.	d	9.	d	14.	c
5.	d	10.	d	15.	b

Chapter 11 Substance-Use and Other Addictive Disorders

1.	b	6.	d	11.	c
2.	c	7.	c	12.	d
3.	a	8.	c	13.	c

4. a	9. d	14. a
5. a	10. c	15. c

Chapter 12   Sexual Disorders and Variants

1. a	6. b	11. a
2. a	7. c	12. b
3. c	8. a	13. a
4. c	9. b	14. b
5. d	10. d	15. d

Chapter 13   Organic Mental Disorders and Mental Retardation

1. a	6. c	11. c
2. b	7. c	12. c
3. c	8. d	13. c
4. d	9. b	14. c
5. d	10. d	15. c

Chapter 14   Behavior Disorders of Childhood and Adolescence

1. b	6. a	11. c
2. d	7. a	12. a
3. c	8. b	13. d
4. a	9. a	14. b
5. c	10. b	15. d

Chapter 15   Clincal Assessment

1. b	6. a	11. c
2. b	7. b	12. b
3. a	8. a	13. c
4. a	9. d	14. b
5. b	10. d	15. d

Chapter 16   Biologically Based Therapies

1. b	6. a	11. a
2. a	7. d	12. d
3. b	8. d	13. b
4. c	9. a	14. c
5. c	10. d	15. d

Chapter 17   Psychologically Based Therapies

1.	c	6.	c	11.	a
2.	b	7.	b	12.	d
3.	b	8.	c	13.	b
4.	a	9.	c	14.	d
5.	d	10.	c	15.	c

Chapter 18   Contemporary Issues in Abnormal Psychology

1.	c	6.	b	11.	d
2.	a	7.	d	12.	b
3.	a	8.	c	13.	a
4.	b	9.	c	14.	c
5.	b	10.	b	15.	c